GIANT LVE SONG

GIANT LVE SONG

A MEMOIR

MAUREEN MULDOON

Giant Love Song

Published by Mad Ramble Press

ISBN: 978-0-9989340-0-6
eISBN: 978-0-9989340-1-3

Cover and Interior Design: GKS Creative
Author Photo Credit: Kevin Fox

"Poets and mystics have always known that the world of imagination is a real world—a third kingdom between the physical universe and the higher realms of spirit—and that it is possible to travel there and bring back extraordinary gifts"

—R.M., DREAMGATES

Table of Contents

Foreword

I met Maureen Muldoon while on my book tour with *The Awakened Woman*. She made it known that we would be friends. Thankfully, I felt the same way, or I may have needed a restraining order. It's interesting to cross paths with a soul sister from across the globe and discover how similar our journeys, how universal our struggles, and how kindred our spirits. It's beautiful to see that when we walk the good walk, life carves for us a path that is not meant to break us, but to wake us, and it peoples that path with helpful hands.

We rise and awaken, not just for ourselves but for the betterment of all. This does not mean the journey will be easy, but we will be guaranteed that our willingness will leave a legacy for those who still struggle. This has been my own life's work, and this is also the theme woven so beautifully into *Giant Love Song*.

Beneath every brokenhearted story is a love song, a lesson, or a blessing. These experiences are an invitation to find our most authentic and helpful voices. We are each responsible for delivering our stories and finding our own voices. Grandma Gogo used to remind me of the importance of owning a voice that matches our dreams: "Until the female lion becomes the historian of her OWN story, the tale of the hunt will always glorify the hunter."

In *Giant Love Song*, Maureen Muldoon has become her own historian. She has found and honors the voice of resistance, the voice of fear, the voice of willingness, and finally, the voice of resurrection. No matter what our stories are, we all must learn to rise.

Enjoy the journey through this giant love song and allow it to crack you open. Find that place, that open wound, travel to your tender spots, and let it inform you. Be willing to wait and listen. It is in these universal classrooms of love and loss that we will find our redemption and healing. We become more awakened.

The truth of our universal potential lies deep within the heart of the individual. However, it does not hurt to have some mighty companions along the journey. If you are looking to be reminded that we are each an essential and Divine thread in love's tapestry, this book is for you.

May it help you hear and honor your own giant love songs.

—Dr. Tererai Trent

1

Middle of the Night

IN THE MIDDLE OF THE NIGHT THERE COMES A SCREAM. Shrill and sharp, it rips me from my dreams. I open my eyes to darkness interrupted by the glow of the corner stoplight, which makes its way in and gently dances on my bedroom wall, pulsating softly from green to yellow to red. Each pop of light visits briefly and fades away, colorful ballerinas making a grand entrance and then gracefully bowing out.

The night is still for just a moment, the moment it takes for her to breathe in before her scream shatters the silence again. Next comes the shuffling of all of my aunts' slippers against the floor. Eight feet scamper to her side. Eight hands press her arms; their love carried by their whispers, every action purposeful and meant to settle her pains and pleads. I want to run downstairs and help her too, but I don't. My body is awkward around the heavy hospital bed and the humming machine that she is hooked up to. My hands don't know the pills to reach for, and the sweet words used to comfort her get stuck in my throat. So I lie still in my bed and wrestle with my uselessness as a tender tear trickles down the side of my face.

It's May 1, 1981, four years since Cancer first entered our vocabulary. It's unsettling the way it has snuck up on us. First as little murmurs that floated from the neighbors' porches, then followed after us as we made our way down the aisle at church. It slipped from the covered mouths of other mothers who sat in distant pews. It showed up in hushed conversations as my mother held court on our front stoop with her lady friends. Then it began to arrive before me in every circle I joined on the playground. It seemed to be waiting in every classroom I entered, smiling back at me in the blank stares of my normally expressive classmates. It winked at me in the kindness showered on me by the normally crabby cafeteria ladies. Cancer was not just having its way with my mom; it cast a spell on everyone.

Now it lurks around our home like a drunken uncle that no one wants to explain. I get to know it by watching its ways.

Cancer is thoughtless and greedy. After stealing her breast, it reaches for her hair and strips her slowly of every strand. She fights back with colorful turbans and fancy wigs, but that doesn't stop Cancer from nibbling on her plumpness and draining her strength. It rests every once in a while, long enough to lick its fingers and smirk at us. It gnaws on her memory and devours her laughter. In the pit of her throat where her laughter once lived, Cancer left blood-curdling screams that rip us from our sleep and leave us searching the ceiling for answers. So far none have been found.

I strain to make out the words my aunts whisper. They have been staying with us, coming and going with morphine and wine. When they first arrived, there was much more to carry, but now they have it down to just two things; morphine and wine. One is for my mother, and the other is for the rest of them. Three of my four aunts are nurses and they know how to navigate the situation. The fourth is my Aunt Rita who is a schoolteacher and she seems as helpless as we kids are. She fumbles for words and reasons, as she stands confused at her little sister's bedside. For a math teacher, it's all the more unsettling when things don't add up. I want to tell her that things don't add up for me either. I want to tell her about the way letters float off pages, the way the world seems to blur and shift too fast for me to keep up. But I don't. Instead, I watch her frail fingers grasp the metal bar of Mom's hospital bed. The whites of her knuckles, the stillness of her stance, the focus of her gaze tells me to give her time. I watch her wrestle with Mom's cancer, and because I have seen this match before, I know she's very likely to get pinned.

I close my eyes to listen to the soothing voices float up the stairway, gentle whispers of mothers who know about nightmares and frightened children. "Okay, Rosie," I hear them coo. "We're all here; it's okay," they assure her. But even from the second floor, I can tell they don't really believe "it's okay." I try to imagine her tucked in her hospital bed as they stroke her head and hands. It's strange to hear my mother spoken to like a baby, yet also oddly comforting. I see them holding her wrapped up in a pink blanket. They crowd and coo and beam down at my baby-mom. Their loveliness wraps around her as well; it is warm and gentle and it makes her cheeks go rosy and her eyes open and she is healed.

Next, I hear the door slam, and I stare at the ceiling of my bedroom again. The odd sound continues. It sounds like an old car turning over. It stops and goes and stops in a way that tells me someone is out there trying to work something out. Like the first few notes of a song plucked out on a piano and played over and over at different intervals. I wonder who it might be and what they're doing.

It's like someone is sawing or digging or dragging metal against cement. I pull the blankets to my chin, stretch my body out and find warmth in knowing someone is out there in the cold early hours of the morning being productive despite our current events. Maybe it's the Giant digging a hole to China for his escape.

The dragging comes and goes in an odd pattern. A million images float by. A parade of possibilities crowd in on me, and I try and forget about the odd sounds from outside and focus on the sounds coming from Bridget, my sleeping sister beside me. Her heavy inhale and exhale through closed mouth then a small burst of air that pushes out of her mouth. Then it repeats, inhale, exhale and the small burst of air at the end. I like patterns; I like finding them, figuring them out. Patterns comfort me and tell me what to expect next. Now her breath mixes with the sounds from outside and it all begins to sound like the ocean. The waves. The sucking in, the drawing up, the crashing down. There is a pattern. I have found it—sucking in, drawing up, crashing down.

I open my eyes now, but all I see is the sound. It distracts me from everything else. It pulls me from the warm bed. I push back the covers and place my feet on the cold floor. My bony body shivers as I stand and make my way to the window.

I pull back the curtain and raise the shade. Because of the blinking stoplight on the corner, we need this much protection so our room doesn't feel like an all-night disco. I see him immediately and lean back on my heels so that I can take it all in without getting caught. It's the Giant; my father. He is outside shoveling snow. It's still coming down and about two inches thick on the ground. From my second-floor view, he still looks massive. His broad shoulders and dark jacket move slowly with each thrust of the shovel like he is lost in thought. I feel guilty spying on him when all he needs is a little peace and solitude. The street is quiet. Like a Christmas card even though we are six weeks into spring. There is not a soul in sight, just the Giant and his shovel trying to clear a safe path for us. Push, lift, dump goes the shovel. Push, lift, dump goes the wave. Push, lift, dump goes her breath, and I get lost in the symphony that is playing out all around me.

There is something peaceful about watching him. Distant church bells chime in, giving their nod of agreement. He hears them too. I can tell because he dumps the shovel of snow, and instead of continuing with the next push, he stands his shovel in straight up and down by his side. Resting one arm on the handle, he bows his head. Hot breath swirls from his lips and evaporates into the air. I can almost see his prayers floating from him. Hot pleading prayers in search of a miracle. I watch his hand come to his face. Is it the sign of the cross or is he rubbing his face? It's hard to tell. I feel my breath go still, and I am suddenly frozen and stuck like the shovel in the snow because I realize that he is not just bowing his head or making the sign of the cross or rubbing his face. What he is doing is crying. I feel the heat of his tears as they roll down his cold cheek. This is all too much, and I am suddenly holding a snow globe that has my father trapped inside. I want to smash it on the floor to free him from this hell. But I don't. I can't, because there is no snow globe. This is reality.

I step back from the window, letting the curtain fall on its own and make my way back to bed. Bridget lies buried beneath a mountain of covers and sleeps like a dead person. I crawl in, careful not to touch her with my cold feet even though, more than anything, I want to wake her and tell her about the screams and the snow and the Giant and the shovel. Her head pokes out from the mountain of warmth, and she purrs like a cat, her two paws tucked up under her chin. In the peace of sleep, she seems even younger than her eighteen years. Her blonde hair circles her head like a halo. I let her sleep. She will have to get up soon enough. She will see for herself what I don't want to tell her.

2

The Nightmare

UP ON THE CEILING THERE LIVES AN OLD MAN IN A wizard hat. He looks off toward the corner of my room and he winks at me. I know that no one else can see him because he is made of cracked plaster. But if I pointed him out, you would see him clear as day. He has put me to bed every night, and he is there to wake me in the morning. His is kind and consistent like a wizard should be. Sometimes he whispers wisdoms to me. "Don't worry so much, everything will be okay," he offers in a dry and crackled voice.

My sister gives me a sharp kick and rolls to her side. I spy her with envy. I wish I could fall asleep, drift off to where troubles melt like lemon drops. It's usually easy for me to drift and doze and check out. I am a dreamer, and despite what John Lennon says, I do feel like the only one. I am more comfortable in my own mind than I've ever been in my own skin. It's nicer and softer, and everything is possible there. Here in the real world I can't seem to think straight, my mind goes in circles and sideways and little distractions call to me from every corner. Sometimes I seem to get lost for hours, days at a time. At school, the teacher is talking and the children are nodding, and everything is making sense to everyone. But for me, the words are pleasant little puzzles. Black squiggles that wiggle and giggle on the page, dying to spring free. They lift off and fly out the window, and I have no choice but to chase them. Once I am gone, I am gone for good, off where the wind blows, where the music rolls, falling down rabbit holes and tap dancing up stairwells in fancy dresses with long flowing hair.

Mom calls it "my own little world." I never tell her that it's really not so little. My sister, Bridget, calls it daydreaming, and my teachers call it sleepwalking. What they call it doesn't matter because I couldn't stop even if I wanted to. I've tried to buckle down and stay focused, but the world is so loud and busy and hard to take in. It's best to check out.

The smell of cut grass drifting through the window, the rusty squeak of the mailbox slot and the thunk of the envelopes that hit the floor, the rough skin of the potato as it peels off under the sharp knife are all little invitations for me to slip off. The smell of my mother's lipstick on my cheek, the hum of the refrigerator that ticks off and on as if it is in a secret conversation with the wall, the warm vibrating sighs of the cat as it curls on my lap, the pattern in the curtains, the way my sister Annie's hair stands up on its own like one hundred little antennas. The slightest thing will transport me to Neverland. Especially with music, it takes only a few notes to drift by from a passing car or a singing sister or a distant TV, and I am lost in the clouds.

Our home is so full of music on a good day it can feel like a love song. The house is old, and it creaks and snaps and pops all day long. My five older sisters join in the concert, spinning record after record in their attic bedrooms, Billy Joel, the Beatles, The Eagles, Linda Ronstadt. My mother plays her musicals down stairs, *The Sound of Music, Finian's Rainbow, West Side Story.* And the Giant will not be denied his Irish barroom songs. He taps the jelly jar filled with wine on the top of the table to keep time as he croons out songs about dying mothers and sons going off to battle. William and Owen, my two younger brothers, play their parts as well by memorizing every word of every advertising jingle and every theme show ever made. I mostly make up songs. They bubble up and flow through me like a river and sometimes it feels like they are singing me instead of me singing them.

Lately, with all the crying, there hasn't been as much singing. *Bye bye, Miss American Pie, drove my Chevy to the levee but the levee was dry. And them good ole boys were drinking whiskey and rye singing this'll be the day that I die.* The song swims around me as it leaks from Bridget's clock radio and mingles with her breath and the rhythm of the Giant's shovel. I don't miss a beat. I hear them all, at the same time and in equal measure. When I say that I need to escape and just tune out every once in a while, I mean it.

I turn onto my side and groan like a 100-year-old lady even though I am fourteen. Things are changing. I don't want them to, but they are. Mom no longer gets out of bed, our house has become a hotel, and worst of all, I need a bra. If I could change one thing, not having breasts would be on the top of my list. I've seen all the terrible things that having breasts can do to a person.

I try to will my breasts not to grow and yet I can't stop thinking about pretty white bras with little pink bows right in the center, where the cleavage is supposed to be. White and clean with that little pink bow. I want that bra but not the breasts. All the girls at school wear the same exact one, clean and white and with that little pink bow...

They flock around me like birds. Flying bra birds flap around my head as I crowd into my locker to change for gym, still wearing an undershirt. I dream about having my own bra but I am not sure how to get one. With Mom off her feet, I'd be too embarrassed to buy one for myself. So I wear these old undershirts and try not to make eye contact in the locker room. A wet heat washes over me as I try to protect myself from being pecked to death by a swarm of angry bra birds. I imagine myself fighting them off as I go screaming down the hallway of my school.

Back in bed, my heart is racing, because even though the birds are like the snow globe--not real--imagination makes it all feel so very real. My thoughts are slippery. I try to steer them to something happy, but thinking about bras makes me think about breasts, which makes me think of my mom. Before I can stop myself, I am reliving the day that Cancer came...

It's sixth grade and I am home from school. Standing on the front stoop, one hand on the handle. Someone is crying. It's off in the distance—someone familiar, someone I know.

I open the door and step into the front hallway. The dining room looks blurry and out of focus like it has been crying too. It breathes in and out, and I hear the room sighing, heavy and tired like someone has given up. The map of Ireland hangs on the wall, and the long table is sprinkled with cereal bowls and newspapers. Then I see them, draped in all directions like discarded wet bath towels, lifeless, heavy, and weeping. I step closer, and they turn to look at me; they are my sisters. There is Marian who is seventeen, the firstborn, the oldest, the one named after the Blessed Mother. She sits at the head of the table where the Giant usually sits. Her slick black hair has a thin braid that frames either side of her face, and she looks like a young blessed mother as she cups her mouth in her hand and looks off into the nothingness. Next to her is Bridget, who is fifteen, the second oldest. I don't see her face, but I can tell that it's her from the waterfall of blonde hair that flows like a golden river across the top of the table. She is bent over her folded arms, and her back is rising and falling in heaves and starts. Annie, eleven, is the fifth of my older sisters, and then comes me, the sixth. She is only two years older and not much bigger. She sits by the window; all I see is her back, as she stares out at the world. Her wild red hair pokes in all directions.

They are crying, weeping really. It's slow, almost silent, and rocking. It stands me still, like walking into a dark forest. I wait in the cold stillness and listen for clues. I want to back out the door, slip silently from this land mine, but my feet have taken root in our front hall.

Julia comes down the stairs and moves past without noticing me as if I am a statue. Sometimes I feel like a statue. Julia is like a lion, her full auburn mane frames her face, her yellow eyes are cold and regal. She sits at the table in the middle of the heartache. She doesn't cry. She rests her porcelain face in her porcelain hands. Her round little body perches on the edge of the bench where we usually sit for dinner. A wave of red hair falls over one eye as she looks around the room for company.

"Riddle is up there taking it pretty hard," she announces, but no one stirs. Riddle is taking what pretty hard? The words bounce off the walls and echo around the room. I look down to check my hands because I feel like a wet bath towel, like I am absorbing the heavy feelings in the room. I want to lie down in my bed away from all this damp sadness.

"What happened?" I ask, even though I don't want to know. My voice sounds oddly high and unfamiliar, like hearing it for the first time on my sister's tape recorder. I don't recognize me. Who is that funny voice saying my words?

"Mommy is in the hospital," someone says. This other voice is also oddly high.

A hard crease forms between my eyes, and I hear myself ask, "Why?" I sound like a cartoon character or someone who swallowed helium from a birthday balloon.

"Should we tell her?" Bridget asks as she lifts her head and tucks a blonde strand behind her ear. Her soft green eyes are moist and red as they take in the room like a cat. Bridget is my only sister with blonde hair. She is like the Barbie that got tossed in the bag of Raggedy Ann dolls.

"It's her mother, too," Annie replies. Her short wild hair casts an eerie shadow on the wall as she stares out the window like she is waiting for rain.

Julia turns to me and tilts her head as if to say, "Didn't you hear?" Her hair falls away from her face so I can see both of her eyes. "Mom has to get her boobs chopped off." Her words come with the sharp and sudden sound of metal chopping into wood, and the room begins to shrink.

Annie snaps her head around. The shadow of her hair on the wall turns into a monster that raises its long claws to grab at us. "Julia!" she says in a hushed tone like she is in church. I look to Annie for answers but she returns to staring out the window again and the shadow monster sits back down. This time it's not just rain she is waiting for, but a whole holy hurricane.

The shrinking room begins to shake as Julia's words ricochet off the walls, and my sisters continue weeping. The little room, the long table, my weeping sisters, the monster shadow, and the words blur and spin and swirl.

I push my way up the stairs. It's hard to move under the weight. The heavy news has climbed upon my back. Through the walls I hear Riddle sobbing or drowning—I can't tell which. Several short gasps and then long silence and then a gasp, like she has gone underwater but then fights her way up for air. I want to get up the stairs and help her even though I am not sure exactly how I would do that. She gasps again, and I take a step. Then another gasp and a sob and another step. I continue on as her sobs grow louder and louder, like a growing storm.

Then there is coughing, wheezing and hissing, like the radiator kicking in on the first cold night of winter. I shake myself from my memory and return to my room with my sleeping sister, but now I see that Bridget is not sleeping. Instead, she sits at the edge of the bed, her blonde head of hair like a human sunrise. Riddle sits beside her, still crying, just like in my daydream, but now it's real life. At least I think it is. You can never be too sure.

Her name is actually Rita, but as babies we all had problems making the "t" sound, so she ended up being called Riddle, and it stuck. Somehow it's perfect; Riddle is pretty complicated. I rub my eyes and sit up to take it in, the whispering of secrets, the tender tears, and the gentle scraping of the shovel against the walkway. Yeah, this is real life. This is prom day.

3

Sunrise

THEY'RE SITTING AT THE EDGE OF THE BED. Their backs to me, one blonde the other brunette, and somehow they blend together. I wipe the sleep from my eyes. But they remain blurry, melting into each other like an odd abstract painting of light and darkness. I wonder about the names of the two very different paint shades that color my sisters. What would I call them if I had invented these colors? "Straw at Sunrise" for Bridget and "Mahogany Morning" for Riddle. I imagine myself standing off to the side with a long paintbrush making swirls and strokes of my sobbing sisters.

Bridget's arm drapes around Riddle's shoulder; Riddle's head is low and resting in her hands. She cries in a way that gets me to drop my brush and sit up on my elbows.

"What happened?" I ask.

Bridget answers with a dismissive wave of her hand. Riddle

makes a choking noise and begins to explain. The words are hard for her to speak, but she doesn't let it stop her. She takes big gulps of air and pushes them out a few at time like she is tossing them from a sinking ship. "I should be allowed to go. It's my only senior prom," Riddle pleads with me as if I have a say in the matter.

I don't. But I sit all the way up to let her know that she has me fully convinced of her argument. I nod my head at her. Of course she should go to prom. How could she not go to the prom? Even the hideous life of Cinderella included a ball. The unnamed heavy feeling returns, and I wish I could go back to sleep, not that it would help. I lean against the headboard and look on, stuck between two nightmares.

Riddle is a senior and I am a freshman at Saint Elizabeth's, an all-girl prep school. My wild haired sister Annie is a sophomore, smack between us in age, but she goes to Oak Knoll, where Marian, Bridget and Julia have already graduated. Saint Elizabeth's is a little farther and less prestigious than Oak Knoll. Riddle and I go to Saint Elizabeth's because we didn't get the scholarship to Oak Knoll. The nuns can only give out a certain number per family, not that we would qualify anyway. For Riddle and me school is not our first choice. She likes boys, and I like daydreams. Neither of us is willing to give these things up any time soon.

"You're not going to the prom?" I ask.

Bridget answers for her by shaking her head no.

"The Cat won't let her go?" I guess aloud.

Bridget rubs her chin, as she turns her light greens eyes toward me. They are soft and sad and searching for words.

In the silence Riddle fills me in. "It's not the Cat, it's the Aunts.

They say it wouldn't look good." She does this thing when she cries, or rather when she tries not to cry. Her face gets hard and shaky and her eyes turn black as night. The tears come anyhow, but it's not for her lack of trying to hold them back. It's like her whole body is invested in keeping them at bay.

She turns back to be consoled by Bridget. They huddle together. They are on my team, "The evens." Bridget, the second oldest, is in college. Riddle is the fourth, and I am the sixth. *Two, four, six, eight! Who do you appreciate? The Evens, the evens, go evens!* I imagine us all in short skirts and pompoms cheering each other on.

There are eight kids in my family, so to make things easier my mother has split us into two groups: the evens and the odds, depending on what number child you are. "Divide and conquer," I imagine her whispering to the Giant before they both fall off to sleep. "Divide and conquer."

This division is helpful when it comes to creating teams to tackle jobs around the house, like raking the leaves or folding laundry. Bridget, Riddle and I will do the dishes while Marian, Julia and Annie, one, three and five--the odds--will shovel the snow.

Sometimes the division can cause a civil war where we scream from across the room, "Odds are the clods!" They reply, "Evens are the heathens." And it's not just that the words rhyme, the accusations are sort of true. The odds, Marian, Julia and Annie are all sort of bookish, cloddish and quirky. The evens, Bridget, Riddle, and myself are the heathen rule breakers. The youngest two kids are the "the two boys" William and Owen. Though they are only two and four years younger than I am, they are in a group all their own. "The two boys" is what we call them.

William, our little man, and Owen, our extra little man. We love them like rag dolls and treat them with the same care. They've been joined together by their same sex and similar age, stripped of their names and rechristened "the two boys."

Riddle turns back to explain her plight.

"The Aunts say I can't go. It wouldn't be right, with mom being sick. It wouldn't look good." Riddle lets out a growl of disappointment, and goes on crying. The Aunts showed up last week and before we knew what hit us, they'd taken over. It's like the ant invasion we had last spring…

Billions of them swarm the place to dismantle a plate of maple syrup and pancake crumbs left on the floor of the sun parlor. I crouch down and study them as my sisters freak out. They are beautiful as they march in single file carrying off their food, slow and steady, bit by bit, as I hum to them. *"Just what makes that little old ant, think he'll move that rubber tree plant? Anyone knows an ant can't move a rubber tree plant. But he's got high hopes, he's got high hopes,"* Frank Sinatra pops off the jacket cover of his album to crouch beside me and sing, *"He's got high apple pie in the sky hopes…!"*

This time, the Aunt invasion is not so different. They are also quite amazing even though they don't have a bit of high hopes. They are my mother's sisters, here to care for their Rosie, my mom. And as much as the Giant tells them that he has it all handled, they won't hear of it. They have their roles to play and they march in single file and carry out their duties. Except for Aunt Rita, the school teacher, they are all nurses; caring for the sick and dying is their territory. It's what they do, their purpose, what they've been trained for. And they will not hand this duty off lightly to just anyone. They came with rosary beads, medical supplies, and cots and set up camp in our living room, surrounding my mother's hospital bed. They have an unending supply of morphine stolen from the hospitals where they work, and they keep their sister so far from the fingers of pain that she can't be reached at all, not even by us. At her hospital bed they confess how they acquired the goods, cackling like witches over their cleverness. My beautiful blue-eyed cousin Robin and my oldest sister Marian are both in nursing school, nurses in training, so my mother has round-the-clock quality care.

It's not too surprising that the Aunts don't want Riddle to go to the prom. Since they've arrived, they have put a stop to almost everything. They say our mother is dying. Every day they tell us in one way or the other, and it's hard to argue when they have all the power. They came with their history, statistics, and ways of doing things that are familiar to all of them, but foreign to us. Most of what they do and say makes no sense at all, especially the part about mom dying. It's like they're speaking a completely different language but don't realize it. Plus, they moved in so quickly and covered so much ground, "Move in the hospital bed, hook up the morphine, someone is dying, send out the word." I don't even try to keep up with them. They have come like a steamroller, and it's no use hanging around and asking them to explain what it all means because you run the risk of getting flattened.

They're all pretty stern, but who can blame them? I am sure I would be sharp, too, if I thought I could save my sister some pain. Besides, they're good to my mom. Real good. They crowd around her and speak in sweet voices like she is a sleeping little kitten. "Rosie?" they call to her. "How ya doing, Rosie?" they say sweetly as they rub lotion on her hands or lift her head to give her water.

But as far as us kids, it's best to steer clear and not ask too many questions. 'Cause the answers, if they do come, are confusing and never what you want to hear. The Aunts play out a strong marching song that keeps them moving forward. I wish someone would stop and take the time to make sure we all know the tune, but "time is running out." And there is no time for explanations.

I stand at the foot of my mother's hospital bed and watch as my Aunts march in and carry pieces of our life off bit by bit. They wrap up and dull down anything that the Cancer has not pillaged. I look around for Frank Sinatra to jump in and cheer me up with his, *"High Hopes,"* but the record player has been moved to the dining room to make space for the oxygen machine, and as hard as I try, I just can't seem to remember the song on my own.

4

First Light

I LAY IN BED TRYING TO DROWN OUT RIDDLE'S TEARS, and I think about my Aunt Caroline and her travel clothes. I wish she was here and not off in India or Italy or Indiana or wherever the heck she's fled. She would explain it all to me. She is our father's sister and one of my very favorite people. She is an artist and spends long hours at her sewing machine, swigging back Budweisers in her polyester shorts, knee high stockings, and tennis shoes as she whips up fancy pillows, curtains, and wall hangings. She creates miniature dollhouses fit for a little queen and king, and she turns used greeting cards and leftover wrapping paper into shellacked works of art. Everything she comes across has a secret second life that it didn't know how to live. Paper clips become stick figures, thimbles become little footstools in her dollhouse, and one of my mother's earrings is transformed into a miniature chandelier.

Aunt Caroline works for the *Newark Evening Newspaper*, and she loves to travel all over the world and collect new words. When she travels, she leaves her faded tee shirts and tennis shoes behind and she dresses like a peacock, all colors and feathers and bangles and dazzle. Her traveling clothes even smell different and just seeing her dressed in the shiny fabric and colorful scarves transports me to exotic places where people ride elephants and walk with umbrellas even when it isn't raining.

Aunt Caroline is not married and has no kids, just her cat, Dolly. So she can live the life of Riley if she wants and collect all the words there are in as many languages as she can. Because more than travel and making art, Aunt Caroline loves words and riddles best of all. She uses them all and loves them like us kids, completely and without rules. I've even heard her use the real bad ones, but she says them like they're pretty and you might even forget they're bad. "*Damn!* That's one *hell* of a cup of tea, Rosie," she says to my mother with a smile. And Mom doesn't freak out; she just smiles back, raises her cup, nods her head and says, "Thanks." Like she has just had someone hold the door open for her.

I lie back on my pillow and think about Aunt Caroline…

"Do you know what that word means? Do you know what that word means? Do you know what that word means, Maureen?" She is making lunch in the kitchen. The record player is going, and she's singing along to *Finian's Rainbow*. "*On the day I was born, said me father, said he. I've an elegant legacy, waitin' for ye. 'Tis a rhyme for your lips and a song for your heart to sing it whenever the world falls apart.*" I know some of the words so I sing along. "*Follow the fellow, follow the fellow, follow the fellow who follows a dream."* Mid-song she turns to me, "An elegant legacy, Maureen, do you know what that means?"

"No," I answer, and my thoughts start running, cause I know the word game has begun.

"'Elegant' means fancy, and 'legacy' is something that comes to you through your family."

"Elegant means fancy," I repeat and think about the fancy pants I got to wear when I was potty trained.

"You're off to kindergarten in the fall. Do you know what the word 'kindergarten' means, Maureen?" She is standing over me as she sweeps her hands against her apron. On the mantle behind her is the display of show dolls she brought from all her travels. We are not allowed to play with them. But she also brings us words and these are for play, and she always has the game going. When she got back from France she invited me to have a "tête-à-tête," which meant she wanted to talk to me. From Ireland she told me about "blarney," which is sort of like saying "baloney," and ever since she got back from Germany, all she talks about is how she's been afflicted with "wanderlust." Wanderlust means she has a strong desire to travel. But I already knew that. Sometimes she will even sing in Irish, and it sounds so beautiful, yet also like she has marbles in her mouth. She told me that when we say "so long" we are really saying "goodbye" in Irish, "Sl`an."

I think about the word 'kindergarten' as I stare at the frozen dolls. My little brother William sits beside me picking his nose.

"Kindergarten means school," he announces.

"It's my word, William!" I protest.

"It's Maureen's word, William," Aunt Caroline repeats. "You'll get your own word."

"Kindergarten," she leans in and repeats slowly, letting me know there is more to kindergarten than just school.

"It's my word," I warn William again so that he doesn't try to butt in.

"Kindergarten," she repeats again slowly, like how Mom talks to the old ladies in the back of the church, and I can tell Aunt Caroline is done waiting and wants me to guess. She told us once that "kin" meant "family." So I take a swing.

"Does it mean a family but at school?" I ask. She stares down at me and gives me nothing. Like the face on a clock, I can't read her. Then a little smile creeps onto her face like a shy cat and moves her lips upward.

"Good guess, Maureen. Good guess." I feel like a winner on "*The Price Is Right*," and I sit up a bit to see what I may have won.

She bobs her head. "It's a German word. 'Kinder' meaning children and 'Garten' means garden. So. it means 'a garden of children.'"

"A garden of children?" William repeats, taking his finger out of his nose and pointing it at me. "She said, 'family at school' and that's not close at all!" he points out. He's right, but I don't care because now all I can think of is little children with faces surrounded by petals of all different colors, and I am so excited that I stand up and run in circles.

"Kindergarten!" I scream. This is the best word she has given me so far. William jumps off his chair and runs after me; he is a copycat but I don't mind. We circle the living room a few times, knocking into the couch and tossing the pillows in the air. William's face is round and lights up like a light bulb without a shade. His eyes twinkle and his freckles dance all over his nose as he laughs and yells out, "kindergarten!" We run into the next room where mom is rocking the baby.

"Mom, good news! I am going to a garden of children!" I yell.

"We're going to kindergarten, mom." William repeats.

"No William, just me!" I tell him and give him a push. He starts to push back, but Mom shushes us and holds a finger over her lips. Her shush is like the end part of a sneeze and it gets our attention. In her arms, baby Owen is sleeping. We stand watching her rock him back and forth. It looks nice to be the baby.

"Babies don't get to go to kindergarten," I say.

"I'm not a baby," William tells mom. He has his finger up his nose again and I feel a sorry for him, because he is not the baby and he is not going to kindergarten.

"You know what else about kindergartners?" Mom asks looking at me.

I draw a blank. I don't know anything else about kindergar-teners aside from the fact that they look like flower children.

"Kindergarteners don't wear uniforms."

"They don't?" I ask, a little disappointed 'cause a uniform means you are a big kid, and I've been waiting so long to wear the uniform like my sisters.

"Do they go to school in their underpants?" William asks.

Mom smiles and my face goes red with giggles 'cause kids in underpants are just funny.

"No, they don't go to school in their underpants," she tells us, and William and I fall over laughing 'cause Mom said "under-pants." She smiles, rocks the baby gently, and says, "They wear school clothes."

I stop giggling. "School clothes?" I repeat, not liking the sound of it.

"Yes, school clothes," she nods. "We'll need to get you a nice first day of school dress."

"A first day of school dress!" I imagine myself walking down the block to school dressed in a ball gown covered with feathers and beads by Aunt Caroline. The two of us decked out in our traveling clothes struck by a mighty case of wanderlust. My feet start itching and I want it all to happen already. The only place I can roam is around our living room, so I scream and go running around the house again, William following close behind. Before the baby wakes, Aunt Caroline steps in and grabs us both by the shoulders.

"Go color on the stoop and give your mother some peace," she tells us as she hands us paper and a cup of broken crayons.

Out on the stoop, William gets busy drawing fire trucks, his favorite thing. I watch the old ladies walk to church, and the milkman bring the milk, and the hippy kids drift by. Mr. Rogers from the TV waves at me from the sidewalk and sings, *"It's a beautiful day in this neighborhood, a beautiful day for a neighbor, would you be mine? Could you be mine?"* He comes up my sidewalk and offers his hand, and we go dance all around the yard with our feet hardly touching the ground. I smile and hum along as my hand begins to draw out the most colorful picture; it's always the same. There is a castle with hearts in the windows and a princess with long hair. There are flowers in the yard and a big sun up in the corner.

This is the same picture my sisters draw, and the picture my friends draw, and so it is the one I draw too.

When we give our pictures to Aunt Caroline, she covers her mouth and tells us she is in awe of our talents.

"What does awe mean?" William asks.

"Awe is a feeling of reverence," she explains. We stare up at her confused. "When you stumble upon something sacred; like fairies, or a well-tended garden, or artwork like yours, and you are filled with feelings that make you want to laugh and cry and shake your head because you just don't even know what to say." Her words make me see fairies and mermaids and rainbows, and I wish I had more paper to draw them, too. William and I stare up at our aunt with our mouths open in awe. The record player sings to us, *"Look, look, look to the rainbow. Follow the fellow who follows a dream…"*

Back in my room, Riddle wipes her nose on the back of her hand and looks to me for some answers. "How am I not supposed to go to prom? I have a dress and a date and…" Her brown eyes search my face for answers but I have none to offer. "Garden of children" I want to say, just to say something. But I don't. In the absence of answers, she bows her head and returns to her tears.

5

Morning

I WISH I COULD HELP RIDDLE, PAY HER BACK FOR ALL THE
ways she has been so nice to me. Because of her seniority at
school, she is entitled to give me the brush off and ignore me
completely, expected to do it really. But she doesn't. Riddle does
very little of what's expected of her. She takes me under her wing
and tells me everything I need to know to survive high school.
We walk to the train station every morning and she plies me with
secrets about boys, shortcuts and secret handshakes. She lays
out in detail how to sneak behind the forbidden doors at school
and confiscate a cold soda from the off limits vending machine
without paying or getting caught. "You just slide your arm all
the way up the slot, pull back the lever and then grab the can."
She is my very own beautiful "Artful Dodger," and she makes
walking to school, even on the coldest mornings of January, the
best part of my day.

"You know, you should always have a boyfriend, even in between the ones that you really like. It's okay to date a boy if you don't like him, because no matter what, you should always have a boyfriend. It's just nice, you know? They take you places and buy you things!" I listen to her go on about boys and I know it's her favorite song. She sings it over and over again and never gets tired of it.

I've actually never had a boyfriend or even kissed a boy. So I have to take her word for how great a boyfriend is even if I find it confusing. She talks about boyfriends like they're handbags, a useful place to stash your lipstick and get your money from. Her adoration seems to be mutual; I watch men and boys turn to stare at her as we go by. She's a looker, but she pays no mind to the wake she is leaving. She already has more boyfriends than she needs and this makes the "no prom" news all the more upsetting.

Prom is a big deal. She has been giving me the details for months. "We're renting a limo and my dress is mauve with a handkerchief bottom and everyone will be there."

My sisters have all been to many proms. Bridget has her prom pictures lined up on our dresser like little trophies. She didn't just go to the proms at her school, she made the rounds; Seton Hall, Delbarton, and even Columbia High School, the local public school. Columbia boys have more than enough pretty girls to ask to the prom, but Bridget and Riddle are very distracting, and prom is kind of an extracurricular activity to them.

Any prom will do, but senior prom at your own school is the night not to miss. I look over at the prom pictures lined up on Bridget's dresser. Bridget in a white dress with a boy with long hair; Bridget in a blue dress with a boy with glasses; Bridget in a pink dress with a very tall boy. The photo of the tall boy next

29

to Bridget makes me think of my parent's wedding picture. My mother's smile and sweet button nose lines up with my father's elbow. My father seems to be ducking so that he can fit his head in the frame of the picture. He is a Giant. In their wedding picture, my parents are next to each other outside a church. We point at the picture and ask her, "Why are you sitting down?"

She shakes her head and smiles at the photo. Her hand comes to her mouth and her cheeks turn pink. "I'm not," she confesses with a giggle.

We stare back at the photo and try to figure it out. He seems too big next to her. My sisters sing, "Short people got nobody to love" as she chases them around the table trying to swat at them with a dish towel. They all laugh and fall over each other and we know that she doesn't really care that she is so short and he is so tall. The song has got it wrong. Short people do have somebody to love and in her case it just happens to be a Giant. When we watch him lean down to kiss her goodbye at the door each morning, we can see for ourselves that they have not let their height, or lack of height, get in the way of their love. Our mother is a half a head taller than a midget, and our father is an inch shy of the ceiling. He smells the way you would think a giant should, onions and wine. He wears dirty work boots and torn flannel shirts. In the heat of summer he raises his arms to my mother to show the large holes beneath his armpits. His lips turn upward as he speaks the words, "Air conditioning," and lets loose a deep laugh that seems to rattle the house. He doesn't know that he smells, so it's not really his fault. His nose doesn't work from when he got mugged.

I try to pull myself back into the room and focus on my sister's prom pictures, but the memory of the mugging has me, and before I can escape it begins to pull me down the rabbit hole.

His nose doesn't work from when he got mugged. From when he got mugged, he got mugged. The old TV in my mind clicks on. It starts out silent and grainy like old news footage or an old forgotten family movie. Some details I remember, some get filled in by my imagination. What is real and what is my dream get all tangled and mixed and it's hard to keep them separate. Like carrying shaved chocolate bits in your warm hands, the details melt and merge into each other...I remember carrying shaved chocolate.

Two bad guys, dressed in black begin to circle the van. Yes, there must have been two. With the Giant being so big, it would take at least two to take him down. They didn't need much strength though; they used a brick to knock him over the head while he slept in our van, waiting for my mother to finish her grocery shopping.

I watch the bandits with bandanas strung from ear to ear, dark eyes, dressed in tight fitted suits, like trapeze artists, or menacing mimes. They move like storm clouds, swift and light, as they whack the Giant, grab his wallet, and fly off into the night.

The Giant's picture is in the newspaper like a famous person. The headline whispered around the house, "Father of eight looks like he won't make it." It's hard to imagine that the Giant "won't make it" because he can make almost anything. He has a room full of tools. I think about the bandits and the Giant and my mother—her day already full with the breakfasts, the dishes, the ironing of uniforms, wiping of noses, and her weekly vacation to the grocery store, to shop alone in peace—ending this way. She screams, an actress in a horror film, frozen still, hands fluttering about her face. A line of worry creases her brow, her mouth screams a silent "No!"

It's always black and white; it's always slow motion and silent. Only in this way am I able to think of it. I would never be able to handle it in full color and sound.

My Uncle Harry came that night. He is not a blood uncle but my father's best man and co-worker. He usually shows up on Easter with a huge chocolate bunny the size of my brother Owen.

Uncle Harry hands the chocolate statue to the Giant, and we kids line up in age order as he sits with the bunny and a butcher knife. "Youngest to oldest," the Giant instructs as we push and shove to get in order. Then he calls to us, not by name, but with the word, "Next."

"What piece do you want?" he asks. We point and he cuts.

"Get the ears, get the ears!" my sisters whisper down the line to me. "The ears are solid."

As I approach the Giant with the butcher knife, his immense nature frightens me and I completely forget my sister's advice. I reach my finger out to tap the bottom of the bunny, because it's the closest part to me and the farthest part from him.

"You want the rabbit's foot?" he asks with a smirk as a groan of disappointment bellows from the Greek chorus behind me. I nod, keeping my eyes on the rabbit's foot. I watch the knife cut into the bunny, the pieces break and splinter.

"A rabbit's foot is good luck, Maureen," he whispers down to me, as I shuffle away with my cheeks full of heat and hands full of shaved chocolate bits.

But on the night of the mugging, when Uncle Harry comes

to our door, there is no chocolate bunny, no lucky rabbit's foot. We find him on our stoop standing against the night, like an unprepared actor in a black box, no backdrop, no props, and no rehearsal, his lines delivered cold and unsure.

"Your mother's at the hospital. You kids should pray for your old man." We gather around the heatless fireplace in our PJ's and tuck into each other. Some on the couch, some on the chairs, and some get stuck on the cold floor. I am four or five.

Marian hands out the rosary beads. Something bad has happened, but what? Something about the Giant who eats supper with us. He is somehow in danger of never coming home. So we pray the rosary, an unending chant of "Hail Mary mother of God" and "Our fathers" that run on and on without end. When we get to the part about our father being in heaven, I wonder if he is. I wonder if I'll miss him.

When our mother comes home she tells us that our father got hit so hard that he went running around the emergency room singing "Choo-Choo!" like a big crazy train and the nurses and doctors had to catch him and hold him down. She has read us the book *Gulliver's Travels*, about how Gulliver was captured by the little people in the Land of Lilliput, and I am not sure if she is making this one up too. If it is true, how many nurses and doctors did it take to hold him? Sounds like maybe an army. I cover my mouth and grin at my sisters who listen to my mother tell the story about the Giant who thought he was a train. But my sisters are not grinning. They look up at my mother like they are watching the fireworks on the 4th of July, their expressions part scared and part wonder.

She tells us that our father was in heaven for a little while, and when he came back he told our mother that heaven was like a garden and that there was an angel who met him at the gate and said, "Welcome, James." But he told the angel that he had eight kids to raise, so she let him come back to Earth. Now he has to stay in the hospital for a while.

I like the angel story even better than the train story and my sisters and I sit in silence as we think about garden angels and Giant trains...

6

Still Morning

RIDDLE BLOWS HER NOSE AND LETS OUT A DEEP SIGH.

"How am I supposed to cancel my date? The prom is tonight. Ron already has the tux and everything." She says Ron like we are supposed to know who she is talking about. But Riddle goes through boyfriends faster than her mood ring can change colors.

She is not just popular with boys, she is popular with everyone...

Riddle! Riddle! When we reach the train station to take the train to school she is met by a small mob of fans that cheer, "Riddle!" She even has a cool nickname. The Delbarton boys who wait for the train with us send sad, strained, sideways glances. She is out of their league. She stands amid admirers, lights a cigarette, and begins to tell a story that I've heard a hundred times, but like a groupie to a rock star, I can't wait to hear the tune again.

"That's right," she nods, "backstage passes to Van Halen. I told them I was Valerie Bertinelli's first cousin." She lifts her white button-down uniform shirt to reveal a concert tee shirt. Not that anyone needs proof; she looks just like Valerie Bertinelli, the spitting image. *"Dance the night away! Dance, dance, dance the night away!"* The Riddle mob begins singing, and she leads them in some spontaneous dance that they all know the moves to as the Erie Lackawanna pulls into the station. The old train coughs and spits like a sick old man as it comes to a stop with one slow moan. We climb aboard without a bit of sympathy for the miles he has traveled.

Even if she didn't look like Valerie, you would want to mistake her for somebody. She has a way of standing out, like an orange in a bowl of apples. The other girls wear loafers, bright cardigan sweaters and matching ribbons in their tightly pulled pony tails. Riddle in her fringed moccasins, faded jean jacket, feather earrings, olive skin and orange backpack, is not like anything you have seen before, and she makes you want to stare. She is long hair and laughter in a cool cloud of cigarette smoke.

Even as I watch her now at the edge of my bed, wiping her nose and cut at the knees as she rocks away her woes, I am still mesmerized. I lie back on my pillow and try to fix things in my head. I try to figure out the combination, the things that led to this moment. I think about the day, the weed, and the locker. The combination. If I could just figure out the combination that would set her free...

I am rushing down the halls of our school. This time I get to her faster and I'm able to follow her instructions. I get the locker open and find the bag of weed. And then I panic. What would I do with the bag of weed? What would I do? I continue to retrace my steps as numbers float by. 8, 6, 7, 5... 8, 6, 7, 5... 8, 6, 7, 5.... What would I do with the bag of weed? What would I do?

Sandie Arne rushes into the classroom and whispers in my ear, "Your sister is in the nurse's office, she needs your help." I raise my hand to go to the bathroom and rush out of the room before the teacher even gives me the noble nod.

At the nurse's office, Riddle is in the waiting area hunched over and crying. Through the glass window I can see into Nurse Mitchell's office. We call her Nurse Ratched 'cause it's just perfect casting. The nurse is on the phone, wide eyed and pursed lips. Like Nellie Oleson, her shiny pride smeared all over her face. Riddle grabs my hand and rattles off numbers. "8-6-7... Go to my locker, get my backpack. The combination is 8-6-7-5-3-0-9... wait, no that's a song." She's right, it is a song, and in the back of my mind it begins to play. *Jenny, I got your number, I need to make you mine. Jenny, don't change your number, 8-6-7-5-3-0-9.* "It's 8-6-7." I try and widen my eyes to stay present and focus on helping her. She shakes her head, stops and looks at me like it's for the first time. "Maureen, you gotta go to my locker and get my bag. 86-77...oh wait!" She closes her eyes and her hand moves as if she is actually working her lock. "86-77-05!"

"Okay," I say. "86-77-05," I repeat, all while remembering how very horrible I am at opening lockers. I am so bad at combinations and locks that I don't even bother to lock my own locker.

"Go to my locker and get my bag," she pleads again. Nurse Ratched saunters into the waiting room.

"What are you doing here?" she asks me. Before I can answer, she adds, "You can't help her. Go back to class." Her eyes are beady and cold, and I catch a chill from the tone of her voice. I suddenly feel ill in this place of health.

I look to Riddle to tell her I will do my best. But somehow I can tell that my words in her ears will be as useless as her numbers in my hands. I make my way down the hall that leads to the stairs that will take me to the senior locker area.

The Cat's voice echoes up the stairway. We call Sister Cathleen "the Cat" because of the way she can sneak up on you and attack. I learned this nickname from Riddle on one of our morning walks to the train.

"Open it!" she orders. My heart sinks as I realize they've gotten there before me. I lean against the wall and peer down the stairway at Riddle's locker-mate Maryann who is so pretty even as she fumbles with the lock. She steps back and shrugs.

"Maybe she changed the combination," she whispers. On cue Nurse Ratched shows up with Riddle by the arm, still crying and confused. It's like watching a terrible soap opera where I know all the actors.

"Open the locker," the Cat instructs Riddle. Riddle cries and shakes her head. I feel my heart beating against my chest.

"I can't... I don't remember... I can't," she mumbles.

"Open it!" the principal yells again, this time loud enough to make me gasp. I see their heads turn up toward me and I scoot back against the wall. "What's the matter with you?" I hear the Cat ask... "What's the matter with you?" I blink my eyes open to see my sisters staring back at me from the foot of the bed.

"What's the matter with you, Maureen?"

7

More Morning

"WHAT'S THE MATTER WITH YOU?" THEY ASK AGAIN AND continue to stare down at me as I bite my lip. Sometimes when I eat, I hum; and sometimes when I hear music, I sing; and sometimes when I daydream, I fall so deep that I begin to talk to myself or laugh or gasp. It's embarrassing. I shake my head and slip beneath the covers and say nothing till they turn back around.

Annie enters the bedroom with a flurry of energy. It has been a while since I have seen her so revved, as though she has been raised from the dead. She heads straight to the window, and we watch with wonder to see what she is up to. She pulls up the shade and turns to us with an extended hand, like a show host on *The Price is Right*. "It's snowing!" she says and smiles back at us. "It's snowing!" Out the window, thick flakes flutter past our windowpane. Bridget, Riddle, and I sit up to watch them float by, and I wonder if the Giant is still out there.

"It's a sign," she says as she beams back at us. One of our aunts had asked to see snow, as a sign that our mother will be okay. And there it is…snow…in May! It's a sign all right.

"Blossom of snow, may you bloom and grow. Bloom and grow forever."

For a second I am standing by the kitchen door watching the Giant sing as he fries up Taylor ham on the grill, and a sudden wave of hope flutters over me. I feel it land like cool little snowflakes all over my skin. "It's snowing. It's a sign," I repeat back at her. But then I sit back deep into the pillows because I am not so sure that I believe in signs. Even if they are rare and wonderful, like snow in May.

Annie presses her hand to the window. "It's a good thing the prom is not outdoors today." Her breath leaves a cloud on the glass, and Riddle folds in on herself and begins to cry all over again, and the hopeful feeling of snow on my skins melts away.

"But it's a good thing, Riddle. It's snowing," Annie says again, this time with less joy and more concern. She stands beside Riddle, just as I had seen her do a few weeks earlier, when Riddle had to tell the Giant about getting caught with weed in school. Annie is a steady Eddie, a solid choice for all things scary, because she is the bravest of them all, fearless in fact. If I ever had to face up to the Giant, I know Annie would be my first choice as a co-pilot, too.

"Hey Riddle, snow is a good sign," she says again, this time with more of a plea. She reaches her game show hand out to pet Riddle's back. As much as Riddle cares about boys and navigating forbidden doors, Annie cares about getting good grades, telling the truth, and making things right. I watched her unravel the weed situation without a drop of sweat or furrowed brow. Her hand moves over Riddle's back, and I am back there two weeks ago. They sat just like this on the edge of my bed as Riddle unraveled the story for us…

"I somehow accidentally took a Quaalude at school," she confesses. Annie stays unflappable. I feel my face pinch up as I try to figure out how you can "somehow accidentally" take a Quaalude.

Annie leans forward. "Okay, what exactly happened?" she asks.

"I don't know! They caught me with a dime of weed in my locker. I am suspended," Riddle confesses. My eyes grow big on their own and I mouth the word "wow" without meaning to.

"A dime bag, jeez!" I say shaking my head. I am not actually sure what this means, except that a "dime bag" is obviously bigger than a "penny" or a "nickel bag" and yet not as big as a "dollar bag." But I really don't know anything about drugs and their measurements, and besides, I am pretty sure that when it comes to being caught with drugs in school, the exact amount is not all that important.

"The Cat wants me to tell Mom and Dad, but I told her that Mom is too sick to tell, and that I didn't want to upset her." We nod our heads at her in silence. That was a good move in a sea of bad choices. And then we all just stare at the floor to think and I can tell we are all thinking the same thing. "Mom is too sick to tell." The words are true, but still so hard to hear, so hard to admit. And there is a part of me that wishes that Riddle didn't say them at all, I don't want the confession to jinx her. I get nervous that saying the words out loud will make them come true.

"Well, what did the Cat say to that?" Annie asks, staying on task.

"She said 'fine,' but I still have to tell Dad, and she wants him to call her after I do," replies Riddle.

"Geez," I say again and start to feel like a Richie Cunningham. "What are you going to say?" Her face goes hard and I watch her wheels turn. "Maybe you should practice," I suggest. Her eyes begin to water, but she shakes it off and takes a breath. She looks up at us, her eyes big and innocent.

"Dad, I was holding some weed for a friend, and they found it in my locker at school," Riddle says.

Annie jumps in. "Don't say, 'weed'. Say, like, 'marijuana'."

"Yeah, and mispronounce it or something," I add trying to be helpful.

Riddle turns to Annie, "Will you come with me?" Without hesitation, Annie stands. I watch them walk to the door, and as often as I have begged them to take me places, this time I am happy not to be invited. They slip out of the room, tap on the Giant's bedroom door and call softly.

"Dad?"

"What?" he answers, tired and impatient.

"I have to talk with you," Riddle says, as I bury my head in a pillow.

I try not to listen by staring at the creepy painting of the clown on our bedroom wall.

He has a long face and sad eyes. *Sad eyes, turn the other way, I don't want to see you cry.* The songs starts playing in my head, but I can't remember the words so I make up my own to distract myself. *Sad eyes, turn the other way, I think my sister Riddle is going to die.* I wish I could remember the words 'cause my song just makes me feel worse.

Before long, Annie and Riddle are back in the bedroom beside me, both a little paler than before. It's odd to see them so still. They look like they just escaped setting off a bomb, but that any second, it still might blow.

"He took it pretty well," Annie offers, and Riddle just shakes her head. I am glad Riddle asked Annie and not me. Annie is the one you want when going to battle.

Back in our room on prom day…or rather no prom day, I watch Annie continue to pat Riddle on the back as she looks around at us for answers. I pull my knees to my chest to sit up and watch the snow.

"She's not going to the prom," Bridget offers up again so that Riddle doesn't have to.

"Oh," Annie says and tilts her head to try to make eye contact with Riddle. She waits and lets the silence have its way. I think Annie might say something about the prom, that she might come up with a thoughtful solution. If anyone would know the right words to say, it would be Annie. But she is silent, saying nothing. She just sits there with Riddle, watching the snow and letting her cry, and my stomach gets heavy and sad when I realize there are no words to say. Out the window the snow falls, drifting and swirling, and I go too. I am out the window, in the snow as it flutters all around, and I stick out my tongue to take the heavenly treat…

"In the meadow, we can build a snowman, and pretend that he's a circus clown. We'll have lots of fun with mister snowman,

until the other kids knock him down..."

We're on the front lawn surrounded by the snow, like a winter wonderland. Bundled up and ready to play. Bridget is packing snowballs and leading us in song. It's not a holiday tune, but a love ballad that we all know the words to.

"Like walking in the rain and snow when there's nowhere to go and you're feeling like a part of you is dying and you're looking for the answer in her eyes. You think you're gonna break up. Then she says she wants to make up. Ooh, you made me love you."
We sing at the top of our lungs, only taking breaks to nibble the ice balls off our frozen mittens.

The snow has been falling for days. We have mounds of it. It meets us at the front door; a huge drift has swallowed our whole front stoop. We stand on the highest step of our front porch and leap into the cool white drifts. Annie rolls around like a dog; when she stands, she looks like a human snowball. "Snow monster," Bridget yells, and with two words, a game is invented.

The sidewalks have been cleared, leaving all the extra snow on our lawn in big piles lining our property. If someone were to hide in these piles, they could jump out at the exact right moment and scare the pants off whoever would be coming down our street. This is how you play snow monster.

William is the smallest. With the enthusiasm of a leprechaun, he climbs into one pile, and we bury him up good to hide him away.

"Wait till we give you the sign," Annie tells him, "then jump out and scream like mad." We do a few practice runs just for fun. He gets louder and faster each time until we're ready to try it out on a victim. Once more we bury him, leaving a little hole for air. When I peek inside to check on him, I can see his little smile grinning back at me. His cheeks are bright and rosy from the chill and the thrill. His eyes sparkle as he waits with excitement to make his entrance. I smile back at him. "Good job, William!" He smiles back at me like a happy little snow monster.

The first to come down the block is a young hippy couple. They stroll hand in hand. At our walkway, Annie calls for William and he jumps out with such force that the hippie guy jumps back and the hippie girl screams. Her hands fly to her hat as she twirls in delight. It's like Candid Camera, but without the camera part. "We got you!" we all scream and laugh, "We got you!" They brush themselves off and nod in agreement.

"Oh man, you sure did!" they say while shaking their heads and clapping their hands. We howl like hoodlums and can't wait to do it again.

Next comes an older man who wears a Sherlock Holmes hat and a plaid scarf, his hot breath puffing out little clouds as he makes his way toward us. "William!" We call in unison. With the timing of a deranged cuckoo bird, William pops out with a roar, and the man falls backwards into the snow. There is even more laughing and cheering, but the man just lays still. We go silent as we watch him searching for his hat and struggling to get up. His exposed head is small and bald, and his face is not happy. He beats his jacket and pants as he gets to his feet.

"That would be very funny except to someone who just had a heart bypass!" he screams suddenly and clutches his gloved hands to his heart.

Like frozen snow children, we watch him make his way up our front walk, ring the bell, and then bang the door. Our mother appears in her housedress. Owen wants to see who is at the door, too, so she lifts him to her hip. Owen is six and too old to be lifted, but he is the baby, and so we all baby him. The reflection of the snow brightens their faces. Like the Madonna and child, she looks so young and little as the angry man leans in on her.

"Do you know what your kids are doing? Do you know your son there almost killed me? I just had heart surgery; do you want a dead man on your front lawn?" He doesn't give her time to answer any of his questions before he storms back down the steps followed by a thick trail of hot breath. His anger stays with us all day. My mother and her cold pot of tea sit at the end of the table. She stares at her crossword puzzle and never lifts her pencil. She just sits in shame and silence, shaking her head trying to figure out where she went wrong.

"What am I going to do with you?" she asks in desperation.

"Throw us in the garbage," I suggest. Because it seems like the perfect answer to the question, especially the way she asks it. If something is bad, you throw it in the garbage like rotten fruit. But my answer only makes her more upset.

"I am not going to throw anyone in the garbage," she barks at me. I stop trying to answer her questions and just stare back at her with the rest of my siblings, our faces red and sweaty with guilt.

For the rest of the day, we try to stay out of her hair. I decide to build snowmen, one for each member of my family. I use up all the top snow on our lawn. But I still have one last snowperson to make so I roll a small ball over to the Garofalo's lawn to use some of their snow. A sharp voice snaps out at me. "Put it back, Maureen!" At first I think it's Mr. Garofalo, who is even scarier than the Giant. He is chief of the fire department, and before that I am pretty sure he must have been a pirate of some sort. He has one twitchy eye and walks with a limp. When he's not spitting up brown jam, he's drinking beer and smoking. And when he isn't drinking and smoking, he's cursing at his family.

"Ant'ny, get your goddamn ass inside and clean up that dog shit." Or "Vinny, you son of a bitch, where the hell is the goddamn ketchup?"

All I see is the snow covered bush that lies between me and a cloud of cigarette smoke and a rough voice.

"Put it back, Maureen, that's our goddamn snow." It's Vinny Garofalo, Anthony's oldest brother. He has come outside to smoke on their stoop. I freeze from embarrassment and try to figure out how he is able to see me. Mrs. Garofalo's voice comes to my rescue, fighting through a coughing fit as she growls out the door at him.

"Let her have the goddamn snow, Vinny, it's not like you're the one who's been shoveling." With that I back away slowly leaving half of my unfinished snow person right there on their lawn.

Uncle Harry pulls up from work with the Giant, and I scurry inside. The Giant's legs are long, so he enters close behind me. Mom is rattling on to him as she moves around the dining room, juggling dishes and silverware and frustration. She sets them down on the tables and begins to lay them out. The main course is how William almost killed a man.

The Giant's neck is red, and he rubs it as he points a finger at William.

"You, up to my bedroom. Five whacks with the belt." William stands motionless. "Now!" the Giant growls. William turns and begins the long climb up the stair, silently keeping his eyes on his feet. My sisters and I are not invited to join him, but we follow anyhow and file into the bedroom, like morbid onlookers at a town hanging.

The bed is made neatly with a white bedspread. Above it hangs a wooden cross with a little Jesus. I don't even think to pray to him, he seems too helpless hanging there with enough problems of his own. The furniture in my parents bedroom is all so big, a big bed, a big dresser with a big mirror for her, and a big dresser with no mirror for him. There is an order to this room that has not made its way to the rest of the house, or maybe it's the chaos in the rest of the house that has not penetrated these walls. No clothes on the floor, no melted crayons on the radiator, and no drawings on the walls. The wood furniture is the same color as the pews at church, and the room smells like wood polish and hair spray.

William steps into the room. The back of his head is shaved up in a crew cut like the Giant's, but William's head looks so small above his little shoulders. As much as I try to fight it, my chin beings to wrinkle and my eyes begin to fill with warm tears. I think about him sitting in the snow mound smiling out at me. We put him up to it. I know it is not his fault. A shoulder shakes beside me. I hear the sniffs and sighs of my sisters. We lean against the wall in my parent's room and try not to cry.

The Giant's work boots climb the stairs. My stomach flip-flops, and our crying grows to the point that we can almost drown out his footsteps, but it does not prevent him from coming. He moves into the room as his shadow falls on us. I squeeze into the pack.

"What are you crying about?" he asks us. We wipe our eyes and answer with more sorrow and sobs. He shakes his head and moves to the bed as he reaches for his buckle and begins to remove the belt from the loopholes of his work pants.

"Take your pants down and get on the bed," he tells William. The bed creaks and the crying grows louder.

"What is the matter with you?" he barks back at us. There is a movement beside me as Annie steps away from the group and toward him. Her hair pokes out in all directions. She still wears the jeans that she rolled in the snow, the seams and ankles still dark with dampness. She stands at attention staring up at him.

"I don't want you to hit William," she announces. The Giant stares down at her, William lies like a dead boy, and the room goes silent.

"Are you willing to take his punishment?" he asks. I shake my head "no" for her as she nods "yes."

"I will hit you just as hard, and just as many times," he warns, staring down at her. William turns his head to look at her. His face tucked against the mattress. Without hesitation she nods again. The Giant takes her in. "Five whacks with the belt," he reminds her. "You're gonna get five whacks with the belt." I want to pull her back into the group, but my arms don't move and again she is nodding.

"Yes, sir," she confirms. The Giant stands holding his belt like a statue; the room is still, not a breath. William's tears drip off his face onto the bedspread.

"Get up," the Giant mutters without taking his eyes off her. William follows the order, and I close my eyes to pray or flee, I am not sure which I am actually doing. Maybe both. The crack of the belt against her skin makes me jump.

There is a moan in the mattress, and the salty tears and snot drip into my mouth. I open my eyes to be with her, but keep my blurry gaze on the well-worn hardwood floor beneath my feet. I want to run to safety, but I am not really sure where that place would be. So I stay and count out the cracks of the belt. Two, three, four, then silence. I wait for the next but it never comes.

"That's it," I hear him say, but it's so soft and strange that no one moves. "Go on," he repeats. The bed creaks again and we follow her out the door in single file. In the hallway, I look back. His head is hung as he fumbles with his pants and begins to re-loop his belt. Keys rattle in his pocket, and his buckle clicks against itself, as he stands all alone in his room.

Downstairs, dinner is served. She sits across from me, only two years older, but I know I will never measure up. Her head is bowed as she moves her fork around her plate. Her slanted cat-shaped eyes glance up at me and then return to her dish. I am not hungry, and even the smell of the food makes me feel sick, so I try not to think about it, as I watch her chase the peas around her dish and lift them to her mouth. At the other end of the table, the Giant sits with his jug of red wine. He lifts his glass and drains the drink. The table is unusually silent 'till Owen sings out, *"Knick-knack paddy whack, give the dog a bone!"* My sisters giggle and pat him like a dog. He is so sweet and little and he hardly ever speaks, so when he does we always celebrate.

"Good boy, Owen, good boy," my sisters coo.

But I am still stuck on Annie, the wild haired girl who sits on the other side of the salt shaker. In the middle of the laughter and chewing and drinking and sweating, we sit.

I can't make sense of it. I am baffled. I can't imagine laying myself down to save my brother. Her deed was more than just kind, it was courageous. More courageous than I will ever be. And although she is the one who will carry the marks, I am the one who has been struck still.

8

Still More Morning

IN OUR BEDROOM, I LOOK AROUND TO FIND ANNIE CURLED up at the edge of our bed sleeping like a cat. Her wild hair circles her face like a fiery crown. Riddle is still staring out the window and plotting her exit, and Bridget is tucked under the covers with a well-worn copy of *Gone With The Wind*. From the clock radio, Olivia Newton-John is singing about believing in magic. *"You have to believe we are magic. Nothin' can stand in our way. You have to believe we are magic. Don't let your aim ever stray."* She sounds like an angel floating just above our heads. *"You won't make a mistake; I'll be guiding you."*

I think about Olivia Newton-John guiding me like that angel, and it makes me want to get up. I swing my feet to the floor, and I stare down at the wavy pattern in the cold wood-grain floor. I feel like there is a secret message in the wood for me, but I can't figure it out. "What are you doing?" Bridget asks.

"I'm thinking," I reply, standing and crossing to the corner of the room.

"Thinking about what?" she asks.

"Nothing," I mumble as I grab my uniform from the chair where I left it the day before.

"Now what are you doing?" she asks.

"What does it look like?" I answer.

"Where are you going?"

"No place," I lie as I pull on my skirt.

She bends her well-worn book towards her face. She has read this book three times. "You know you don't have to go to school."

I nod. I know. These days everyone stays home from school. Bridget transferred to a nearby college to help take care of the two boys and me. Riddle is suspended from school because of the weed. Annie's been home for a week mostly sleeping. Marian took a break from nursing school to help care for Mom and Julia got called home from college a few days ago…

Julia picked Longwood College in Farmville, Virginia for three reasons, and she taps a finger on her left hand for each one to show us how simple it is. Her thick red hair cascades over her left eye. Her skin is clear and fair, and she looks like the little doll that Aunt Caroline brought home from one of her trips. Julia ticks away reasons for her college choice on her pale little fingers.

"One: Is it far enough away from this hellhole? Two: Can I afford it? And three: Will they do my laundry?" She packs up her bags along with the clippings from the Vogue magazine. Pictures ripped and taped to her wall that will serve as her "new image" for her college adventure. The models are all long and lean with straight blond hair. Peasant skirts, ruffled blouses, riding boots, and velvet blazers. There is one where the model leans back against a convertible and looks off in the distance. Her skin is a glow of pink and gold, her hair a river of blonde. The model looks inches from dead in a pale, wispy, shallow way. It's a wonderful image, but I am not too sure it's within Julia's reach. Julia is more of a pin-up girl, curvy and strong and vital. There is nothing laid back or wispy about her.

For the last few years, she has been going through a "rough patch" as mom put it. "It's just her way of dealing with things," Mom says. Her way of dealing with things is beating the hell out of the rest of us for any little thing, and telling Mom that she doesn't even care if she does die. So, needless to say, I am not too sad to see her go, but I am honestly surprised by how happy she is to leave us. She has a plan and a new image, and she is ready to take her show on the road. As she loads her life into the car and takes off, I imagine her fighting the urge to flip us all off on her way out of town. My mother watches her leave, waving from the front stoop, till her car is long gone.

It's almost a year when she returns from Longwood College. The scraps of magazine inspirations did not take hold, and she shows up pretty much the same way she left, except now she has a traveling companion—a short, fat girl named Trinket, who sports a mohawk and black combat boots. I stand on our stoop waving my homemade "Welcome home" sign as they move past me into the house. Instead of the ruffled blouses and peasant skirt, Julia is sporting an ensemble best described as angry.

"Welcome home! Welcome home! Welcome home, Julia!" I chant, doing my best to reenact all the TV reunions I've ever seen. She looks past me and goes to say hello to Mom. Trinket with the mohawk hangs back with me in the front hall. We stare at each other, and I think she might bite me. She peeks her head into the living room but then she pulls back.

"Is that your mom?" she asks. Trinket has a pug nose, and the thick black liner beneath her eyes makes her look dangerous. But there is a softness to her huge yellow eyes. It's buried deep, but the longer she waits on my answer, the softer they get. I don't answer right away, because I am not sure if it is a trick question. Is the lady lying in our living room our mom? Who else would it be? Do people keep random women in hospital beds in their living rooms? I peek into the room to check too. Julia is standing by the bed, and Mom is smiling. I turn back to Trinket.

"Yeah, that's my mom," I confirm.

In a few minutes, Julia returns. She looks more fired up than usual, and I hold up my sign to try and distract her. "Hey Julia, welcome home!" She grabs the sign and moves out the door. "Hey!" I scream and follow after her. On the steps, she rips the cardboard in two and then four and then again, and when she can't rip it anymore, she throws it to the ground.

"I am in shock," she screams. "Can't you see that? When I left she was walking around and now she can't even get the fuck out of bed." I am not sure what to do or say. My artwork lies on the floor, and her curse word hangs in the air. I feel my face grow warm, and I try not to cry. Trinket is staring at me, so I just gather my artwork and try to act casual. Julia turns to her, "Come on. Let's go."

I hate her for not playing along, and I hate myself for forgetting that on TV the warm homecomings never include a dying mother in the living room. A car pulls down the street; a song blasts from the radio leaving a trailing of questions. *"Are you ready? Hey, are you ready for this? Are you hanging on the edge of your seat? Out of the doorway the bullets rip to the sound of the beat...Another one bites the dust...Another one bites the dust."*

9

Getting Ready for School

"YOU DON'T HAVE TO GO TO SCHOOL," BRIDGET REPEATS. "Everyone is staying home today," she offers as she sits up and turns up the radio. *"Hey, Mr. Tambourine man, play a song for me."* I continue to get dressed. I am going to school, what else is there for me to do?

"I'm not sleepy and there is no place that I'm going to." I button my dingy white school shirt. *"Hey, Mr. Tambourine man, play a song for me, in the jingle jangle morning..."* The song runs through my head, followed by a parade of tie-dyed dancers with bangle bracelets and tambourines and rattles made from dried up gourds. Rattles made from dried up gourds. I am in the Connor's backyard with my little friend Jenny swinging to the music...

"It's party-time for Satan down at that Connor house, a real circus of hippies is what they have there," my mother's voice drifts in. According to her, Satan is holding parties all over town, and the hippies and long hairs are the worst offenders. It's pretty easy to see why. Jenny's mother doesn't wear a bra, and her dad has a ponytail like a girl. They wear braids in their hair, colorful tee shirts and puka shell necklaces. I watch with Jenny as they gather in Jenny's backyard, playing music and dancing. *"Hey, Mr. Tambourine man, play a song for me, I'm not sleepy and there is no place I'm going to."* Jenny and I sit on her swing set and watch the show. It's the best show ever! They dress in flowing dresses and share cigarettes that they pass around the circle. They sing songs and dance, and sometimes they even include us in their show. They'll roam over to the swing set.

"Hey little kid, you want a push?" They swing us so high in the air that they can run underneath us and smile at us as we drop back to earth. My heart goes to my throat as we scream, "Stop!" But if they do stop, we always beg for more.

When I leave, they pat me on the head. "See ya later little kid," they say, like they would like to see me later, even though they don't even know my name. They have christened me "Little kid," so I matter. I love sitting and watching them even more than I like sitting on the lawn of the Elks on Saturday afternoons and watching the brides tumble out of the church. Brides are beautiful, but I am pretty sure that when I grow up I want to be a hippie, cause hippies are pretty and cool, and if you are a hippie, it doesn't seem like you have to grow up at all. Just hang out and enjoy the music, nobody asking what you're doing or where you're going. Because when you're a hippie, "the best place to be is where you're at, man."

They dance and sing and hug each other hello and goodbye,

and it's hard to imagine that this is Satan's idea of a party when everyone is so nice to each other...

I pull on my socks, and Bridget turns a page. She has read this book at least five times, and she reads it like she could read it five hundred more. I slip out of the room and make my way downstairs.

In the living room, Mom is asleep in the hospital bed and plugged into a morphine drip. This I had expected. The thing that takes me back is my sister Marian, curled up in bed with her, like John Lennon and Yoko Ono. My sister is wrapped around my mother's body, which just lies there straight as a board, light as a feather. It is hard to look at them and hard to look away. Marian has the monopoly on my mother. They have a special bond that can't be infiltrated. I have watched them for years in their intimate tête-à-têtes. As I stand at the bottom of the stairs, staring at my sister in bed with my mother, my mind goes off, and I am suddenly standing in the dining room trying to figure out how to get her attention...

She sits at the other end of the table; she licks a finger and flips the page. I watch her slowly licking her way through a book. The two boys are in the living room watching the boob tube. Here in the dining room, it's just the two of us. It's quiet. I can hear the Brady Bunch theme song drift in... *"Here's a story of a lovely lady who was bringing up three very lovely girls."* The two boys sing along as I try and imagine my mother as Carol Brady and me as Marcia or Cindy. I try to think of things to say that will pull her from her book. Something to get her to notice me. "Hi Mom, I'm home," I practice saying in my head. But from there, I can't figure out where to go; it seems too hard. I clear my throat and get ready for my cue. I wait for her to look up and put down her book. That's what Carol would do. I wait. They never show this much silence on TV. It's quiet; I can hear her throat gurgle as she swallows her tea.

Maybe I should start. Maybe I should just blurt out, "Hi Mom, I'm home." But the thing is, I didn't actually go anywhere so it might not make sense, and she might look at me like I am crazy. There is a sound at the door and I turn to see who it is. Like a stunning explosive firework, she calls our attention with no need to beg or barter for it. She claims it only because she is completely entitled.

"Hey Mom, I'm home," Marian's voice crashes in on us from the front hall. "We're learning about breast examinations," she says as she tosses her jacket on the chair. This is my mother's favorite part of the day, when Marian comes home and tells us about nursing school. My mother takes her in like she's some kind of medical genius. Marian puts her book on the table as I shake my head and fold my cards. *"You got to know when to hold 'em, know when to fold 'em. Know when to walk away, know when to run."* She has taken my opening line, stolen my part and followed it up with "breast examinations." I would have never come up with that. Marian goes on talking about lumps and bumps and poking and prodding. Mom has her fingers to her lips, and she is taking it all in like a dry sponge. Her eyes are narrow, her face a little pale and something has her thinking. She starts to ask something.

"Marian, I have this thing…I think I might…" She turns to me as if she sees me for the first time. "Maureen, go upstairs,

I need to talk to your sister." It is a mild decapitation, and I blame Marian, "the mom hog."

I know Marian is the reason Mom found the lump. It was the size of a golf ball, so it's not like it was a major mystery. Marian walks my mom through the whole thing, she goes to the doctor appointments with her, she reads the prescriptions and explains the diagnoses. She is like having a personal interpreter for this new language that mom has to learn called Cancer. Marian is her girl.

I want to be mom's girl, but even now, as I watch Marian's body wrapped tightly around my mother's in the small hospital bed, I can't even begin to see where I might fit in…

Every day, I watch my mother's face light up at the sound of her savior's voice. Marian is the rooster, who is credited for waking the sun. I want her beheaded, plucked and roasted for dinner. Mom closes her book on the table. I don't even think she saves her page. She cranes her head and calls out.

"Marian?" My mother's voice is filled with such hopeful expectation that I catch my breath. And Marian does not disappoint. She swirls into the room with a pile of thick dog-eared books and thicker pile of wild black hair. Her face is blushed and vibrant, her eyes, how they twinkle. She smells of Ivory soap and grass. She is so vital that there is no room for argument; she will save us all for sure. Not just from death, but from the black-and-white world of home life. She brings stories and color and music, sometimes even bits of sweets or leftover dessert that she has saved for my mother. If my mother loves Marian more than the rest of us, it really makes complete sense. She is big and magnificent in so many ways, and I am small and disappointing. I fade into the wallpaper as my mother begins her inquisition. It's never about her own Cancer that she wants to know, always about other people's diseases. She loves to quiz my sister with symptoms of neighbors and friends to see what she comes up with.

"Rhonda Byrnes has had vomiting and stomach cramps for twenty-four hours straight. What do you think?" She asks, while holding her chin.

"Most likely food poisoning," Marian replies.

"Food poisoning? Really? Well, I'll have to let her know." My mother seems so happy to know she is not the only sick one. "That boy, Bob, came by looking for your sister this afternoon. Had one of those sores on his lip. What would that be?"

"A sore on the lip? Well, I would have to diagnose that as herpes. Medically known as Herpes simplex virus 1."

"Herpes," Mom repeats as she bobs her baby-bald head. In the heat of the day she has taken off her wig.

"It's not too serious, but it could spread. It's pretty contagious and it can be painful," Marian continues.

"Herpes," my mother repeats again, this time shaking her head and sucking on her teeth. "I'll bet his upper lip rots right off his face."

Bob is dating my green-eyed sister, Bridget. Mom does not like Bob because he is Jewish, and Jewish people don't believe in Jesus. Mom loves Jesus. But I love Bob. He makes my heart pound. Bridget and Bob are both so beautiful. Watching them kiss and hold hands is like watching a never-ending Pearl Drops commercial. On Saturdays, Bridget tells my mom that she is going to take me to the park to help me with math. I am in sixth grade, and math is not one of my best subjects. The thing is that we never go to the park. We go through the park, and then we continue on up the big hill, where all the big houses are. I watch her blonde hair get swept up in the wind as she ushers me away on these adventures to Jewstead. The place is called Newstead. But everyone in my neighborhood calls it Jewstead 'cause that's where all the Jewish people live. We go to Bob's house, and Bridget and Bob go to "study" in Bob's room and I get to play Pong and eat all the candy I want in their family room. I am not sure why it's called the family room. No one from Bob's family is ever there. I think they should call it heaven. If it weren't for the Jesus thing, it probably would be heaven. I love Jewstead. I can't tell anyone; it's a secret. Bridget tells me lots of secrets, and I am good at keeping them. My days of being a tattle tail are over, no more Brenda Starr for me. Brenda Starr is the nickname my sisters gave me for my bad reporting. I have been doing my best to live it down.

Mom and Marian are now sharing a knowing look and bobbing their heads together. They seem to have reached an agreement that, "Yes, it would definitely be for the best if Bob's lips were to rot from his face." This whole idea seems horrible to me and I want to save Bob from their terrible curse.

"Hey Mom," the words explode from my mouth and hang there in mid-air, grotesque and unsupported.

"What?" she asks, rationing out her words like a miser. She has been put upon and I am her baggage. Cancer has made her impatient and tired.

My mind is reeling with possible ways of keeping her attention, but time is of the essence, and I need to return the serve or she will move on.

"What...what's herpes?" I finally manage. She looks over her glasses at me. I am crumbs on the bed sheet. She shakes her head disapprovingly before wiping me away and turning to my sister.

"Should we tell her?" she asks Marian.

Now they're both looking at me like they're weighing onions at the Shop-Rite. What's so big about herpes that they don't think I can handle? Not that I really care, I don't. I just want to be included in the conversation.

I sit up in my seat and try to look worthy. They are deciding if I will be invited in. Mom doesn't talk to Marian the way that she talks to me. And with Marian she listens. I want that. I hold my breath and wait.

"It's a social disease," she snaps at me like I'm a bad dog on the good couch. It's all so abrupt. I don't get it. Carol Brady would have said, "Well honey, it's a social disease." Carol Brady would have explained what the heck that means.

Now, my mother is glaring at me with a look that carries a warning.

"It's what happens when you're too social," she gives one last bob of her head, and I am dismissed for good.

Too social? Oh my God, I wonder if I have a social disease.

"Miss Muldoon, this is not social hour," my teachers remind me. "Little Miss social butterfly," they say. And suddenly I am realizing that I may have a social disease.

I examine my lips every day in the mirror, waiting for signs that they will rot off my face. I've found an old tube of ChapStick at the bottom of Mom's purse. I pray that the ChapStick will keep my social disease from disfiguring my face. I like my face. I could stand in front of the mirror for hours just looking at me. I especially like my hair. It's long. I've never had long hair before because Mom always cuts all our hair short so that we won't get lice. All the other girls in the neighborhood tease us and call us the Muldoon boys. But now it's long. Mom being sick has made it hard for her to keep up with the haircuts. My hair is feathered like Farrah Fawcett. I take my comb out of my back pocket to flip it a few more times, just for fun. My comb turns into a microphone and I'm singing.

"See that girl, watch that scene, dig in the dancing Queen." It's the "ME" show, and I enjoy every episode. Out of the corner of my eye I see my Mom. She is coming. My singing is so good, she has to come and see for herself. I smile at her without missing a note to let her know that I see her. She is staring at me, and I close my eyes to belt out the high notes.

"Feel the beat from the tambourine oh yeah!"

I open my eyes to a stranger. I don't recognize the girl in the mirror. With two quick and badly aimed swipes, my mother has lopped off the entire front of my hair. Both wings. I am wiping all the loose hair from my face; it's in my eyes and mouth. I no longer have bangs, the whole top and front of my head is just very short bristle that pokes straight up like a very bad mullet. A haircut you would have if you had gotten lots of gum stuck in your hair, and had no other choice.

"Your hair was in your eyes," she explains as she returns the scissors to her housecoat pocket and goes to dispose of my beautiful Farrah hair that she has clutched in two handfuls.

William comes through the door and slows down like you do for a car crash.

"Holy shit, helmet head, what happened to you?" I shake my head 'cause I don't know, and when I see the ugly girl in the mirror, I get no answers either. She looks even more confused than me. I almost feel sorry for her. But I can't keep looking, 'cause that hair keeps screaming at me the same question that William has asked. The same question comes from my sisters' eyes. And I know all the kids at school will be asking, "Hey helmet head, what happened to you? Who did that to you? What did you do?" I am confused by all the questions, 'cause I know stuff like this never happens on the Brady Bunch, or the Walton's, or anywhere. The questions run around my brain and beat me into a ball. It seems like my whole life is just a series of questions that I don't know how to answer.

I stare at my sister's body curled around my mother's, and a knot tightens in my gut. I stare like I am looking at a window display, looking in at something that is out of my reach, something that I will never afford.

I study my mother sleeping, and I imagine her waking up and turning to me with arms extended. "Come here, Maureen," she calls, and I go and curl up in her lap. Even now after getting burnt, I can't help but long for the warmth of the oven.

"See that girl, watch that scene. Dig in the dancing queen."

10

Down Stairs

"WHAT ARE YOU DOING? YOU'RE NOT GOING TO SCHOOL, are you?" I scan our living room to try to see where the question is coming from. The room is crammed with cots filled with sleeping relatives. The Giant is in one. He snores the loudest. Passed out from his early morning shoveling, the melted snow from his work boots has left a little puddle on the floor. The rest of the cots are filled with the aunts and a few cousins. It is like an orphanage for grownups.

Above our fireplace mantel is a picture of a lady in a yellow dress reading a book. She is lit by two fake candles that Aunt Caroline calls candelabras. They hang on either side of the pretty lady reading.

At the end of the room there is a bench between two bookcases filled with books: *Moby Dick, Swiss Family Robinson, The Jungle Book.* When we were little, Mom would read them aloud, making up different voices. Mowgli sounds young and curious; Akela, the mother wolf, is soft and kind; and Ahab, who lost his leg to Moby Dick, sounds angry and gruff. Next to those books are the encyclopedias that my mother bought from a man at the door. In the one marked D there are a few pages missing. The pages about dolls, cutout dolls to be exact. I took a pair of scissors to them one rainy day. When Mom found me, she went through the roof. "This is a book!" she screamed and slapped my face. "You don't cut into a book!" she barked in her best Moby Dick voice. But that time I knew she was not playing a part. The encyclopedias now sit high above the rest, away from curious children with scissors.

Above the bookcases and the encyclopedias are two more fake candles, and this is what lights our living room. Out the windows in the front of the room, it is still a bit dark, and the snow is still falling. There is a glow every few seconds of the stoplight on our corner that blinks red and yellow and green. In the early light, the colorful blinking lights are less like Christmas lights and more like an ambulance with no sound.

But I don't want to think of silent ambulances, so I sit on the bottom step and begin to pull on my shoes as I think about Christmas lights.

"Don't put your finger in the socket. Don't put your finger, don't put your finger in the socket the socket. Don't put your finger in the socket." I am five years old as I watch the Giant wrestling with electric cords. I stare into the little black circle that the Giant calls a socket. "Don't put your finger in the socket." He warns me. He sits back on his heels with a pile of tangled glass bulbs and electric cords. He is twisting little bulbs in and out of the sockets. Some light up, and some stay quiet. He has a small pile of dead soldiers, "Toss the dead soldiers in the garbage, Maureen," he orders. I come close to gather the little baby bulbs--like fragile little eggs--I scoop them gently into my palms.

"Don't put your finger in the socket," he warns, and I nod up at him, even though I am not sure what a socket is. Could it be that empty light bulb holder that looks like the perfect place to poke a finger? I place the dead soldiers back on the floor and slowly slip a small finger into the little cap. Suddenly, I am up on my toes shaking like a cat in the tub. Annie rushes by, swats my finger away, does a high jump that turns into a cart wheel, ends in a round off and moves on like a crazed super hero. I'm frazzled but free. I desert the dead soldiers as I climb onto the couch and lay down, trying to shake my brush with death. From a safe distance, I take in the scene.

They open boxes of ornaments and decorations wrapped in old newspaper and dance around with each new discovery like a Christmas morning dress rehearsal party. We have so many different nativity sets. Some are missing a king or a Joseph. Bridget tells us that we should use them all. And since she is also the one to invent the "Hide the Play Doh game" as well as teaching us all the words to "Boom boom, ain't it great to be crazy," (one of our favorite songs), we trust her. *"Boom boom, ain't it great to be crazy? Boom boom, ain't it great to be nuts like us? Boom boom, ain't it great to be crazy? Giddy and foolish the whole day through. Boom boom, ain't it great to be crazy?"*

We line the little nativity players up together and have them traveling from one side of our living room to the other. Over the encyclopedias, under the reading lady, a wonderful ceramic parade of wise men, and sheep and drummer boys and angels and, if William has his way, a few army guys and Batman join the pilgrimage to Bethlehem, which happens to be located on our mantel. Every day we move the cast of characters an inch closer, trying to get our kneeling Mary to balance on the back of a porcelain donkey. We tuck Joseph up against Mary's donkey to hold her up, and he plays out his supportive role perfectly.

Baby Jesus comes on Christmas morning with the presents, and, until that day, the manger is empty. We tuck the little baby behind the little barn house where the sheep and shepherd boy wait for him. He'll need to wait patiently, like the rest of us.

This show plays out in slow motion across our living room, as the Advent candles get shorter and shorter, and we creep our way to Christmas day. *"Come, they told me, pa rum pum pum pum..."*

I pull on my other shoe and watch the stoplight send a flickering red and yellow and green glow through the room. I can't remember this past Christmas…just don't remember. Now the porcelain parade is tucked away in the attic somewhere. Wrapped in newspaper and waiting for us to invite them back out next December. I wish they were still up. I wish the little figurines were here with us now to help us in making this uncomfortable pilgrimage. Seeing the Blessed Mother trying to balance herself on the donkey would sure make me feel better for some reason.

I steal one more glance at Marian in bed with Mom, and I wish I could be brave enough to climb into the bed, too. But I don't, and besides, there is really no room for me. I imagine shrinking really small and snuggling between the two of them like a little baby Jesus surrounded by two Mother Marys.

Being that small would allow me to do tons of things. I could join the holiday parade across our living room to make-believe

Bethlehem. I'd like to be the angel who hangs out above the stable. I bet she has a pretty good view. I try, but I can't seem to picture myself as the angel. Instead, I'm the little drummer boy. I am there beating my drum as the beautiful kings lay their gifts at the baby's feet. The angel smiles down on me, the Blessed Mother nods at me, the ox and lamb keep time. *"Pa rum pum pum, rum pum pum pum, rum pum pum pum."* The angel winks at me. "Good morning, Maureen," she says, and I smile back without missing a beat.

11

Make the Lunch

"MAUREEN?" MY COUSIN ROBIN SITS UP ON ONE ELBOW; her voice is warm and crispy like buttered toast. "You're not going to school, are you?" I realize that my cousin is talking to me and not the angel that hangs above the stable. But I still feel the patter of my heart. *"Pa rum pum pum pum."*

"Why are you dressed for school? You're not really going to school are you?" I don't answer her because I don't want it to become a thing and wake everyone else up. I just scan the room again; my eyes fall once more on my mother and Marian. It's like I am a moth and they are my candle, and I want to get close, even if I get burnt.

Robin follows my eyes. I can see her trying to make heads or tails of what is happening in my mother's hospital bed. In her distraction, I slip from the room.

I head to the kitchen and push open the heavy door. It whines at me. *Hee haw, hee haw.* I am alone in the kitchen, listening to the door mock me on its hinges. *Hee haw, hee haw, hee haw.* It sings in an annoying "told you so" way.

The kitchen is a mess, so I close my eyes, but I can't close out the sound of the door. On the stovetop, there are three apple pies. The cinnamon wraps around me like a warm scarf...

"Tell your mother one hat is enough," I hear her say as she unwraps the scarf from around my neck and pulls the second from my head. "Tell your mother, one hat. One hat is enough." I am standing in Penny's front hall wearing many layers of clothes. She unravels each item as if I am a doll, and Penny mimics her words. "Too much, Maureen. Too many hats!" We giggle as the items fall to the floor, and I am happy to be free from the weight of it all. "Oh my, there is a child under it all!" she exclaims and we giggle some more. "How old are you, child?" she asks with amused exaggeration. I giggle out my answer and try to cover my laughter with my hands. I am seven. I tell her. "Seven! I had thought you were a grown up with all those layers...but under it all is just a child!" I fall back in laughter as my friends and I roll on the floor at her play acting and mistaking me for an adult. She reaches in to tickle me again, and I can hardly contain myself. She smells of cinnamon and soap. She is my best friend's mom, Mrs. Levi. Her house is warm and welcoming and smells of burning wood and grilled cheese. She loves to make pies and pet rocks and crocheted oven mitts. She is an artist.

"One hat is enough," she says again. My hair stands straight up in the air from the static electricity. She kneels when she talks and smooths my hair back down with a gentle stroke, and part of me wishes she would go on petting me forever. Her long straight hair hangs to her waist, and she looks like Cher, but prettier. I imagine her standing at the door singing through a crooked mouth, *"Then put your little hand in mine! There ain't no hill or mountain we can't climb. Babe, I got you babe."*

It's very easy to imagine Mrs. Levi as Cher. She is an artist and wears scarves in her hair, hoop earrings, and bell-bottoms. She paints rocks and puts little googly eyes on them and calls them pet rocks. They line up on their windowsills and mantelpiece. We play Fisher Price and house, and my favorite is the baby carriage. The baby carriage is magical. I wish I had one of my own because all the girls on my block have one.

It's hard to play strollers when you don't have one. I followed the stroller parade with my naked baby wrapped in an old towel, but the other girls scream, "Maureen, go away! You need a stroller to play."

"Mom, I want a stroller," I beg.

"And the man on the moon wants ice water," she tells me from behind the pages of her book. "What do you think, strollers grow on trees?" I tell her that I'll be asking Santa then, and she tells me that Santa has plenty to deliver and is not always able to fit it all in, even when it comes to good kids like me. So I tell anyone who will listen that I want a stroller, and one day, one shows up.

"Maureenie! Yoohoo! Maureenie? Look what I got." Maureen McMartin warbles down the block in shiny black high platform sandals, bright yellow gauchos, and hot pink lipstick. She is loud in every way. She is older and has taken a liking to me, maybe because of the same name thing. I like her right back because she is beautiful like a Barbie doll, if Barbie was really fat. I don't talk to her though. She's too much, too bright, too loud, too beautiful. Like Glinda the Good Witch, if Glinda was really fat. Plus, the cat always gets my tongue.

Maureen is one of the neighborhood kids who comes to the beach with us in the summer. She dresses me up like I am her doll and puts makeup on my face, naming each color and paste that she pulls from her bag. Blue eye powder that is cold and wet against my eyelids; the brush that feels like a cat's tail against my cheeks that she calls blush. To top it off, she rolls a glass tube over my lips with a round plastic ball that leaves behind a thick shine like a snail, except the shine on my lips tastes like strawberries, and she tells me it's called Love Potion. I want to tell her that she doesn't need a potion, I've already fallen for her. But I am afraid if I do, she will stop rolling the little ball and brushing the cat's tail, so I just smile and say nothing.

She comes up to our stoop where I sit, calling to me like my name is a song.

"Maureeeeenie!" she sings. I can hardly look at her. She is carrying something that looks like a basket. It's big and white. I sneak a peek and my heart starts pounding. It's a baby carriage! She's putting it down in front of me. It's white wicker with a thick pink ribbon that has been threaded all the way around the basket and ends with a big fat bow by the white wooden handle. I reach out to hold the handle, and I can't seem to breathe or talk or anything. I stare up at her; my mouth is open but no words come out.

"Maureenie! See what I got for you?" I try to form words, but the only sound that comes is "Haa?" I nod my head up and down. I don't know where all my words have gone.

"Yeah, I got it out of the garbage. Your little friend, Penny, tossed it out. Or her mother. Either way, I saw it, and I thought of you. I pulled it home, painted it, and found this bow...but it don't have no wheels, Maureeenie. But maybe your daddy could put some on. Ya like it?" Again the sound "Haaa" squeaks out, and I nod up at her. My whole body is smiling. I grab my baby doll and toss her into the carriage. We don't need wheels. I can just hold it up, and if I run fast enough, nobody will know. It's a little tricky, but I manage to get it up as I run screaming in the direction of the stroller parade.

"Penny, wait up!" The carriage is bouncing from one wooden corner to the next. Baby is getting a pretty bumpy ride, but I keep going. My arms are getting weak, and it's hard to keep it up. It keeps jumping and bumping and bouncing into my legs. I hit a crack and the carriage stops short, the wood meets hard with my shin, and a sharp pain shoots up my leg. Still, I have a stroller, a real live beautiful stroller, and I am almost there. I can see them just houses away. So I pick up the carriage again and go charging down the street. I am caught up in the eye of a great storm that pushes me forward, taking no toll of the damage. I can't stop, even when everything begs me to. The sore arms, damp forehead, blood running down my shins and my sister, Riddle, who calls after me.

"Maureen, that carriage needs wheels!" I turn to her, but she is just a blur of orange standing beside my sister, Annie, who is standing on her head with both legs pointed in different directions like a human Y.

"It's fine!" I scream back. My carriage hits another crack in the sidewalk, the wooden stumps get stuck in the mud and the doll goes flying into the air. In slow motion, she twists and turns, free of her blanket and lands face down in the dirt.

I stop to gather her up. I am left like a ravaged landscape—exhausted, defeated, deflated, and in great need of a Band-Aid. My beautiful stroller is worn down from being pushed over the cement. I drag it the rest of the way home and carry it up our stoop and sit down.

Maybe I will ask the Giant to put wheels on my stroller. He is the only person I know who could do it. He has all those tools in the basement.

As I sit there thinking, Penny comes up our walk. She looks at me, her face is hard, like she's playing tic-tac-toe and losing.

"Ah, hi, ah, Maureen, you, ah, got that stroller out of our garbage."

"No, I didn't." I search her eyes.

"Ah, yeah, ya did," she continues.

"Maureen McMartin got it," I confess, shredding all loyalty held for my fat fairy godmother.

"Yeah well, ah, my mom wants it back."

"What?" I hear the words, but I am not sure what she means.

"She wants it back," Penny repeats.

My mind reels with possible ways of stalling, but I come up blank.

"Her friend saw you running down the block with it and she told my mom that it could be an antique and worth some money 'cause it's old, and you were just gonna ruin it anyways. So she wants it. Besides, she didn't really mean to throw it out to begin with. It was just on accident."

"On accident?" An accident is something that happens by accident, something you can't help. I try to imagine Mrs. Levi opening her door and getting taken by the wind. Her long hair flies wildly in the great gust. She grabs for something to hold on to and lands on the carriage. The wind is so strong that she and the carriage get lifted and carried out to the street. Finally the wind lets up, and she lands with the carriage among all the trash. She lies there a moment completely dazed, and then only after gathering her wits, she runs back inside, forgetting all about the precious carriage in the trash. So it ends up, left there on accident. Penny stares back at me impatiently.

"Could you get it for me?"

I want to shake her and scream, "No, you can't ask for something back after you've thrown it out, especially after somebody else painted it and put a bow on it and gave it to someone else as a gift. That's not the rule! The rule is: If you throw it out, it's out." But I don't say that, because I get the feeling Penny knows the rule by the way she's not looking at me. And I'm pretty sure that her mom knows the rule too, but she's a mom and you don't argue with moms. I give Penny back the stroller that was given to me as a gift. I take the big pink bow off though 'cause that part was mine for sure.

Mrs. Levi takes it from me at the door. The cinnamon scent washes over me, and makes me feel sick…

I open my eyes to the messy kitchen. I am here to make lunch. Stay focused, Maureen. What's next? Get the bread. Avoid the landmines. PB&J. Play it safe. Keep it simple. PB&J.

12

Make the Breakfast

IN THE KITCHEN, I MAKE A BOWL OF CEREAL FOR BREAKFAST, puffed wheat in skim milk. I am not really hungry, but this is the next thing that I know to do after I get ready for school. I spread a spoonful of sugar over the puffed wheat. *"Just a spoonful of sugar helps the medicine go down."* I bring the spoon to my lips and fill my mouth. Stick with the plan, stay the course. Despite the band of gypsies who have set up camp in our living room, I try my best to stick to the normal schedule, even if everyone else has thrown it out the window.

A square patch of sun is starting to form on the floor from the kitchen window, and I can tell the snow won't be staying long.

On the side of the house, I hear a rattle and go to see who is in our garbage. From our side kitchen window I see Morris. He pushes a cart around town and collects things. Sometimes bottles and cans and sometime stuffed animals and newspapers. There doesn't seem to be a method to his madness. But he is definitely mad. That is what my mother said to Miss Miller when they talked about how on bitter cold mornings, Morris sometimes steps inside the kindergarten to warm his hands. Miss Miller didn't like it much, but she'd let him stay a bit before shooing him out the door. "Poor Morris is mad," they'd say. Which is funny cause I have never seen him mad at all. He is always happy and humming and sweet.

He is the person I think of when mom talks about "those less fortunate than us." Sometimes I save up things that I think he would like; a plastic ring I got from the gumball machine or a shiny object that I slip in my pocket at Penny's house. When I give him these trinkets, his eyes water up and he says, "Or Mree, Orr Mreee?" which I think means "For me?" When I nod my head yes, his hands get shakier than normal, and he smiles and shows me his gums where his teeth used to be.

There is a thin layer of snow on the back of his coat as he bends to root through our garbage. He digs around to the rattle of wine bottles. Our garbage is filled with empty bottles and empty morphine bags. "The garbage man will think we are having some party," the aunts joke to keep themselves from crying. "What with all the wine bottles and morphine bags," they say, shaking their heads and blushing. Sounds like "Party Time for Satan" to me, I want to add, but I am not sure they would get the joke. Or if it is even funny; I have lost track of that sort of thing.

I look down at the PB&J that I am making for lunch and think about Morris. "If you give something away that you love, to someone in greater need, it will be returned to you tenfold." I hear my mother's words, clear as day. They echo back at me from the floors and the walls and an image of a pink baby stroller rolls through my mind. Then I see her standing over me as I stood on this very spot in the kitchen so many years ago. "Tenfold," she whispers. I know she is right because I saw the magic myself. But I'm in no mood for loaves and fishes miracles. I step back from the window. I don't want Morris to see me, and I don't want to see him. I just want to be left alone. I tuck my sandwich in a bag. But I can't tuck away her words. "Tenfold Maureen, Tenfold, Tenfold." She is bargaining with me in the kitchen again. "Tenfold."…

It is Christmas morning, and I am seven. I have spent the night, and many before this night, imagining this moment, Christmas morning, stroller day. We wake before the sun and stare down from our bedroom windows trying to find reindeer tracks in the snow. The radiator hisses at us to be careful, don't stand too close. Marian and Bridget are in charge of securing us upstairs till they get the word that it's time to come down. Marian threatens that she will lock us back in our rooms if we don't pipe down, and Bridget tries to distract us with a game, "Who can hold their breath the longest? Who can cross their eyes?" Neither the threats nor games work. We want our Christmas, and we hoot and holler and hop from foot to foot like Indians trying to bring forth rain.

Over the deafening pitch of our war cries, we hear the thunder of the Giant's orders come booming up the stairs at us. "Single file!" With those two words he is able to do what Marian and Bridget had not. Instantly we settle and fall into line. "Single file," we repeat. "Single file, youngest to oldest."

Turning the corner from the stairway to the living room is like going from night to day. The Giant has a camera with a light so bright that it blinds us. I feel the heat of the bulb like a bright summer's day, and I smell the scent of burning dust. My siblings and I smile and wave at the camera through squinting eyes as we try to find our way to the tree.

My sisters are all jumping around and yelling. There are bows and ribbons, toys and bikes and there, in the middle of it all, is a sight for sore eyes. I blink a few times to make sure I am seeing clearly. Could it be? A real Christmas miracle, right there in the middle of the blinding, bright light and morning haze and bobbing sisters?

"He fit it in! Santa fit it in!" I scream. My head is shaking and my body starts to dance, hands flying in the air, feet up on my toes. My sisters push and shove me to get out of their way, but I don't care. It's so wonderful to be pummeled in the rough sea of Christmas.

The baby carriage is better than my dreams. It's pink! A pink stroller with a pink-and-white-striped hood and white wheels! All four! They are so bright and clean. Nobody has ever played with this stroller before. It is brand new and glows like the light around baby Jesus' head.

I grab my baby and place her in the beautiful new stroller. We can stroll around the block for as long as we want without Mrs. Levi taking it back. We can play strollers every day for the rest of our lives if we want to.

The snow is still thick, so I make do with the living room. I've been strolling around the living room for days. "You're wearing out the carpet," Mom calls from her throne at the end on our dining room table. But I keep going. There's a knock at the door and Jenny Connor shows up with her beautiful hippy mother.

Except that Mrs. Connor looks thin and tired. I don't need to look at her mood ring to tell that she's blue. She lifts her hands to pull her hair back from her face. Her bangle bracelets send out a beautiful jingle as she takes my mother in her arms and thanks her with a big hug. My mother steps back from her smiling and nodding and holding her hands like she is afraid that Mrs. Connor might be sick and does not want to catch it. Then Mrs. Connor leans down to kiss Jenny. She smells like the cut grass and a smoky grill and, even in the middle of all this snow, she makes me think of wet summer nights catching fireflies on their lawn. I stare at her, hoping she has a hug for me too.

"Okay kitty cats, have fun." She smiles and ruffles my hair. My eyes roll back and my heart begins to purr.

After she leaves, Jenny gets a load of my beautiful new stroller, and we go a couple rounds.

"No, Jenny, I just got it for Christmas."

"Please?"

"No."

"Please?"

"No."

My mother makes the call from the other room. "For crying out loud, Maureen, you let her play with that stroller, she's the guest." I sit on the couch and wait my turn. Jenny takes the stroller and follows my well-worn path. Each time she crosses by me I call out to her.

"Are you done yet? Are you done yet? Jenny, are you done yet! Ahh!" She won't even look at me. She's just looking at my naked baby. Like I'm not even here. She's circled the room about a hundred times. "Your turn is up, Jenny." She won't let go of the handle.

"My baby is sad," she finally blurts out. "Her mommy and daddy are splitting!" It sounds horrible, and I think about a mother and father being split right down the middle, cartoon style. It's a weird story for my little friend who is usually humming and twirling her hair that is pinned to the sides of her head with plastic rainbows and flowers and bunnies.

"Splitting?" I ask.

"They're not gonna dance together anymore, can't work it out, and my mom has to move away." She stares down at my baby, and holds tight to the carriage. I stare at her head as it hangs over my stroller and think about Jenny's mom and dad dancing barefoot in their backyard. He has taken his hair out of its ponytail and it swings about his face. Her mom's is swirling and twirling as she throws her head back to laugh. She raises her hands in the air, and there is more hair beneath her arms. They both seem so hairy and wild and beautiful. I've never seen my parents dance like that, so I am not sure I would miss it, but for Jenny it's different. Her parents' dancing is always the main show. I want to ask why they have stopped dancing and where will the mother go? But I don't. I don't know what else to do to make Jenny happy, so I let her stroll my baby for the rest of the day until her mom comes to get her.

When Mrs. Connor returns to our door, I jump to my feet and grab the warm handle of my carriage, as Jenny gets lost in her mother's arms. Then Mom calls me into the kitchen.

"Maureeeeeeeen." The heavy kitchen door whines in pain as I push it open. *Hee haw, hee haw.* I find her standing, one hand on the counter, one on her hip.

"Jenny was pretty sad today," she whispers.

"Yeah," I nod and look at the door wondering what the secret is all about.

"Her parents are getting a divorce. Her mother and father are not going to live together anymore, and Jenny is going to move."

"Why?" I ask, but Mom doesn't answer, just goes on.

"Maybe we could do something to make her feel better?"

"Okay. Maybe we could make her a surprise or something. Maybe candy?"

"I know she sure likes to play with your stroller." An alarm goes off in my head. *Danger Will Robinson! Danger!*

"My stroller?"

"She's less fortunate than you. If you give her your stroller, it would cheer her up." I imagine the unfortunate Jenny strolling my baby carriage next to Morris and his shopping cart. It's so sad an idea that I shake it from my head.

"But I just got it. I haven't even taken it outside."

"Jesus says if you give something away that you really love, it will be returned to you tenfold."

"Jesus?" At the mention of his name I know I am done for. Mom thinks Jesus is like God or something and whatever He says, goes. I am not really listening any more, just watching her mouth move.

"What's tenfold mean?" I finally ask, stalling for time.

"It means ten times. It will be returned to you ten times."

"But I...I don't want ten times more strollers. I just want the one I have." She's not listening. She leaves the kitchen on a mission. Our kitchen door swings back and forth, making fun of me. *Hee haw, hee haw, hee haw.*

"Maureeeeen," she calls to me, but I stand frozen, staring at the kitchen door.

"Maureeeeen!" I push open the door; it feels tenfold heavier. My mother stands looking out the front door; I don't see my stroller anywhere.

"Mom?" She's standing in our doorway waving goodbye. I look out the door with her. Jenny and Mrs. Connor wave back at us. The car radio is singing *"To everything turn, turn, turn, there is a season turn, turn, turn..."* But I don't turn; I can't.

"Say goodbye, Maureen."

"But Mom..."

"Say goodbye."

"But Mom."

She's not listening to me; she's just smiling out the door and waving. So I wave too. I wave goodbye to Mrs. Connor and Jenny. They look like fairies, their long wild hair blowing in the wind. Jenny and her heathen hippie mother, with her two pendulous breasts that sway freely, unencumbered by bra or Bible. She helps Jenny into the car with a hug. She didn't seem less fortunate than me. Mrs. Connor loads my beautiful pink stroller into the back of their station wagon. It fits right in. *Hee haw, hee haw.*

13

Pie for Breakfast

HEE HAW, HEE HAW, HEE HAW. THE KITCHEN DOOR SWINGS open, and my Aunt Gabby comes and puts tea on. I duck into the little bathroom off the kitchen cause I don't want her pestering me. I close the door on the little room. It is not really a bathroom, just a closet with a toilet. It used to be a pantry. The Giant put the bathroom in for Mom when she couldn't make her way up the stairs anymore. I sit on the lid and wait till I hear the whistle of the kettle, the click of the spoon against the mug, and finally the squeal of the kitchen door to let me know that it is safe to come out of hiding.

I can see the electric coils are still red beneath the tea pot. The rest of the stove top is covered with the apple pies and half scavenged containers of other packaged desserts brought by the neighbors. It's an odd variety of muffins, coffee cakes, and cookies. The refrigerator is the same–layers of unfamiliar bowls, tins, and pans filled with other mothers' cooking.

Most of the dishes are desserts. Maybe they all know about Mom's sweet tooth. I am not sure which tooth it is, but I think it might be one of the teeth that she keeps in a glass of water on the side of her bed at night. When she's angry with us, she screams out to no one in particular, "Nothing is sacred! You kids would rob the teeth right out of my head!" When she says this, I think of those floating teeth and how at first I wasn't exactly sure what they were. I think of how it felt both unsettling and bizarre to see someone's teeth in a glass of water. Hearing her accuse us of wanting to rob them is equally odd. On a list of a million items that I would think to rob, my mother's teeth would be nowhere in sight.

She loves candy and sweets so much that she hides them around the house, secret stashes of sweets. Even with her own teeth sleeping in a glass of water by the side of her bed, she still can't seem to stay away from them. Her favorite is Necco candy wafers and black licorice. When she can't get her fix of choice, three heaping spoonfuls of sugar slide into her tea and it settles like a wet beach at the bottom of her mug. Besides, it's not like she's fat. Before Cancer came, she stayed in shape, thanks to Jack Lalanne and her boxes of Ayds appetite-suppressant candies. They came in chocolate, butterscotch and caramel. My favorite is the caramel.

I'd find and devour them by the handful. The Ayds candies start off tasting like sweet chewy caramel. But then they turn medicinal tasting and by the time I swallow, my tongue feels like it's coated in chalk.

Maureen McMartin tells us the reason Ayds candies work

is because they have worms in them. I don't get why wormy candy would make you thin, but I don't understand most of what Maureen has to say. She runs to our home from her house next door with a hand blender stuck in her hair. She got too close while mixing a cake, and comes screaming for help while blobs of lumpy batter run down her face.

"I was just trying to test it," she admits between tears. It's hard not to laugh at her sweet confession. We know all too well about her not-so-secret love affair with *"Sugar. Oh honey, honey. You are my candy girl, and you got me wanting you."*

Maureen McMartin is not so secret about any of her love affairs. She's dating a guy who works as a toll collector. She comes by daily to trade us dollars for coins so that she can drive through and see him. She drives off the next exit and then drives around and gets back on the freeway so she can continue talking to her tollbooth boyfriend. It seems like an expensive way to carry on a conversation, but she says it's worth it. Sometimes when she is short on cash, she'll trade us Hostess cupcakes or Ding Dongs, 'cause she knows we like the sweets even better than dollars and her mom keeps their kitchen stocked with all kinds of snacks and treats. When we see her coming with the Tasty Cakes and Twinkies, we rummage through the couch cushions and search the bottom of our mother's purse for coins. "You're wasting your money," my sisters tell her as they hand over lost change for Ding Dongs. Maureen McMartin just smiles and sings, *"I don't care too much for money, cause money can't buy me love."*

My sisters pull off the wrappings, bite into the Ding Dongs, and smile back at her. Everyone seems super happy with the exchange. We are all little candied apples that have not fallen far from our mother's tree. When mom sees we have cleaned her out of her change, she throws her hands in the air and yells, "Nothing's sacred anymore."

I look over all the pies and cakes lining our counter top and wish my mother could make her way in here to see it all. It would be a nice payback for all the candy and coins she's been robbed of.

There is a plate of chocolate cupcakes with M&M's pressed into the icing. She would have loved those, and suddenly I feel like she's been robbed all over again. I see her sitting at the end of our long dining room table. She is pale and shaking her head and mumbling. "Nothing is sacred anymore...."

The memory swells like a growing wave, and before I know it, I've gone under... *"Trick or treat, smell my feet, give me something good to eat."* The song vibrates through the house and pours out onto the street. I am seven, and it's Halloween, the highest of holy days in our home. Our yearly goal is to be the first ones out in the neighborhood.

"Clean up in the candy department! Clean up in the candy department!" Annie screams through an empty tissue roll while running around the house dressed as a hobo or clown or scarecrow. It's hard to tell exactly what she is, but her wild hair looks perfect for the part. The costume is not so important. My sisters like to be hobos, rubbing leftover coals from the summer barbeques on their faces and raiding the Giant's work clothes. But hobos are ugly, and I can't imagine why you would be one if you had the chance to be a princess, which I am, every year. With one of my mother's beautiful lacy slips and a tiara made out of cardboard and tin foil. I wish I could wear my first Holy

Communion dress but that would probably be sacrilegious or something.

I pull up my mother's slip and make my way next door to try to score some early sweets before the real hunt begins. I knock on the Gabiola's door and Mrs. Gabiola leans out at me without opening the door all the way. She holds her cigarette close to her face and wrinkles her nose like I am an ant at a picnic.

"Maureen, you can't just come out here in your mother's pajamas and some twisted Reynolds wrap. You won't get a single piece of candy from me till you put on a decent costume." She flicks her ashes and my lip starts to quiver and my eyes begin to sting. The screen door shuts but her words make their way to me on clouds of smoke that billow out of the screen. "Go get a decent costume."

What is a decent costume? One of those shiny princess dresses that come matching and new? I know we don't actually have that type, and I begin to worry that my mother's slip will keep me from getting any candy at all.

"Mrs Gabiola is a jerk," I tell Riddle, who is sitting in front of a mirror with a piece of coal, making her face dirty like a bum. She has wrapped an orange scarf around her head, and she is going as some sort of pumpkin hobo. She squints her eyes at me like she is doing math and something about me is not adding up. Then she nods her head, and a light goes on behind her eyes. A twinkle and a smirk crawl up on her face.

"You just need some makeup is all. Go get Mom's purse." With a sense of relief, I run off to gather the recommended ingredients. Riddle is an artist. She can draw just about anything, so I am in good hands. She sits me down and begins her work. Large pink circles are drawn on my cheeks with mom's lipstick.

She covers my eyelids with blue eye shadow, smearing it all the way to my hairline in little points so that I look Chinese. Then comes the black liquid eyeliner. With a steady hand she does her best to outline my eyes. I look into her deep brown eyes as she works her magic. She is lost in her art. The final touch is a dollop of thick red lipstick all around my mouth. "Smack your lips together," she tells me while demonstrating the movement. I imitate her, pushing my lips tightly together and rubbing them against each other. I look like a painted China doll, heavy on the paint. I grin at my reflection. In the mirror I see a China doll and a magical pumpkin hobo grinning back at me. Just when it can't get any better, we hear the Monster Mash song drift up the stairs from our record player and Riddle and I grab our pillow cases and scramble down the stairs.

I take my new look to the streets and skip Mrs. Gabiola all together. There are already enough evil witches on Halloween.

So I gather my mother's slip and follow after my sisters. The thing about my mother's slip is that, as short as she is, I am still much shorter, and so her slip is too long. I wish I could cut it, but after the encyclopedia event, I back away from anything having to do with scissors and Mom's things. I try to tie the slip up with some odd belt or scarf but even still, it's called a slip for a reason. Eventually it trips me up, and I fall. It happens every year, smearing my makeup and leaving red marks and real blood dripping from my lips, but that in no way slows me down.

At most doors, people just look at me kindly and hand over the loot. But at other houses they try and guess. This is the worst. I stand shifting from foot to foot, ignoring my full bladder as they smile like happy game show contestants hoping to win.

"Oh, look! The bride of Frankenstein," they yell and clap their hands.

"No," I snap and shake my head. They lean out with drunken smiles.

"But you are very spooky," they add, trying to pry a clue.

"I am not the bride of Frankenstein," I tell them, "I am a princess." And I watch their faces change from scared to sad. At one house an older man comes to the door. There is a party going on and he is trying to pass out the candy while holding on to his drink.

"What are you?" he asks. His eyes hard, his hands shaky, the ice clinks and the amber colored liquid swells like a mini tidal wave that splashes over the edge of his glass. I don't answer, just hold up my pillowcase and try to avoid his eyes and the spray of his drink. I am not here for conversation; I am here for candy and with only one night to cover as much ground as possible. I can't stick around making small talk. "Well," he continued, "you look like a streetwalker."

"A streetwalker?" I glare at him and shake my head in disgust. "I am not a streetwalker, whatever that is!" I've heard this word from my mother and am pretty sure it's not good.

"You're not going anywhere dressed like that!" she screams at my sisters. "You look like a streetwalker!" The word reminds me of a bug—like a daddy long legs or a roly poly, and I wish Aunt Caroline were around. I hold up my pillowcase. I have stayed on the sidewalk all night except when I used the cross walk. But I don't need to explain myself to him.

"Dad!" a women calls from inside the house. Suddenly she is beside him, followed by a group of cheerful dinner guests. She is tall and slim and wearing a long green gown that goes to the floor, but not like the fluffy prom dresses that my sisters have worn. Her dress lays flat against her body, and her hair is twisted up in a bun. She has peacock feathers and gems pinned to her head, and she looks like a beautiful lady from the old-fashioned movies. "She's not a streetwalker," the lady in green laughs, coming to my rescue. "She's a...," she pauses to look. Her face bends and sways as she tries to narrow in on me. "Well she's a...a sleepy little clown, aren't you baby?" Baby? I am not a baby, and I am not a clown.

"I am a princess!" I shout. She turns her head to cover her face in the old man's shoulder, and it seems like the two of them may fall right over from trying to control themselves as the rest of the group bursts into laughter. I shake my head, gather my rage and ragged slip, and run to catch up with my sister. I know about dealing with drunken adults, no matter how pretty or kind they seem at first, it's best to just keep moving. I don't need to be abused for a Tootsie Roll. They are not the only game in town.

My sisters and I troll the neighborhood until late into the night. After we cover as much ground as we can on foot, we pile into the van, and the Giant takes us to a different neighborhood, one with short lawns and big houses. If the getting is good, we pile back in the van, trade costumes and circle the same block again. We're professionals. The Giant sits in the driver seat and sings. *"And we're all off to Dublin in the green, in the green, where the helmets glisten in the sun. Where the bayonets flash and the rifles crash to the rattle of a Thompson gun."* He has a lovely voice and he sings like he enjoys it, but also like it's sacred in some way. How my mother says the prayers is how the Giant sings his songs. And when he is done singing, he asks for a piece of chocolate, and he seems like a big kid who is just as excited about the free candy as the rest of us.

When the last porch light goes dark, we head for home, our bodies spent and buzzing on sugar. Our mother waits at the door for us to hand over the bags. Even though we know it's coming, the sight of her standing there gathering up the candy always comes as a shock. I do my best to walk as slow as possible while shoveling sweets into my mouth and pockets.

"Aw Mom, why can't we keep some?" we beg through mouths full of half-chewed chocolate bars.

"You'll rot the teeth right out of your head," she barks back at us, and having the evidence to back up her warnings, we do as we're told.

After all the bags are gathered, she begins to dump them on the table and sort them out. It's heartbreaking to see all my hard labor tossed into the melting pot, never getting to really take in what a good job I've done. But this is how it is, how it's always been. After sorting, she begins to count all the Hershey Bars, then all the lollipops, and on and on. When she has a tally, she reaches for the kitchen phone—the one with the extra-long extension cord so that she can keep an eye on the candy, and she calls her friends to give them the update.

"Ninety-five Snickers, 165 Mounds Bars, 140 licorice sticks!!" The count goes on like this for a while interrupted by squeals of, "Well, how do you like that? For crying out loud." We all stare on at the mountains of brightly wrapped treats that cover our dining room table. After a while, she looks up at us and covers the mouthpiece. "It's late, get up to bed," she instructs. As we slowly back away from the table she adds, "And don't forget to brush your teeth!" Back into the phone she is cackling again. "Oh, they'd be out there till the cows come home if we let them!"

I hear her joke as we head to our bedrooms sucking on the left over jelly beans and hard candy stuck in our molars. It seems a shame to brush away the only candy we have left, so the tooth brushes all go unused for the night.

In the morning the mountains are gone, and we know it's all locked away in the basement in the old freezer with the padlock. She wears the key around her neck and holds a powerful carrot that definitely has our attention. If we're good, she'll dole out little treats to us from the freezer.

The next day we head out to school on our best behavior as she waves victoriously from the door.

But before the end of the week, there has been a break in. Some unknown goblin or hobo has taken the lock right off the freezer with one of the tools from the Giant's workroom. My mother is in shock and in need of a Plan B. Once the freezer is no longer an option, she takes to hiding the sugar stash around the house. She's pretty good at first, but no match for eight candy addicts. We followed her for clues. Candy wrappers in her pockets, smears of chocolate on her lips.

It's her loose lips that sink her ship. The habit of talking to herself finally catches up with her. She carries on long detailed conversations with herself while folding the laundry or burning the dinner. This particular time, she's in the bathroom audibly congratulating herself.

"Ha, I got them this time," she laughs. "Those kids will never find the candy down in the basement bathroom in the garbage cans. How do you like that?" She asks no one in particular. But wild-haired Annie is patiently waiting her turn in the hallway. Annie has only one answer,

"I like it very much." With winged feet and a lusty smile, Annie quickly makes her way to the basement.

No one liked to go to the basement, especially not alone. The basement, like all basements, is dark and spooky. But our basement excels at being creepy. There is the Giant's workroom, the boiler room where the old freezer sits with its broken lock, the laundry room with its mountain of dirty clothes, a bathroom with a toilet, and a rusty shower filled with cobwebs and a sign on the wall that list the bathroom rules in a poem: *"Please remember, don't forget, Never leave the bathroom wet."* The poem goes on about how to take care of business while in the bathroom, ending with a gentle reminder: *"When other folks are waiting one, please remember it isn't done."* But other folks are never waiting one for that bathroom. In fact no one ever uses this bathroom. It's cold and smells of wet cement and moldy drywall. If, during a game of hide and seek, someone goes to the basement to hide in the bathroom, they can be sure that they will never be found. The only time this creepy cave of a bathroom is used is during one of the Giant's yearly meatball parties when the line for the other bathroom makes its way down the stairs. That's when you plead with a sister to please come down to the basement with you. And you beg them to stay in the room so they can be there to witness or run for help if killer spiders suddenly attack or if you get carried off through the basement window by boogiemen.

But fearless Annie is on a mission and it doesn't take her long to find the sugary treasure. In even less time, she manages to put a substantial dent in the haul. For several uninterrupted hours she lives in the basement in blissful solitude among piles of discarded wrappers. By nightfall, she begins to feel sick, or guilty, or both and invites Bridget and Julia to join her. In the light of morning, all that is left is a few loose candy corns and some root beer barrels.

When the crime is discovered, you can hear our wailing for blocks.

"You ate all our candy?" The news of the crime leaves us white as ghosts, our mouths hung in shock, the idea too heavy to digest. Wild haired Annie and her tribe of giggling banshees crowd in the corner and joyfully rehash the breach.

"You were the one who told me, Mom! You were the one to spill the beans!" At the head of the table clutching the empty pillowcases our mother sits in shock. She sways her head gently back and forth repeating the same question over and over:

"It's gone? It's all gone?" I feel bad for myself, but worse for my mom. It isn't just the loss of the candy, and having those hoodlums giggling at her. This marks a definite turning point; she has been outsmarted. They've turned on her, disregarded her wrath, and she is losing control. And worse yet, she will have to go on quenching her lust for sweets on chalky Ayds candies.

I witness it unfold, the unjustness of it all, salted with my greedy sisters' laughter. I would gladly trade a few rotten teeth for the rotten apples that stand in the corner celebrating their cleverness, and I know my mother is right. Nothing is sacred anymore.

In the kitchen, I grab a fork and dig right into the middle of a pie. I chew it around in my mouth and feel like a criminal doing time, but the pie doesn't bring any of the peace I hoped it would.

14

Moonshine

OUT THE WINDOW, MORRIS MAKES HIS WAY DOWN OUR driveway. Little puffs of warm air drift from his mouth like he is smoking an invisible pipe, but it is just his hot breath in the cold air. He bends to pat our cat, Crazy. We named him Crazy because he is a bit of an attack cat. He pounces out of corners, and under stairwells with claws drawn and thirsty for blood.

I watch as Morris reaches in his pocket and gives Crazy something—a bone or a piece of food. He settles down to enjoy it and I feel even worse about my stinginess. Especially when our kitchen is bursting with food.

The dinner ladies from church are religious about bringing the meals. They come to the door and try handing it over with the least amount of exchange even though their eyes are hungry for information. Like actresses auditioning for a role, they deliver the same parting line, "If you kids need anything. Anything. We are here for you. You call us." Some fight back the tears, some with calm assurance, each more convincing than the last, and then they are gone. Their words echo from every cookie and casserole. "If you kids need anything, we are here for you. We are here for you, we are here for you." It feels so good to hear, but then I watch their cars pull away and wonder where they are going.

I imagine a room of church ladies cooking and praying and waiting by the phone for us to call to let them know what we need. It makes me feel safe for a moment, until I realize that, for the most part, I don't know their names, and they haven't left their numbers. They are someone's mom, and I am pretty sure I wouldn't know what to ask for even if I could contact them.

Among the stacks of desserts, there's a gathering of bottles; wine, whiskey, beer. Mostly empty. They're lined up like little soldiers who will help us through the battle.

"Moonshine oh moonshine oh how I love thee, you killed my poor father, but dare you kill me."

The cap from the whiskey bottle is resting on a stack of dirty saucers surrounded by used teacups. I pick up the bottle of whiskey to replace the cap but before I do, I bring it to my nose. One whiff and I am back in first grade.

I'm on the couch, sick to my stomach. It started with a hot dog that came back up onto my lap and lands me on the couch under a pile of blankets. After a while, it's not just the hot dog. It's the oatmeal. The toast. The soup. Even the water, once nothing else is left to come up. When that happens, I start to cry, because the water seems so harmless going down. When it comes back up, it's the most painful of all, and Mom is upset because I keep missing the big pot that she has put by the couch for me to throw up into. Now there's a pile of smelly blankets in the laundry room waiting to be washed. I haven't been able to keep the food from coming back up for so long that Mom looks my way and tells the Giant, "She's wasting away to nothing. The doctor says she needs to keep something down or we'll need to take her in." I am not sure where she means when she says the word "in," but it makes the Giant more silent than usual, and then I hear him tell her that we need to get some food in me.

"What do you want?" she asks in a sweet voice. She leans down to me by the couch, her eyes are soft and tired. "Hmm? You can have whatever you like."

Whatever I like? No one has ever offered me "whatever I like," and so many things come to mind.

"Anything?" I ask, to make sure I am not being fooled or tested. She nods, and I smile, because I can't image anything better than an ice cold Coca Cola. I've never had one, but I've seen them on TV, and it always looks wonderful.

There is a blizzard outside that taps against our window and a wind that whistles like the kettle and moans as if it has a bellyache just like mine. I look out the front window, and all I see is white snow blowing in the dark night. Bridget and Julia are sent to Lombardi's Delicatessen to get me the Coke. Lombardi's is closer than Leo's candy shop but still far enough that they stand in the vestibule and tell my mother that if they go out in the storm, they will freeze to death. My mother wraps another scarf around their heads to shut their whining and to keep them warm. They look like the two astronauts about to walk on the moon. When they open the door, the wind blows in a blast of cold air and snow and I hide beneath my warm blankets on the couch and dream about a cold Coca Cola just for me. *"I'd like to teach the world to sing in perfect harmony."*

The clock ticks, the cat cries, and the evening news hums in the back of my dreams. Finally, my sisters come back through the door with another blast of freezing air. They are bitter cold. Cold from the weather and bitter at me for having to walk in a blizzard for a Coke. Julia comes to the couch with the Coca Cola in a nice glass. It looks just like on TV, and my mouth gets all wet and juicy. Her cheeks are like roses, her yellow eyes watery and tired. She hands me the glass, and I drink it down in almost one gulp. It prickles my nose and tickles my throat and leaves the most delicious taste of liquid caramel in my mouth. The jingle jangles in my head, *"Have a Coke and a smile."* So I do. I drift off to sweet dreams.

The next morning, I feel sick again. The Coke is empty, and the pains are back. Marian, Bridget, Julia, Riddle, and Annie line up at the door in their school uniforms.

I watch from the couch. All the little blue knee-high socks take their places at the door. The lucky ones have a pair with no holes, and elastic still holds them up. Those little knees will be cold out there. I watch the calves and shins slowly slip into view. The dance of bending to pull up the socks has begun.

Mom comes at them with a dirty washcloth. She holds my sisters by the neck and wipes off breakfast. They plead with her as I sink deep into the couch.

"Oh Mom. No."

"Oh, stop that. Stop your complaining and say your prayer."

"Jesus, Mary and Joseph, be with us on our way. Holy Spirit inspires us. In the name of the Father, the Son and the Holy

Ghost. Amen." She holds her cheek out for kisses. They each deliver one as they rush out the door into the cold.

I pretend to be sleeping, just in case she might have the need to wipe my face, too. She uses this rag to clean the stove, wash the dishes, wipe the table, and then each of our faces. It smelled of cold grease and mildew. Most days, I didn't mind that it had been in the dirty sink and over the dirty table. It's the idea that it had wiped the crumbs from all those noses before mine that bothered me. We lined up oldest to youngest, and with the two boys not yet in school, I am always the last one to get the rag. And really, it's not surprising that I am sick. Mom's hand on my forehead feels soft and warm and chubby. It makes me open my eyes. I couldn't help myself. I look up at her like an abandoned dog at a pet fair.

"I am going to make you some tea," she tells me and heads for the other room.

"Tea? Like a tea party?"

I pull myself up a little. I've seen movies where a mother cares for her poor dying child, putting wet towels on her forehead and bringing tea. This is great, a tea party for Mom and me. Little clouds of smoke twirl up from the mug. It's so hot I grab bits of blanket and make oven mitts so I can hold it. It's tea with lemon. There's a pit floating on top. Honey too, thick at the bottom, and something else.

"What's that smell, Mom?"

"It's a Hot Toddy, Maureen. It's good for ya. Drink it all, you hear me?" I nod my head and watch her go.

"Mom? Ma, Mom?"

She settles into her throne at the end of the table and pulls open her book. If I take my two little fingers up to my eyes and look at her, I can squash her. But I don't, this will make it very hard for us to have a tea party.

I wonder what she's reading as her eyes move back and forth beneath her glasses. She licks her fingers to turn the page the same way our cat Pebbles licks her newborn kittens. Pebble's has given birth all over our house, in our dryer, in the socks box, and once under my dresser. I watch every time. After they're born, she licks them clean till they're soft and fluffy. Her tongue is warm and coarse, and I wish my mom would lick me. I know that sounds strange, but just around the neck and ears. I think it would be nice. The kitties sure like it. It makes them hum like a church choir. It's about the best sound I've ever heard. It sounds like the static that comes from the TV when you don't hold the hanger the right way, except it's coming from the cat's heart saying, "I'm in love, I'm in love. I'm in love."

The hot clouds float up at my face. I'm all sweaty. My lips suck in a small sip, and it's hot. Firewater! Firewater! I have to catch my breath and shake my head to make it cool off.

It's feels like Vicks cough rub, hot and prickly on my nose. It slides down my throat, leaving a path of warmth and comfort. It is firewater. That's the name I would use, but only because I don't know the name for whiskey.

Before the mug is half drained, everything has changed forever. The room is bright, and suddenly there is music. It floats in and gets louder and louder like a parade is marching right up our block. My face is warm, and I feel better. Actually, I feel so happy that I want to dance and sing.

"I'm a rambler. I'm a gambler. I'm a long ways from home."

It feels like I am dreaming, but I am awake and feel like I

slipped down Alice's rabbit hole. I'm floating like that lemon seed in my mug, just floating.

"I'm a rambler. I'm a gambler. I'm a long ways from home. And if you don't like me then leave me alone." Then I start spinning, or is it the room? Or both. I am a spinning top on a merry-go-round. We are spinning together but not in sync. I close my eyes and drain the rest of the Hot Toddy. It feels so good, like a hot bath or a warm hug, and I raise my empty mug to my mother

"Can I have some more tea, please?" But she is gone, lost in the newspaper, and there is a wall of print where she used to be.

"Mom? Ma, Mom?

"If you don't like me then leave me alone. I drink when I'm thirsty. I drink when I'm dry. If the moonshine don't kill me, I'll drink till I die."

I like that tea. Hot Ta Tea. It makes me feel cozy and happy like my cat's hum. So I lay back and slip in all the way, and I drown. With a smile on my face, I drown.

"Moonshine oh moonshine oh how I love thee, you killed my poor father, but dare you kill me." How can the light of the moon kill anyone?

I hear my mother's voice scolding the Giant.

"Jim, you don't need to be teaching 'em those barroom songs. They're just children."

"If the moonshine don't kill me, I'll drink till I die. If the moonshine don't kill me I'll drink till I die!" I raise my mug to the wall of newspaper, "More hot toddy please?" But she can't hear me. She's as lost in her words as I am in my tea. So I let myself drift off in funny thoughts of talking rabbits and juggling bears and Carol Burnett pulling on her ear and singing, *"I'm so glad we had this time together, just to have a laugh, or sing a song. Seems*

we just got started and before we know it, comes the time we have to say, 'So long'." My Aunt Caroline pops in to say, "So long is an Irish word that comes from Sl'an."

I stand with the cap in one hand and the bottle in the other and think about taking a big slug to wash down the pie. I hear my father singing, *"Lord preserve us and protect us, we've been drinking whiskey 'fore breakfast."* The past and present are fighting for air time, and I stand in stillness and try to figure out how to clear the static.

15

Tea Time

I TWIST THE CAP ON THE BOTTLE AND PLACE IT ON THE counter among the bottle brigade. The teapot is hissing and calling out, "I am ready." The Aunts answer by pushing open the kitchen door and searching around for clean cups or mugs to have their tea. As they move about the kitchen, they are talking to each other about my father's snoring, my mother's medication and my sister's prom. When they can't think of things to say, they pick up old conversations and begin again, as if for the first time. They are never at a lack for words. They lean against the dirty counter with their steamy mugs and groan about the uncomfortable cot or laugh about an odd dream they had. If a moment of silence sneaks in, it comes with a reminder of why they are all here. No one wants to listen to the hard message of the silence, so they pick up their words again and fend off the pain with witty banter. I try to make myself invisible, just to stay on a bit to hear them.

Their voices remind me of my mother's voice. When I hear them talking and laughing, I remember how long it has been since I've heard her. A hard knot grows in my throat.

Aunt Jody puts a couple pies in the oven to warm. The smell of pie and the sounds of their voices make it feel like a holiday party. That's usually when the Aunts come. They come for the first Holy Communions, baptisms and birthdays. They show up in station wagons packed with wired kids and wiggly babies. They come to the shows at school and my mother's glee club performance.

Our mom has the grand finale, and they are there early to help her get ready. 'Cause there's no business like show business and it's their business to make sure she looks great. They will save her from the "Rustia girl" raccoon eyes. That was her last name before she married the Giant.

I think about my mother coming up the block, as I try to swallow away the hard knot in my throat. I can see her walking; her lips are moving as she practices her song, her hair is hard and shiny. We press our faces to the window and can almost smell Aqua Net and hear the singing.

"There's no people like show people, they smile when they are low." We run to the door to see her shiny new hairdo. Today is the day she's been singing and talking about for weeks. Our mother will be performing on stage just like Cher, except not on TV. She'll be on stage at the school auditorium with the rest of the glee club ladies. There is so much to do. There's a special dress, new stockings, and a trip to the beauty parlor.

"I want to look extra snazzy," she tells us as she heads out the door. Half a day later she comes back home up the block, her short dark mane curled up and shiny, like a pretty new hair hat. As if that's not enough, my aunts arrive, pulling into the driveway honking horns, waving bottles.

They are here to help her get ready for the big show. They are all dressed up too, to support their sister. Seeing them smiling in lipstick makes it feel like an unplanned Christmas. They follow mom upstairs to her bedroom, and we tag along behind, jumping the steps two at a time to keep up. We crowd into Mom's bedroom, which is too small, so we kids jump up on the bed. The two boys pad into the room in their pajamas.

"Where are you going, Mommy?" they ask as they tug at her hem.

"She's going to the glee club," we all answer in unison.

"What's a glee club?" William asks, smiling and getting caught up in the excitement. Mom's mouth twists up and her eyes search the ceiling.

"Well, it's a singing club that brings glee to people."

"But what's glee?" he asks again.

"Glee is happiness," she says.

"So it's a happiness club?" he asks again.

"That's right, it's a happiness club," she nods as my aunts laugh and shake their heads.

From the bed, I watch my shiny mother take the time to explain the word to us, and I feel like I am seeing the most beautiful version of her. I want her to stay like this forever. I wish she never had to make pancakes, wear a housedress, fold laundry, or wipe our noses. I wish she could always be with her sisters wearing makeup and talking about happy things.

"I want to go to that, too," William says as he pulls at her hem again.

"Me, too!" Owen agrees, and the room lights up with ooos and ahhhs, cause Owen hardly ever talks, and when he does, it sounds so sweet.

Marian and Bridget lift our brothers and take them back to their room. "Not tonight," they say. "You guys need to stay here." Out in the hall we can hear their protest, but the real show is in the mirror, so we all go back to watching Mom like she is on television.

In the big mirror in her bedroom, she puts on her lipstick.

"I like it," Aunt Gabby nods approvingly. Aunt Gabby is the prettiest, so they all trust her and look to her for her approval. Her pale blue eyes sparkle like diamonds, her hair the color of brick and her skin an unripe peach, golden rosy and pink. She crosses her arms and leans her weight on one leg. Her shirt sways as her round hip moves away from her body. These sturdy hips, which have birthed my seven cousins, sit beneath a small waist that sits beneath a large bust that sits beneath a well-boned face that always wears red lipstick. All of her parts stack up to building a powerfully beautiful lady. On our summers at the beach, she comes out of the ocean like a lady in the movies, her wavy wet hair pulled back away from her face. She moves like a bear, slow and dangerous, even the water seems to drip from her in slow motion. On a crowded beach, she makes everyone else fade to sand.

"I like it a lot," she added, making my mother's face glow, like she has pinched her cheeks.

"It's called Crushed Rose," my mother whispered in a high pleasant voice that she usually saves for new neighbors and priests. She smiles, replaces the lid, and smacks her lips together in the mirror.

"Nice," Aunt Rita confirms as she pats her own blonde waves into place. "But you need a little work on those raccoon eyes." Her voice is dry and crackly, probably from a long day of yelling at kids at the Catholic school where she teaches. She sticks out among my other Aunts who are all nurses and speak in the soft tones you might hear in a hospital. Aunt Rita seems to be one volume click down from a scream. It's like she is still trying to be heard over a noisy class, and at any given moment, she might place a bad mark on my head, "D- for bad penmanship and raccoon eyes."

"Oh, Rita, she doesn't have raccoon eyes!" Aunt Jody jumps in to stick up for my mother. Aunt Jody is not as pretty as Aunt Gabby or even Aunt Rita, mostly because her hair is always so short, and it makes her look like a boy. But she's my fairy godmother, and I love her because she is funny and kind, and sometimes, when no one is looking, she will press a small gift or a quarter into my hand. So I think she is very beautiful in her own short-haircut way. The other thing I like about Aunt Jody is that she is a good talker—always ready with a funny story about the wiping of old people's asses in the hospital or of her own kids' asses at home. She has the whole house howling from the time she steps into our home in mid-sentence till she rambles down our block yelling her goodbyes from her station wagon packed with kids as she drives off waving.

"Oh come on. We all have them," Aunt Rita argues, her voice growing louder.

"The Rustia girls have dark circles, it's no secret." She turns to my mother with a smile, "But don't worry, Rosie, I have the answer! A little thing I call magic in a tube." She pulls a fat white pencil from her purse, snaps off the cap and begins drawing pale pink half circles under my mother's eyes as if she is writing an assignment on the blackboard. "Rub it in," she instructs as she returns the magic wand to her purse. My mother dabs at the cream with her fingers. "Abracadabra." Aunt Rita says, winking at the rest of them and raising her cocktail in the air.

"To the magic of makeup." The ice clicks against her glass to signal the lesson is complete and class is dismissed.

In the mirror, my mother looks like a movie star. We stand on the bed to see her over the heads of our aunts. We do our best not to jump, but the combination of excitement, her beauty, and having the perfect springboard beneath our feet makes it very hard not to bounce around a bit.

"Stop jumping on the bed," she calls to us over the finishing touches. Then she turns to our Aunts.

"What should I do with my hair?" she asks, even though it's already perfect. I run to her side and grab a red bow from her dresser. It's actually one of my little brother's discarded clip-on bow ties that he wore on Christmas, but I think it would make the perfect cherry on her Sundae.

I hold it up for her, "How about this?" She takes the bow from my hands and holds it to her hair. In the mirror, she makes a face that I have never seen on her before. Opening her eyes wide and letting her mouth drop open a little, like she's suddenly surprised, and she looks like the pretty lady on the side of the shampoo bottle. I can almost see bright lights flash and hear cameras click. My mother is someone totally different, and watching her light up is better than the fireworks on Fourth of July. I stand back and join my sisters on the bed as we cheer a wordless song of "Ooh and Aah!" My Aunts make a disapproving face at the red bow and shake their heads. My mother nods in agreement with them and the bow is dropped. But she has considered my idea, and so I am somehow a part of the major production of "mirror, mirror on the wall, who's the fairest of them all?" I can't help but stare at my mother 'cause I know without a doubt that she is the fairest of them all.

After her earrings are clipped on and the right necklace picked out, they move like one out the door and down the stairs; a delicious smelling glee parade with my mother as the Grand Marshall. I can see the back of her head floating down the stairway and bobbing as she leads us in song.

"There's no business like show business." We follow her on cue. *"Like no business we know!"* She has been singing this song for weeks; it's her solo number—the grand finale, and we know all the words by heart.

She leaves the house early to meet the other Glee club ladies at the Church. We watch her go, as we stand on the stoop and cheer her on. "Break a leg, Rosie!" Her sisters yell and wave their glass of wine. We join in too.

"Break a leg, Mom." Which seems wrong but feels right. She waves back with a smile, and there is a bounce in her step, and she sure does look extra snazzy. The rest of us walk down after her. In our school auditorium, we sit at large round tables with white tablecloths and slowly sip sodas through little red straws, trying to make them last all night. It feels magical in the auditorium as we wait for the show to begin.

Soon the lights dim, and the curtain opens. On stage, there are fifty ladies, mostly with pale blue hair all done up just like my mother's. They sing song after song. Their shiny red lips mouthing the words, and when the words stop, their lips stay put in bright happy smiles. They really are a happiness club, except for one lady on stage who cries through the whole show. It's hard not to stare at the crying lady as she gulps and shakes her way through each new song.

When we hear the music for my mother's big number begin, we sit up and turn to each other, "Here she comes. It's her turn," we whisper. Then we hear a special introduction.

"To close out the evening we have last but not least, Pee Wee Muldoon." The crowd starts laughing and down she comes with both arms stretched to either side of the stage like she's welcoming a room full of her dearest friends. She looks so wonderful in the lights, as she marches across the stage, with the crowd laughing and clapping as if she's Dick Van Dyke or something. Then the music grows louder, and she opens her mouth and starts to sing. She sings the song that we have all heard at least a million times over the past few weeks. Now, in front of all these strangers, it's even more magical, and it feels like we are hearing it for the first time.

"There's no business like show business like no business I know." We mouthed the words with her, our hearts filled with pride. We are connected to the beautiful lady on stage. And then the rest of the happy club ladies came in to back her up with

"Nowhere can you get that happy feeling when you are stealing that extra bow." And our mother does a funny bow and the crowd goes nuts with laughter. Even the crying lady perks up a bit. We look around, as if to say, "Hey, that's our mother, we live with her."

Then comes the part about there being *"no people like show people, they smile when they are low. Even with a turkey that you know will fold, you may be stranded out in the cold. Still you wouldn't change it for a sack of gold, let's go on with the show!"* Except she doesn't sing that, instead she sings something like…

"Even when you stranded in the cold with a turkey out in the cold." Then her face changes, and she says something about being cold again, and then the words stopped and she just mumbles something that sounds like *"la la dee dee da da la de de da and a bag of gold."* Her face looks happy but also like someone is sticking her with a sharp pin. And I stop watching and duck under the table with Annie. We hide beneath the long tablecloths that hang to the ground.

"She forgot the words," Annie whispers to me in the dark.

"I know," I whisper back. And the two of us sit Indian style beneath the table and giggle, because we didn't know what else to do. We can hear her trying to save what's left of her performance. We peek out from the tablecloths. *"That day you open and there you are, next day on your dressing room they've hung a star, let's go on with the show!"* We drop the tablecloth and return to the safety of our dark little hide out.

"She forgot the words," Annie whispers again. "How could she forget the words?" I just shake my head, and cover my face. It's all too much to think about. We wait till the show is over and we can hear people moving around. Then we wait till we hear the folding up of chairs, and only then do we sneak out of the auditorium and rush back up the hill to our home.

Mom's face stays red for days, and every time she thinks about it, you can tell 'cause she shakes her head and starts to sing again and then shakes her head some more, and then she laughs a little and says something like, "Oh for crying out loud." And she laughs, not in a happy way, but more of a "Jeez, sure wish that didn't happen!" way. Whenever she thinks about it, it makes us think about it, and when we do, we try not to laugh, because we know that she doesn't really think it's funny. We know from the way she looked at herself in the mirror, the way she led the parade down the stairs, the way she walked out on stage and drank up all that light, that inside of our mother is a real live show person. And she smiles even when she is low…

16

Hand Prints in Cement

STANDING IN THE MESSY KITCHEN WITH MY CHATTING Aunts, I imagine I can hear her singing, loud and proud as she flips pancakes and pours milk. All while the cat runs between her feet looking for a hand out, and the two boys chase each other in and out of the heavy door. I wish she was standing here too and not lying still in the next room. I wish I could hug her and remind her of all the other lines she didn't forget, all the other lines that she got perfect. The more I think, the more thoughts crowd my mind and the lump starts to come back. So, I take my cereal out to the dining room and try shaking it off. I sit down before I notice her at the end of the table with her head in her hands. Aunt Gabby looks up at me. Her pale blue eyes weary, her signature red lipstick nowhere in sight.

"Maureen, why are you leaving for school when your mother is dying?" Her question hits me right in the gut, and I am not sure how I am supposed to go on eating. I keep chewing and chewing till the cereal is liquid, and my sadness turns to a boil and then a quiet rage. I want to tell her that my mother is not going to die, that she has it all wrong, that this is just the way it is, the way it has always been. She will be up in a few days and then down in a few days and then up again. But never down for good. That is not how this story ends. 'Cause that's an ending I can't swallow. I imagine debating my aunt on the finer points of faith and miracles.

"What about the snow?" I want to say to her. "Didn't she ask for it? Isn't it a sign that things will be okay?" I am not the one giving up on signs from heaven. I gotta be the one who holds on to the faith.

I think about telling her how uncomfortable I am with the whole set up of sleeping relatives, no prom for Riddle, the packed kitchen, and all the waiting around. Our home is like a crowded bus stop with everyone just waiting. Days spent waiting for death. Nights spent waiting for sleep. Prayers, fears and morphine tying the two together and wrapping them up in a knot so tight it threatens to cut off our circulation. Rows and rows of rosary beads repeated and repeated and repeated again. Hoping for miracles and asking for signs. It shouldn't go wasted. Someone has to hold on.

It's got me confused. Why would God send us a sign and still take our mother. That's mostly what I want to know. I would tell God not to busy himself with the signs and just get to work on the miracle. And mostly, I want to ask Aunt Gabby about the snow. Why she asked to see it, what it meant when it came. Was it a sign from heaven that everything would be okay? Did she believe in miracles?

Is that what she believes? Is that what they all believe, and is that why they asked? The questions come like waves upon waves, but I let none of them out.

I spoon the soggy cereal into my mouth to try to keep the questions down. Aunt Gabby puts her head on the table, and I go on thinking about signs. What were they again? Who asked for what? Aunt Jody asks for a white dove. Aunt Gabby asks for the snow. Marian asks to see a little girl in white carrying a rose. They share these signs over my mother's bed as they change the bandages and smooth back her hair. I wanted to ask for a rainbow, like the big one in the *Wizard of Oz*. Going where troubles melt like lemon drops makes good sense. *"Somewhere over the rainbow way up high, there's a place that I've heard of once in a lullaby."* I imagine the giant rainbow coming right to our front door and taking us all far away. But I don't tell anyone because I don't really believe that this will actually happen, or that there is a place where we could escape. Besides, nobody asks what sign I wanted.

The Aunts have been here before. They know their parts even if they are reluctant to play them. They prepare the stage, set the props, and go about rehearsing their lines. Checking each beat off. Hospital bed, check. Morphine, check. Asks for a sign, check. Joke over wine and pie, check. Cry during the rosary, check. They know this dance, and have all the moves down pat, just another casual Friday of sickness and death. I want to tell them to stop being so sure about the whole thing. But I don't, I just keep placing spoonful after spoonful of cold cereal into my un-hungry belly. It gets over the lump in my throat and sits heavy in the pit in my gut.

My spoon hits the empty bowl and she looks up at me. "Maureen, you should say goodbye to your mother." She says it in a way that is supposed to tell me this time is for real. The last four years were just a dress rehearsal, and I hate her for it. She is poking at a tender heart, messing with an angry dog. I look her in the eye and as cool as I can, I tell her,

"I already have." It shuts her down like when mom tried to tell me about the birds and the bees.

"Maureen, your body is changing and soon you will be…"

"I know Mom," I cut her off, fast and cold. "They told us all about it in school."

My other Aunts parade by with their cups of tea and plates of pie. I take my empty bowl to the kitchen, dump it in the crowded sink, and head out the back door.

Our back patio is speckled with little handprints pressed into the cement. I scan the pavement to find mine. It's much smaller than I remember my hand ever being. I kneel down to measure, and suddenly I am kneeling beside him, heart thumping, hand pressed to the ground and mind racing…

Dad drill, dad drill, dad drill! Dad drills are like the fire drills we practice at school. For the fire drill, the alarm goes off and we line up cautiously, moving swiftly in single file to the playground. For the Dad drill, one of my sisters calls out "Dad Drill," and we all run and hide as fast as we can, and it is always every man for himself. We practice when he is not home.

He is not the type of dad who sends heads rolling when he walks in the door, like some other dads in our neighborhood, but it's the fear that he could that puts us on edge. The truth is we are more scared than he is scary. He could never live up to our fears. My mother is constantly warning us about, "When your father gets home you're all gonna get it." And the dad drills do nothing to eliminate the myth. Besides, he is a Giant so you can't be too safe because Giants are notorious for being mean to kids.

It's hard to look at the Giant and harder still to make eye contact. Instead, I sneak with my sisters down to the basement. We push open the heavy wooden door and snoop in the Giant's forbidden workroom for clues. It's a cave, dark with cobwebs, and dust and tools, millions of them. Hammers and nails, screws, bits, bolts. He has glass jars filled with all sorts of things and a whole section of odds and ends that he has gotten "off the job." A beautiful chandelier covered in years of dust, discarded light fixtures, and half empty boxes of bathroom tiles. We're not really allowed in there, but we go anyway.

The tools in the dark smell of cold fog and dirt. A shaft of light finds its way in and twinkles on a glass jar of three inch nails or the sharp edge of a saw, and we jump a little and hold on to each other while keeping one eye on the door. If everyone should suddenly run, you don't want to be the one left behind. Being in this silent dirty room so close to these sharp edges is like being close to the Giant himself. So we walk on tippy toes and try not to leave clues that we were there.

The monster of all tools is the cement mixer planted in our back yard, a massive chunk of gray metal that's louder and more terrorizing than the rest. It's big and scary like the Giant as it churns out wet cement with a low deep hum that says, "Stand back, don't get too close." The cement mixer came in handy when he got the idea to turn a section of our backyard into a patio. He calls it our own miniature Grauman's Chinese theater patio, complete with handprints, like we're famous people. After watching Jack Nicholson press his paws at the Chinese theater in Hollywood, the

Giant tells Mom he will make his own. I kneel beside him as he takes my hand in his and presses it down. The cement squishes up between my fingers and feels like sandy oatmeal.

"Don't move," he says, "just stay still." It's exciting. But I stay perfectly still and stare down at his hand on my hand in the liquid sidewalk. I can hear his breathing as my hand gets sandwiched between his cold rough palm and the cool gritty cement. "Okay," he says, "good job."

He pulls my hand from the cement, and there before me is a perfectly shaped handprint. It's so wonderful that I want to tell him. I begin to work my way up to his face. His plaid shirt, his white buttons, his neck with little black hairs. He leans his weight back on to his heels and takes in his work. As I get to his mouth, the back of his hand wipes the drops of water from his upper lip. Then his lips turn to me. "Go wash your hands at the hose," they tell me. I nod my head at the buttons on his shirt and get up to go. I pass my sisters who have taken the clothesline down from one end and are jumping rope with it. Close by, Annie is digging a hole in the mud with one of Mom's good spoons.

"I'm digging to China!" she screams at no one in particular. The two boys watch her as they wait their turns to be immortalized by the Giant.

The rest of the day, we stand around the yard watching the Giant work on his masterpiece in cement—drawing in the numbers and smoothing out the rough bits. Eight handprints and the Latin numeral to show which child is the owner. It's still the most magnificent thing I had ever seen.

I look down at the handprints and think of all the things that did not get pressed into cement, all the things that will not be made permanent.

17

The Swing Set

I WIPE SOME DEAD LEAVES OFF THE CEMENT PATIO. We used to spray it down with the hose and keep it nice and neat so everyone could see. But lately, we've had other things to care for.

I stand and take in our backyard: the compost pile, woodpile, old clothesline and rusty swing set. It all looks abandoned like a ghost yard, and yet I can still see all the stories that lay just beneath the surface of things.

A slight gust of wind sends the swings swaying, and I can hear my sisters scream, "Ghost children!" and run around the yard.

The swing set arrived the same day the moving van came to take my second grade friend Jenny away. A group of long-haired hippies carried her swing set up the block and stood on my front lawn.

My name echoes through the house like a winner on The Price Is Right.

"Maureen! Maureen! Come on down!" I am seven, and by the sound of my sisters' voices, I am sure that I have won some major award. I pass a ten-year-old Riddle in the front hall furiously brushing her hair in the mirror. "There's a whole bunch of cute guys here with a swing set," she informs me while hiking up her shorts.

By the time I get out the door, they're bringing it around the back. With effortless ease they lift it over the fence and place it in our yard. It's the hippies from Jenny's house, and they're giving me her swing set. Their swing set really, cause the hippies got to swing on it way more than she did. And even though they are leaving, I am beside myself with happiness that they have somehow thought to include me in the exit plan. I beam back at them, exposing all my crooked teeth. A whole swing set just for me? Watching it get carried up and over the fence is the best show ever, not just because of the size of the gift, but also because of the friends who bring it. My hippie friends from down the block are moving out today and taking Jenny with them, but they have not forgotten me. I stand without words and watch with my mouth hanging open as the neighbors look on and shake their heads in amusement.

The hippies don't mind the attention. They smile and sing and strut their stuff as they move like a team of dancers carrying a contraption of poles and swings and slides above their heads like they did this sort of thing every day. "Right on, Maureen," they laugh, "Far out huh?"

I blush. The swing set is one thing, but hearing them say my name is a whole other treat. It's so much nicer than "little kid," and it rolls off their lips so sweet and direct that it goes right to my heart. I fall in love with each and every one of them. I can't imagine how my mother could not like hippies; they all seemed like modern-day Jesuses with their sandaled feet and generous smiles. "There you go, Maureen," they say and leave the yard waving two fingers in the air at us.

My brothers scramble up the slide as I follow the hippies around to the front yard where half the neighborhood has come out to see the swing set parade. My mother and Mrs. Gabiola shake their heads and cover their smiles. Riddle sits on the highest step of our stoop and bats her eyes back at the handsome hippies as they head back down the block. It's hard not to run after them and beg them to take me with them. I don't know where they are going, but I know it will be fun—someplace where they will dance and sing and swing and braid each other's hair.

Their songs float back to me and I cling to the words that seem to escape me like handfuls of sand.

My brothers hang off the swing set like little monkeys. Annie joins in and gets some major momentum going as her toes seem to tickle the clouds. She pumps with so much power that she has the thing teetering a bit. "See who can go the highest," she yells at me, her wild hair dancing in the breeze.

I kick a few leaves off the patio as I look out at the swing set, another breeze sways the swings, but this time there is a creak and I step back away from my memories. Ghost children.

18

Around the Side of My House

I MAKE MY WAY AROUND THE SIDE OF OUR HOUSE PASSING the garbage cans and the Gabiola's backyard. The Gabiola's yard is just a big dirt patch where they play basketball night and day. In the summer they cook every meal on their dirty grill. Mornings are always quiet at their house. I pass without incident. Out in front of our house, there are a few people on their way to work. Businesspeople walking to the train, old ladies going to mass, grade school kids walking their dogs before school. William and Owen will be making their way down to Our Lady of Sorrows too, but I take the train, so I leave for school an hour earlier than they even need to wake up. Seeing all the people going about their day like everything is just fine helps me breathe easier. I step in pace with them.

The houses on our block are big and filled to the brim with kids. The average family has six or more. We have eight kids in our family, which could have been more if mom didn't lose the twins after Owen was born. I can't imagine having more than eight kids, but people do, especially the families who go to Our Lady of Sorrows. The Smiths have nine, the Halls have eleven, and the Rogers have fourteen.

There are a few smaller families. The Terrills, whose father is the chief of police, live to the right of us and have five kids. The Gabiolas, whose father is the captain of the fire department, live to the left. They only have four.

The Giant is an electrician. I know firemen put out fires and policemen catch bad guys but as for the Giant, I have no idea how an electrician spends his days. There is a slight connection between the large man who shows up for dinner, the crack of lightning, and the alarmingly jolting feeling you get when sticking a finger in an outlet. They all have something to do with electricity. His connection to this mysterious force makes the Giant all the more ominous.

As I walk the block to the train station, I watch for patterns. The houses on our block are lined up in perfect order like obedient school children. Each one is surrounded by a decent-sized lawn, which runs uninterrupted into the next in an unending pattern of grass, walkway, grass, driveway, grass, walkway, grass, driveway. No one has a fence, and you can run from one front yard to the next without ever stopping till you get to the end of the block. Easy access for trick-or-treating, Christmas caroling, and Ring and Run.

I come down our driveway that sits between our house and the Gabiola house. I turn right and cut across our lawn. Our cat, Crazy, is perched on our stoop licking her paws. I don't blame her; our stoop is pretty much the place to be at any given time and just being near it makes me feel calm. Like looking at the ocean, it helps me breathe.

When mom was still walking, she would head to church every day. When she stopped being able to make the walk, she'd end up settling on the front stoop. For me, the front stoop would always be the first choice…

It's just five steps leading to a landing that is framed by two large, white, paint-chipped pillars. On any given night, it's a kid magnet. Kids from all over would stop by for a game of Spud or Red Rover.

We shield our eyes and count to twenty by Mississippis, ending in the forewarning of "Ready or not, here I come." We learn new versions of songs like, "*Jingle Bells* and *Batman smells* and how *Robin laid the egg*," and "*Baby, baby stick your head in gravy.*"

We melt slugs with Morton's salt and turn steel wool into fireworks, lightning bugs into wedding rings, and garbage can lids into sleds. On summer nights, it's a comedy club that sends laughter and lewdness spewing down the block. It's our Neverland, our grandstand for broken hearts, bloody noses, wishing on stars and mooning cars. And it's so easy to get to. "Meet you at the stoop," we tell our friends and everyone knows exactly where to go.

It's where we learn about the church and the steeple and how, if we open the doors, we can see all the people. Where teams are picked for kickball and we practice yelling warnings of "*Car! Car! C. A. R. stick your head in the jelly jar!*" with red faces and pounding hearts. It's summer nights and Christmas carols all rolled into one.

It's the secret club where I got my first explanation of how babies are made from my whispering sisters who taught me the hand jive of *"Some girls sit like this, and some girls sit like this, but the girls who sit like this, get this, like this."* And where I decode the meaning of the middle finger.

It's the sunny spot where my mother devours her books and washes them down with cup after cup of weak tea. It's the gym where she practices the latest calisthenics from Jack Lalanne.

It's the garden where she waters her potted geraniums and my sisters blossom into teenagers doing fan kicks and singing, *"Who wears short shorts?"* And *"Hey, hey we're the Monkees."* It's the altar where we pray *"Jesus, Mary and Joseph be with me on my way. Holy Spirit inspire me,"* before kissing my mother's cheek each day before school. It's the backdrop for Halloween pictures and first days of school and prom pictures.

It's the cause of my first trip to the hospital when I fall off the side of it one day as the Giant pulls in from work and I decide to act like one of the kids on TV, jumping up and down for joy. I land in the bushes with a broken arm, silently cursing those damn Brady kids once again.

It's the magical place where one night I watched in the shadow of the moon, my mother change into a blushing school-girl as she confessed how she and the Giant got engaged. "He'd kill me if he knew I told you," she began. And then without further hesitation, she unraveled the story of how they'd been dating and he took her out to dinner and asked her to marry him. After she said yes, he drank too much and was too drunk to drive her home, so he put her in a cab. But when he realized that he just sent his bride-to-be home alone on the night they were engaged, he jumped in another cab and followed her all the way, screaming out the window, "That's the girl I am going to marry," just so he could give her a kiss goodnight on her doorstep. That's the type of story you'd be likely to hear on our front stoop. Its darkness and safety brought out the deepest of secrets like an unholy confessional, especially on warm summer nights set with twinkling stars and serenading crickets and the occasional warm whoosh of a car's headlights moving down the street.

It is still the place we go to unravel riddles.

People can tell it's a safe place to spill the beans, and they do. Mom's friends join her for a cup of tea and rehash the latest dramas. Claire, the new girl, tells me about her parents and her secrets. Things you don't think are heavy, get unloaded on the stoop, and everyone leaves feeling lighter.

I give Crazy a pat and think about Claire and her troubles. I don't think they are too terrible or interesting, but I listen anyway 'cause I can tell that it's all important to her. She chips the polish from her nails as she babbles on about boys, being popular, and parties we haven't been invited to.

It's late and getting cold out as she stands to head back to her home three houses away. I start up my front stoop.

"Hey!" she calls out, and I turn to her.

"I need to tell you something else." She jogs over to me and plays with her zipper.

"What?" I ask again.

"See, I lied to you. My dad, my dad is not on a business trip. He is in New York, where he lives. My parents are divorced."

"Oh," I say, grabbing my jacket and crisscrossing it over my chest for warmth. Her light blue eyes are soft and sad, and I think she wants to say more, so I wait.

"I am sorry. I lied. I just didn't want you to not like me," she adds. I shrug.

"I don't care if your parents are divorced. It's not really a big deal."

"Well, except it is. When it's your parents, it is a very big deal."

"Oh," I say again. "Well, you don't have to worry about me not liking you." I tell her. She looks me in the eye and smiles.

"See you tomorrow, Loser," I tell her.

"Not if I see you first, Weirdo," she says, and we push at each other and go our separate ways. We each smile a little because we know something nice just happened, but we're not sure what to call it, so we blame it on the stoop, the magical, wonderful stoop.

I take a moment to try to figure out the magic to these five cement steps that lead to a landing, and a wooden door covered by a screen door that creaks on its hinges and slams on its own. On the landing, by the door, there is a worn mat and an old milk can that my mother has painted blue. I can't figure it out. It doesn't look like anything special really, and yet it is everything for sure.

19

In the Front Yard

DOWN ON THE SIDEWALK THE SNOW HAS MELTED. ONLY the damp pavement is left.

Our neighbor across the street steps out on to his stoop. His wife, Angel, kisses him goodbye as he heads off in his business suit. His two kids come to the door in matching footie pajamas. The little girl has curly blonde locks, and the boy has straight black hair. Their cheeks are round and red and happy. "Bye, daddy," they say over and over again while waving their hands. "Bye, Timmy. Bye, Tiny," he calls. Tiny is actually Justine, but she is so cute and small that "Tiny" is the perfect nickname. I wish I had a cute nickname. But the Giant doesn't use my regular name, so imagining him calling me nicknames seems impossible.

With so many of us, it's tough to keep us all straight. Sometimes he gets so frustrated that he forgets our names altogether. He goes down the list hopping from one to the next like hot coals, and seeing him fumble makes us laugh. So now he just calls us "you." When he needs more than one of us he points. "You and you, it's a two-man job." My sisters and I look at him confused.

"We're not men, we're girls," we want to tell him. But you don't talk back to the Giant. I really don't like being called a man, but being called "you" is not so bad, compared to what he calls other people. His favorite name is "communist bastards," and he has special names for different groups of people. Some are guineas, some are krauts and chinks, and for black people he has a whole list.

Baboons and porch monkeys. Porch monkeys makes me think he is talking about the people who live one town over and keep an actual caged pet monkey on their front porch. We never get close enough to see if it's real, but every time we drive by, we push and crowd each other to one side of the van in hopes that we can catch sight of the porch monkey.

I don't know why the Giant calls black people "monkeys." But I do know it's bad. No one wants to be the monkey's uncle or the monkey in the middle. Plus, Mom always gives us the hairy eyeball when we sing, *"You look like a monkey and you smell like one, too!"* at each other's birthday parties. But it's confusing because the word monkey is not a bad word. You can use it in a sentence at school and no one thinks twice. Neither is Kraut. It could be a nickname for sauerkraut and the word Guinea is just like a guinea pig. So it's hard to figure out if these are real bad words or not. That is not the same for the word nigger.

I know that word is bad by the way most people lower their voice a little. Except for the Tevlin sisters. They have no problem saying everything at full volume. They have "been around the block," as my mom would say. They know all the bad words and the best ways to pair them for the greatest effect. They don't just say nigger. They say, "nigger lover." Like it is the worst thing you could ever be.

Annie and Frannie both have buck teeth and Frannie has a baby hand that never grew and a burn mark on her cheek from when she pulled a cup of coffee on herself as a baby. Frannie is short and sharp and dark, and Annie is big and pink and bubbly. Plus, Annie has a lisp. That makes me want to watch her when she talks in the same way that I like to watch the sprinkler that gets set out on the lawn in the summertime.

They live on the edge of Vailsburg, the black section of town. They walk home from school with Daniel and Doug Walker, two of the few black kids who go to our school. The walking to school is all well and good, but Frannie did the unthinkable and got a crush on Doug. She even held hands with him, with her good hand, on the way home from school.

When the two girls fight, Frannie calls out "Hey TH-upid" and Annie comes back with "baby hand" and "nigger lover." I stand between these warring sisters as they toss word bombs at each other, doing my best not to pick sides. I imagine with morbid curiosity how quickly their razor sharp words would cut me down, and I've been so well pruned already. I pull my lips over my own crooked teeth and do my best to protect my soft spots. "Sticks and stones may break my bones but names will never hurt me," is blarney, or "a load of crap" as the Giant would say.

I look around the Tevlin's front yard in fear that someone might hear them shouting these words. I've only spoken to a black man once. Well, the truth is I didn't actually speak to him. He spoke to me. He comes out of nowhere and runs a circle around my mind.

Right outside my house, down by the sidewalk, Owen sees him first. A car drives by, and now Owen is beside me. He is very little, and I am telling him to stay away from the street. Owen is pointing at something, and I turn to look.

He comes down our block on a shiny ten-speed and looks like a black Mr. Clean. He's the type of person you would notice even if he hadn't been in the middle of an all-white neighborhood. He stops when he hears Owen yell, and everything, including my heart, stops with him. I look at Owen in shock. Not just because he hardly ever talks, but I am not sure I've ever heard him yell either.

He first words actually came out in a sentence, which was, "Get Mauween out of my woom." And our mother fell over herself in joyful relief as she spent the next few hours calling everyone she knew to squash the theory that Owen was a mute. Each call ended with the punch line of, "Get Mauween out of my Woom." Later, the doctor would tell her that he didn't speak for so long because he didn't have to. With six girls falling over themselves to do his bidding, he wanted for nothing.

We were all so busy trying to get him to say some words that we must have forgotten to tell him the words to never say.

Except for the day Michael Gabiola got his bike stolen, and of course, from the Tevlin sisters, I have never heard the word yelled. But Owen's young and hasn't been schooled in the etiquette of racism.

The man on the bike circles around and slowly pulls up to my brother. His brakes let out a cry as he lands his foot on our curb.

"What did you say?" he asks, spitting a little on the "s" and cocking his head for emphasis.

Like a boiling soup wanting to burst from the covered pot, I watch him trying to keep a lid on. But by the look in his eyes, I have every reason to believe that at any moment he will explode and, like Fannie's face, we will all be badly burned.

Owen goes quiet and reaches up to pinch my arm. This is what he does when he's nervous or scared. I stand beside my baby brother who only comes up to my elbow, and this man's knee. I stand still and quietly take the pain. Owen is my responsibility and as much as I want to run, I know I will have to go down with this shipwreck.

My face gets cold and sweaty, and I want to tell the black man that it's not my brother's fault. I want to tell him about the Giant and his way of saying things, like "jackass" and "the goddamn sons of bitches." But as I stare up at his angry face, no words will come. The words are so far gone that I am not sure I'll ever get them back. There is just a vacant warehouse pillaged by fear, and not a word can be found. So we all just stand there in pain, waiting on Owen as he continues to tighten his grip on my arm, his little nails finding each other through my skin. I want to blurt out the word for him just to get him to stop. But I am trapped between my silent brother, this black man's anger, and my own fear.

What the black man doesn't know is that it could be years before Owen spoke again. It had taken him four years to say anything, and since then he's still pretty stingy with the words. But the black man stands firm and crosses his arms like he has all day.

"I asked you a question, boy. What did you say?"

He didn't say the word "asked" like Daniel and Doug say it—axed." He speaks like a teacher. Clear and slow.

"What did you say?"

Owen repeats the word in a squeaky little whisper, but even still the man turns his head, and his foot slips from the curb like he's been slapped in the face with an open palm. Once he gets his balance, he moves back in at us, closer than before. The skin on his face is shiny now, like his bike. The muscles in his arms look like the ones on my brother's G.I. Joe doll. His lips are puckered, and he moves them in a circular motion. I'm not sure if he is thinking or getting ready to spit at us. But as I watch him, I realize that he is not a man at all, but a teenager like my sister, Marian. It's weird because he talks like a man and not like all those hippie teens who shuffled by our house and ask things like, "Hey man, have you seen my dog?" or "Hey man, which way is Band Street?" This boy/man/teenager/guy is more confident than anyone I have ever met, and even though he is out of his territory, he makes those hippies seem like the ones who are lost.

"Where did you learn such a word?" he asks. I think about the Tevlin twins and the Giant and how Michael Gabiola went running down the block with a knife screaming "I'm gonna kill the first nigger I see," after his new bike was stolen outside of Leo's Candy Shop. But I stay silent cause I am pretty sure that ratting people out will not help my brother's cause.

"Do you even know what that word means?" His eyes squint a bit, like he is handing us a riddle, like he's giving us the benefit of the doubt. And when he asks, I realize that I am not really sure what the word means. I know it is something white people call black people, but I am not sure why. I could have asked Aunt Caroline, and she would have given it to me straight.

Owen shakes his head from side to side. His bright green

eyes are a blurry water color, heavy on the water. But like the black man, he does his best to hold it all in.

"It means ignorant. Do you know what that word means?" he asks and then answers without waiting for us. "Ignorant means stupid, and only stupid people use that word. Whoever taught you that word is ignorant, do you understand?"

I nod my head to show him that I understand. Nigger means ignorant, and ignorant means stupid. And being stupid has nothing to do with being black, and he is saying that people who used the word nigger are actually the stupid ones. I like that he has laid it out for us, but I don't like where it leads us.

'Cause when he says "people," he's talking about the twins and Michael and the Giant, my father. He is calling my father stupid. My face goes pink and warm, and I hate the boy/man for telling us that and hate everyone else for not telling us. And I especially hate the Giant for loading Owen down with this heavy ammunition, for leaving this loaded gun around without thinking about how kids could pick things up and someone could get killed. From the way things looked, that someone might be my little brother, Owen. My lip quivers, and a tight ball forms in my throat. I stick my tongue down deep between my lip and my lower teeth to try to keep my skin from showing too much.

"Do you understand?" he asks again, wanting to make sure we get the lesson. Owen and I nod our heads up and down at him. The black man shakes his head from side to side at us in a way that makes me feel heavy and hollow like a big fallen tree or a bad report card. He put his weight on his other leg, takes his foot off the curb, places it on his pedal and begins to rides off.

His arms grip the handlebars as his feet power down on the pedals in smooth strokes. Watching him ride is like watching a large bird take flight. It seems like the boy and the bike are one, and I feel oddly sad to see him go. I want to call after him and ask about all the other words and questions that I don't understand. I'm sure he would give me the truth, no matter how painful. What about communist? I want to yell, "What does that word mean? Will the TV really eat our brains? Will eating carrots curl your hair, and why aren't girls allowed to be priests?"

I watch till he turns the corner, and then I knock Owen's hand away and begin rubbing the tender spot left on my arm.

"You are stupid. Why'd you have to do that? Huh?"

He answers me by letting the tears spill over and down his cheeks and he hangs his head. So I take on the role of the black man, shaking my head back and forth at him in disappointment. We stand there a while; him wiping his eyes, me rubbing my arm. I know this will set him back in the talking business. I feel bad for him and don't really blame him. If everyone you knew drank from the toilet, it may take you a while before you start to wonder whether that was a good idea. But monkey see, monkey do...

20

From Our Side of the Street

ACROSS THE STREET, I WATCH MR. DANIELS GET IN HIS CAR and head off to work. He wears a suit and looks like Mr. Brady from the *Brady Bunch*. I imagine he smells good too, strong and clean. "Goodbye, Timmy. Goodbye, Tiny." He calls one final time as he pulls out of their driveway. "Bye, Daddy! Bye, Daddy!" they sing out, dancing from foot to foot.

Mrs. Daniels opens the door, and they scurry inside like two little baby squirrels, leaving me standing there staring and with one more question for the black man, "Why do some kids get the dads that smell good and remember names and other kids get Giants?

Down at the corner I pass Jenny's house, but a new family lives there now, and an old lady is out early, hanging clothes on the line where our swing set used to be. She wears an old plaid housedress and a bright red sweater and it's like she doesn't notice the snow or doesn't care. "It's May, and in May we use the line," I can almost hear her saying as I walk by. She grabs a clothespin from her pocket and begins to hang a pair of black socks. There is a man's T-shirt and a lady's housedress and a couple of smaller dresses lined up in a row on the line. One of the little dresses has an apron attached. A pinafore. I watch it dance in the wind like it's putting on a show for me. The old lady looks up, and I smile out of habit. She nods at me but not in a friendly way. It's more of a slow nod with still eyes and flat lips that tell me she is still deciding if I am worth it. I turn my eyes back to my feet as they move over the wet cement. If April showers bring May flowers, what does May snow bring? I press my foot into a white snow patches, and it melts to slush under my foot.

A woman walks past me on her way to church. She is pushing a baby stroller, and I move to the side to let her by. As she passes, I smell the sharp sweetness of Jean Nate perfume, and suddenly I am beside my mother, and we are going shopping.

"Back to school clothes" and it's just the two of us. My sisters are at school and Aunt Caroline is watching William and the baby. Mom has on a church dress, lipstick, and Jean Nate.

She takes me by the hand, and we walk to the store, holding hands the whole way. No stroller around to push me to the side. No cold metal bar to hold. I have her warm, soft hand in mine.

The store is called The Children's Cottage and it's a long way from our house. I skip over the little puddles on the sidewalk.

"April showers bring May flowers," she tells me. "April showers bring May flowers," I repeat over and over again, turning it into a song.

The ground is still drying out from all the rains, and the air smells like wet dirt and tree bark. The street is sparkly and wet and quiet with all the kids at school. I can hear the sound that our feet make against the sidewalk. It's like we are walking in a quiet dream. I swing her hand and make sure not to step on any cracks. Don't want to be the one to break her back, especially not today.

At the store, she picks out two dresses—one light blue with pink stripes, and one plaid with a little white apron attached to it. I have never seen a dress with an apron attached. "It has an apron, Mom?"

"That's called a pinafore," a voice calls back. But it is not my mother's voice. It's smooth and sweet like a voice on the radio. I look up to find the most beautiful lady ever. Prettier than Maureen McLaughlin, if that is even possible, and way skinnier and shiny. I have never seen anyone so shiny. She sparkles like the wet streets. Her lips are covered in pale pink, like she just kissed a cupcake. Her eyelids glisten like blue snow.

She gently pushes me into a little room of mirrors. Her dainty hands pull on the curtain, that hangs from a bar above us. Her nails are painted hot pink—the same exact shade as her shoes. She closes the curtain, and all I see are the tips of her hot pink shoes peeking under the curtain at me. Then she is gone.

I am alone with the dresses and mirrors. If I stand at the right angle, I can see ten of me. I move my hands up and down and watch ten hands go up and down. I try going faster to see if I can trick the mirror. But it's dead on every time.

"Don't get lost in there, Maureen." This voice I recognize. "She's prone to lollygag," I hear Mom explain.

I try on the one with the apron. In the mirror, Alice in Wonderland smiles back at me, and I curtsy to her. Then I try the next dress, the baby blue sweater dress with thin pink stripes around the waist. It feels like a cozy warm hug on me. I pull the curtain to the side and step out. The sales lady cocks her head to one side and smiles.

"It looks flattering on your petite figure." I have no idea what these words mean, but I like every single one of them. My face gets warm and I stare at her shoes. They are the prettiest shade of pink, and they make me think of Jolly Ranchers.

"Okay, go change," Mom instructs.

When she is not looking I peek upward. The shiny lady takes the two dresses and winks at me. I gasp. She is so sweet and pretty and filled with possibilities, like a human birthday cake, ready to make my wish come true. Her words repeat themselves in my head like a love song as I change back into my clothes. I watch ten arms struggle through to find the armhole and ten hands pop in to view. It's like my own little magic show. I straighten out my top and pull on my pants and practice my new words in the mirror.

"It looks flattering on your petite figure."

I know I will take these new words home with me and try them on a million times.

I step out of the little room and Mom takes my hand and we head for the door. I pull back a little.

"What about the dresses?" I ask. There is silence, and I frown at the shiny lady and then at my mother.

"We're going to put them on lay away," Mom says.

"Lay away," I repeat, and the shiny lady nods and smiles.

"That means we don't take the dresses home today, Maureen, but we'll make special trips back to the shop and bring a little money each time, and soon we get to take them home."

"And they will be mine for keeps," I inform the sales lady, mostly for my mother's sake.

"Well, they really look flattering on your petite figure," she informs me again. I smile sadly at her, not just because of the hold up with the dresses, but also because even though I like these new words, they seem like the only ones she has. She is like a beautiful broken talking doll, when you pull her string she only has one thing to say. So I wave to her instead of saying goodbye.

Back at home it smells like pizza, and Aunt Caroline is stirring sauce and rolling meatballs, and the record player is singing how *"the moon hits your eye like a big pizza pie, that's amore!"* The two boys are sitting at the dining room table with red sauce all over their faces. I tell Aunt Caroline all about the shiny lady and the dresses and the new words, "flattering" and "petite" and "figure." Aunt Caroline tells me that "flattering," means it looks nice; it's a compliment, which means to complete or fill up. And she is right cause I do feel full.

"Oh and 'petite' is a French word that means 'little,' and 'figure' is your figure." She puts her hands on her waist and shakes her hips a little. "Your body shape. So she's saying that the dresses look complete on your little body." I frown up at Aunt Caroline. "The dresses look complete on my little body," doesn't sound half as nice as how the shiny lady said it.

"Well, they did look nice," I add.

"Then that is no blarney, Maureen. She wasn't trying to butter you up."

"No, she wasn't," I agree even though I am not sure what butter has to do with anything. We stare at each other and she smiles 'cause she can tell I look confused. "'Butter you up' means covering you with unnecessary compliments," she tells me and then, "To compliment someone means to fill them up."

"Flattering and compliments and buttering you up are all the same," I say. And Aunt Caroline's face lights up!

"Yes!" she says and waves a wood spoon in the air that drips sauce on the floor. "By George, you got it!" she says and I smile.

"I guess she did fill me up," I say. Aunt Caroline nods. "And I sort of liked it," I confess. "I did, I liked how she filled me up, it felt nice."

"Sure it did," Aunt Caroline continues, "compliments are nice, but what you have to know, Maureen, is that with or without butter, your bread is already perfect." I stare at her blue eyes, as she looks right at me and sings, *"That's amore!"* and then taps my nose with her spoon, and I smile and feel like fresh baked.

"'Amore' means 'love,' Maureen...Italian for 'love.'" She answers my questions before I even ask them. I wipe the sauce from my nose and lick my fingers.

Aunt Caroline is lit up like a beautiful fairy godmother. In the light of the window, she twirls her wooden wand in the air and conducts the music, humming along with the song about the moon and the pizza and the Italian love.

A horn blares, and she begins to fade as I find myself back on the cold, wet sidewalk. An old blue Chevy drives slowly by with a hand waving out at me. The tips of my ears are feeling the cold, and I wish I had worn a hat. As I track the Chevy, I see Mrs. Accardi ducking her head to smile at me from behind her steering wheel.

Mrs. Accardi, the pretzel lady, playground attendant, and crossing guard lady is also one of the solid regulars at morning mass. The blare of her horn and shake of her hand is less of a "good morning" and more of a "Wake up, Maureen! Get a move on! Stop the lollygagging! Quit your dilly dallying!" Mrs. Accardi would sometimes warm our stoop, up until Mom got too sick to sit outside. But when she still could, Mrs. Accardi loved to stop by and give us the local report: Who's going to church these days and who's not. Who's the worst driver and what kids are always late for school and her theory behind it all. She's a great storyteller, and we love to hear her side of everything. But the downside is that no one, not even us, are spared from her assessments. She gives Mom the run down on each one of us. "This one," she says pointing at me and laughing, "she likes to take the long way to school. She's got her head in the clouds, that one." She looks up at the trees and makes her face dreamy and her voice high. "Meandering to school in her own little world, the school bells could be sending a three star alarm and she couldn't care less." I can tell Mom doesn't think it's all that funny by the way she looks at me with disappointment. It makes me hate Mrs. Accardi a little, and I wish she wasn't such a blabbermouth.

I wave back at her just so she won't go spreading rumors about me being spacey. Across the street, the kindergarten house looks like a pretty face. Two windows for eyes and a red door for the mouth, and the front porch is a pretty lace collar. A shade gets pulled up, and the little face is winking at me. Miss Miller is inside getting ready for the kids.

I love Miss Miller. In her class, I never showed up spacey or dreamy, and she let Mom know that too. "The kid's got smarts, this one. Crackerjack reader." She'd nod at my mother as if to say, "Well done, Mrs. Muldoon. You get a gold star." I wish I could go into the kindergarten and warm myself in the entranceway like old Morris. I wish I could go in and take a nap on one of those uncomfortable mats and watch Miss Miller erase the chalkboard to the sweet snoring of all the little noses all around me.

The shade on the second window gets pulled, and I imagine the sunlight streaming in, hitting the floor and making the dust dance. I loved kindergarten from the very first. I had waited from our stoop for so long watching my sisters go off to school, that by the time the first day arrived for me, I was hot with excitement like Taylor ham on the grill, sizzling and ready to pop. Just thinking about the day and the opening of the shades, and I am back with a package on my lap and Aunt Caroline is over, wearing her traveling clothes. She is off to a great adventure, but first she has come to see me off to kindergarten.

The new school dresses have not come home with us yet, so she brings a package with her from Ireland. "It's for you," she says and hands it to me. "It's for your first day, Maureen, 'cause you gotta look sharp when making first impressions." I grin from ear to ear because it's the first day of school, and now I also have a present to open. I love presents. I'm like Cinderella going to the ball. I open the box. Inside are a beautiful white ruffled shirt and a plaid skirt. It's feels itchy and has a big safety pin on the front.

My mother's hands go to her face and she smiles. "Isn't that something?" she says to Aunt Caroline and then she turns to me, "Go ahead and try it on." I pull off my pajamas and get dressed right there cause I can't remember ever getting new clothes and I don't want to wait to try them on. The buttons are a little tricky, but I get it done and then pull on the skirt.

"The safety pin is showing," I tell them as my mother tucks in my shirt. But they just laughed and Aunt Caroline says,

"This time it's okay, because it's a kilt."

"What's a kilt?" I ask.

"It's what the men wear in Ireland when they play the bagpipes."

A man skirt? Are they kidding? I am going off to school in a man skirt that needs to be pinned with a big safety pin for everyone to see? This is not how I had imagined heading off to the garden of children. But the two of them seem so happy about the outfit, so I get happy about it too.

Aunt Caroline will stay home with the two boys and Mom and I will walk down the block together, hand and hand, and I can't stop smiling. Aunt Caroline takes my picture on the stoop and again as I wave from the front walk.

"Remember, Maureen, the pen is mightier than the sword," she yells from our front door. I just nod and wave like I know what she is talking about 'cause I don't want my first walk to school with Mom being held up by one of Aunt Caroline's word games. I am off to kindergarten, don't you know. That room is packed with tons of words and riddles and if I don't know what they mean, there is a teacher who will tell me everything. I will gobble them all up like a thirsty dog.

My smile is so big now that it hurts. I try to pull down my face and open my mouth to get it to quit, but my smile won't take a break. My feet are skipping and my heart is fluttering, and I practically dance my way to kindergarten.

At school, Miss Miller meets us at the door. She is older than mom and Aunt Caroline, but she seems very nice. She helps me hang my coat on the little hooks on the wall, and then she takes me by the hand and shows me to my very own desk. It's wood and metal and has a piece of paper on it that says "Maureen" in blue magic marker. "That's my name!" I tell her. This is my desk and it has my name on it!

"Well, we knew you were coming, Maureen," she tells me with a pat and a smile. She has a list, and she checks off my name, and I am so amazed by it all. I was on a list? She knew about me? Had she been looking forward to this day and meeting me as much as I had been looking forward to meeting her? It's not possible, but I love that my name was on a list. That there had been some planning involved. I rest my hands on my desk and fall in love with Miss Miller. I watch her move back to the door to help the other kids who line up with their mothers. Some of them are crying and have to be pried away and coaxed to their seats. I can't imagine why. One boy moans so loud in the corner and his wailing makes it hard to enjoy my new desk. He holds tight to his mother, his face pink and blubbery. He is just plain out howling and letting the snot drip. I shake my head and make a face. My mother comes over to my desk.

"Be a good girl," she tells me.

"Why is he crying like that?" I ask

"He wants his mother," she whispers. "He's scared." I shake my head.

"He's a big cry baby," I tell her, without whispering.

"Be a good girl," she repeats. She passes by the teacher, "Bye Eleanor, and good luck," she says. Eleanor? My teacher has a name and my mother knows it. Makes sense with all my sisters who have sat in this room.

Mom slips out the door, and I try not to look at the snotty crybaby. Once all the mothers are gone, Miss Miller teaches us a song.

"Good morning to you. Good morning to you. We're all in our places with sunshiny faces, and this is the way to start a new day."

I hug my desk, and wrap my legs around the metal legs of my chair, cause I love it here and never want to leave. We start our day by singing! And she tells us that we will start every day this way, with a song. I can't imagine any better way to start a day. I look around the room at all the children singing; dressed up in their first day of school clothes, and I know that those German people are right. This is a garden of children.

The first thing we do after the song is to draw. But not just anything! There is a work paper passed out, and the teacher says to draw a big circle on the line. I watch the other kids, and their circles look like jelly beans. This is not going to be as easy as it sounds. I don't want to make a mistake, so I think about drawing a circle. Then I think about drawing the head of a princess, which is something I draw all the time. I pick up my pencil and with one smooth stroke I draw the world's greatest circle. Miss Miller walks around the room looking at our circles. She stops when she gets to my desk. "Very nice, Maureen," she says.

After the drawing we have a snack with juice and cookies. I raise my hand and ask, "Do we get cookies every day or is it just the first day of school party?"

"Every day we have snack time," she says. And I pop an animal cookie in my mouth and look around the room at all the kids eating cookies. I think I could live here, sleeping on one of the mats every night and having cookies and juice for breakfast every day and getting to play with all the toys stacked up in the play area.

Now the shades on the side windows go up, and I know I need to get a move on if I want to make the train.

21

Walking by the Church

I CROSS THE STREET AS ANOTHER CAR BEGINS TO PULL UP to park at the church. Someone else is heading to early mass along with Mrs. Accardi. The car slows to a stop and honks at me. I stand still and wait to see if it's someone looking for directions or just some pervert getting ready to expose himself. Either is an option that I've witnessed in equal measures. The window rolls down, and Patty leans her head out. She smiles and calls to me, "Hey Maureen, look at me, I got a car. It's me Patty!" She calls as if I could mistake her for someone else. Her bold cheekbones, wild eye, crooked smile, and strange stutter set her far apart.

"Patty, you can't stop in the middle of the street. I think you need to pull into the parking lot."

"Yep, yep, I know. That's where I'm headed," she says as she pops back in her window and pulls into the parking lot.

"Hey Maureen, hey, hey, hey Maureen, it's me Patty. I'm

Patty. Your mom's friend. Do you remember me?" She asks me this every week when I see her walking to church, and each time I answer the same way.

"Hey Patty, sure I know you."

"How is she, Maureen? Your mom, your mom is not doing so good? How is she? I would come by. Should I come by? I would if I should, but not so sure. How is she, Maureen? Not so good?" Patty is slow. When I was a kid, I always thought it was because she drank a lot. But even now that she is sober, the same slurry stutter and repeating of ideas seems to plague her.

"Mom is fine, Patty. She's doing fine."

"Yeah?" she asks, smiling at me with all those crooked brown teeth. I nod.

"I am going to church, Maureen. I am going to pray for your mom. She is a good lady, your mom. She's a saint anyhow, so no matter what happens… Okay Maureen, you tell her Patty said hello."

Of course I remember you, Patty. Like an odd family pet that came and went as she pleased, showed up unapologetically like the cat, pregnant, tired and thirsty for love. Scary, sloppy Patty who slept on the couch and stopped by on ShopRite days to get a good meal. ShopRite days are the days we go grocery shopping. We walk with Mom.

A lady in a light blue raincoat and a plastic hair cover walks past me. Her right hand swings like the metronome that sits on our piano, back and forth it goes. Back and forth, like the swinging of a pocket watch for one who is meant to be hypnotized.

My sisters swing their arms when they walk, too. My mother swings her arms, and we all swing our arms when we walk. Suddenly I am six and swinging my arms and trying to keep up with my mother.

"Mom, Mom, Mom." Since Dad got mugged, Mom has taken matters into her own hands. The new plan is that we will all walk to the ShopRite. It's far, but also like an adventure. So we all follow Mom, keeping the pace and swinging our arms as we go. We pass the Church, the Elks, the Jewish Council thrift shop. At Alex Eng's Chinese Restaurant, we take a left. Then we walk down South Orange Avenue, and it's still a ways to go. The last five blocks are the longer ones with all the stores. When we get to the Shop Rite, we follow my mother down the aisles, and when she is done, we help to carry the groceries home. I think she is lucky to have so many children to help her shop.

At the grocery store, we tell her that we have to use the bathroom. She sends us off two at a time. We never go to the bathroom though, it's too smelly. Instead, we drift off to the Brach Candy display and fill our pockets when no one is looking. My favorite is the Raspberry Crème Filled Caramels. The only thing better than candy is stolen candy. The way you need to unwrap it in your pocket and pretend to cough to bring it your mouth, tucking it away in the side of your cheek, the secret sweetness of it all.

At the checkout, she hands us each a paper bag of groceries and we follow her like little ducks. My bag is heavy, full of cans that bang against my shins and the paper edges scrape my skin. We pass a restaurant where people smile out at us. They point and count.

We pass the bagel shop and the bank, town hall and then a big window. I press my nose against the window to peek inside. Little girls are dressed in pink leotards and ballet slippers. Some of them have little pink skirts that flutter when they move. They hold a bar attached to the wall and follow the teachers, just like us, little pink ducklings. When I see them, my breath goes in fast and hard and does not come back out. I am struck still by their beauty. I have discovered fairies, and I try not to move so that I don't scare them away. Soon their faces turn to me and the circle of fog I have left on their window. The teacher shakes her head and waves me on. I look to find my mother. But she is gone. She and her seven dwarfs are now half a block away. I run as fast as I can, the bag of cans bang against my legs as I call out.

"Mom, Mom." They stop and turn as I run past my sisters to find her.

"Mom, Mom, I want to go there," I am pointing and out of breath.

"Where?" She turns and squints her eyes.

"There, to that place with the girls in the pink."

She shakes her head and continues to walk.

"No, Maureen. You can't."

"Why?" I ask, trying to keep up with her. She turns to me and looks me in the eye.

"If you get dance classes, they'll all want them, and we can't afford it."

My heart feels heavy, and my shoulders turn in. I want to tell her that I don't think they will. They didn't even seem interested; none of them even stopped.

"Mom, Mom!" I call, but she is busy with a bag and a baby, and I stop calling and start walking slowly so that my breath can catch up with me. Now my bag seems twice as full, and I watch her drift further and further away. We can't afford it.

I know she is right, and I like her being straight with me. Normally she'd say something like, "You need that like you need a hole in the head!" or "The man in the moon wants ice water." or "There are poor children starving in China." which makes no sense to me. I wasn't asking for a hole in the head, and as much as I knew that I should, most of the time, I didn't really care about the thirsty man stuck on the moon or the poor kids in China.

I fall in line and watch my feet make their way home over the cracked pavement and asphalt. I imagine them wearing ballet slippers, pink and perfectly trained. I see myself spinning up on my toes as the music swells and crashes like waves. I am lifted by faceless men and applauded by thousands as I raise my arms, face to the light. This daydream keeps me thrilled for blocks until chanting crashes in on it.

"William is chewing gum. William is chewing gum." Gum! I nudge through the flock to try to get a better look. "Gum? Where did he get gum?" We all know that the Brach candy display doesn't hold gum. We surround him, as he stares smacking away on a juicy piece of gum, his eyes twinkling like a little rascal. "William has gum, Mom!" we scream and point.

She turns and approaches him. "All right, pipe down all of ya's. Who is the parent here?" she asks, and we all go silent. "Give me that," Mom instructs with her hand out to William. He looks up in confusion, and chews even faster trying to drain it of all its worth before having to turn it over. "Open your mouth and give me that gum." They lock eyes and stare at each other. It's a standoff. We gather closer, a concerned mob of villagers wanting to see justice upheld. Finally, she places a hand on his head, leaning it back, and with her other hand she extracts a watery pink blob from his mouth like she is playing Operation and going in for the sweet tooth. The sugary syrup drips from his down-turned lips. "Where did you get this?"

"Yeah," we echo.

"Where, William? Where did you get that gum?" He says nothing and points to the sidewalk. Mom's eyes grow in disbelief. "What? There? You got it off the sidewalk? Jesus, Mary and Joseph! You're liable to get the plague!" Our jealousy fades to judgment as our eyes bulge and our hands fly to our mouths to cover our grins.

"William!" we smirk in disgusted delight, "you can't eat gum off the sidewalk!"

"But..." he begins through confused and watery eyes, "But..." he continues, "But it was just laying there, and nobody wanted it." He is so small and sad that I want to pet him like a dog. Instead, we laugh and repeat his words a few hundred times before we make it back home.

"It was just laying there and nobody wanted it!"

At our stoop we are met by Patty, the pregnant lady who needs a place to sleep. She is big and slow, and her words slip into each other making her hard to understand. Her teeth are brown and crooked like the sidewalk, and she looks odd. Somehow my mother can talk with her for hours.

Patty will spend the night on our couch again. We will hear her getting up at all hours to get something to drink. In the morning the Giant is furious to find that she has cleaned out the liquor cabinet and then moved on to the mouthwash.

We find her spread out and snoring on our couch, finally lost in the sleep she had been chasing. She doesn't even wake when the Giant storms out of the house and slams the door. She just lies there, like the pre-chewed gum. Somebody's leftovers that have found their way to our home.

My mother brings a blanket and covers Patty's swollen belly.

She spends no time fussing over Patty. She does not tuck the blanket in around Patty or smooth the hair from Patty's face. She just puts the blanket down and goes on to clean the dishes from the table.

In the kitchen, Marian and Bridget are putting away the groceries. They have the music up and are singing at the top of their lungs. Mom calls to them, "Patty is sleeping. Simmer down." But they can't hear her, or they don't care about waking Patty. They hold wooden spoons to their mouths and serenade each other.

"When you're weary, feeling small, When tears are in your eyes, I will dry them all; I'm on your side. When times get rough and friends just can't be found, like a bridge over troubled water I will lay me down."

Mom's hair is tucked to her head with bobby pins, and she starts to hum along, too. She moves about the house picking up socks and newspapers, and soon the humming turns to talking and she carries on a conversation with herself about who-knows-what 'cause I only get to hear half of it. "Well, how do you like that?" she asks no one, and then she shakes her head and begins to laugh. "Well, for crying out loud!"

I watch Patty lost in her dreams and Mom lost in her conversation and my sisters in the kitchen lost in their song, and I start thinking about dancing and twirling and fairies again. And it's okay because maybe we are all lost in our own little worlds together.

22

Still Walking by the Church

PATTY PARKS HER CAR AND SLAMS THE DOOR. A LIT cigarette dangles from her mouth, and she slowly makes her way to church. She looks like Pig-Pen walking in a bubble of her own smog as she makes her way to the Eucharist. She stands in front of the church and maniacally pulls drags from her cigarette. I see her here at least once a week and on Sundays. I think she loves the warm safety of the church, but also she loves the Eucharist. My sisters joke that Patty just loves the free meal and would jump through fire hoops for a swig of the sacred blood also known as wine. But I think there is more to it.

Patty sits at the back of the church and cheers all the little kids on as they make their way down the aisle after receiving the first Holy Communion. She sings *"Let There Be Peace on Earth"* real loud and proud like she is giving a concert, and, as weird as her talking issues are, her singing is pretty nice.

I am in second grade, standing on the church steps trying to smile without opening my mouth. I can hear the sounds of all the whispered prayers and reciting of the sins. My classmates and I have memorized the whole list of sins to know which are the worst and not to be forgiven. I shall not kill, I shall not steal, and I shall not commit adultery or use the Lord's name in vain…

Children's voices sing out *"Let there be peace on earth and let it begin with me!"* In church, all the second graders fill up the pews and we practice our songs. When that's done, we wait our turn to see the priest about cleaning our souls. There are over forty of us and only four confessionals so we sit a long time stewing in our sins. There is one sin that weighs heavy on my heart, and I work out the wording in my head so that I can get it all out as fast as possible and then get the heck out of the confessional. I don't want to be in there too long. When someone stays in the confessional too long we smirk at each other and push out our eyes to say, "Oh my gosh, look at what a sinner they are." I do not want to be that child.

As the line gets shorter, I start to feel a little worried about the sin and the priest and what if he does not forgive me? What if I get sent to hell and never get to wear a lovely white dress like the other girls. Susan O'Malley goes in before me. She is a "goodie two shoes," and before long, she is out again looking extra holy with her hands clasped in prayer and her head bowed like the nuns have taught us.

Now it's my turn, and I step up to the booth and move the red curtain to the side. The material is soft but heavy like a door. Inside the booth, the curtain closes on itself and it is pitch black. In the dark quiet I find a kneeler. It, too, is soft beneath my knees and feels like being in a dark phone booth that smells like old Christmas trees. I kind of like it, even though I can't see a thing. I am not even sure if my eyes are open.

A panel opens in the wall in front of me, and I jump a bit. The panel reveals a very dirty window that I can't see through. It's dingy yellow, like the windows of Patty's car from all her smoking. I hear the priest clear his throat, and I wonder if the priest smokes, too.

"Yes, my child?" I perk up, cause this is my cue. It's exactly how the nuns said it would be, just as we had practiced.

"Bless me father, for I have sinned. This is my first confession." After my delivery, I try not to smile but I am pretty sure I have nailed it. Clear and sincere like the nuns have shown us, and I am the perfect parrot.

"What are your sins?"

"Well I..." This part is not so easy. They didn't give us a script. For this part we are on our own. The event plays over in my head and even though I thought I had it all worked out, I am not too sure where to begin.

"Yes child?" the priest asks. Then comes the silence as I kneel in the dark with the yellow light and take a breath. Maybe I don't really need to confess, or give all the details. Maybe I can just say the commandments that I've broken and be done with it. He clears his throat again and I think about the clock ticking in the back of the church wall.

"I have bored false witness against my neighbor. Well, except that it was my brother not my neighbor that I was witnessing falsely about. And I stole some candy.

"How so?"

"What?"

"What happened with your brother?"

"Well, Father—I was watching them, my two little brothers. My mother was down in the basement. Doing the laundry." I pause and he clears his throat. "My little brother, Owen, broke my mother's vase. It was water-for-crystal. She got it from my Aunt Caroline who went all the way to Ireland just to bring it back for her. He bumped it by accident, and it broke all over the floor. My mom came running up the stairs, and when she saw the broken vase she started screaming, 'Who did this! Who did this?'"

So far, I have told him nothing, but it has taken so long to get here, and I think about the snotty kids on the other side of the curtain pushing their eyes out at me, so I continue telling the story that I don't really want to tell.

"So I told her it was William who broke the vase. And she swept him up with the broom."

"She swept who up with the broom?"

"William. She took the broom and beat him with it, and when he fell on the floor, she swept him up with the glass, and he was crying and trying to tell her that he didn't do anything, but she didn't listen to him." There is silence and I don't know what else to say.

"So who broke the vase?" he asks again.

"Owen, the littlest one, not William," I tell him.

"So why would you tell her it was William?"

"Well, Father, 'cause I wanted William to get into trouble and not Owen."

"But why?" he asks again. At first, I don't answer him, because it will take too long. But he waits.

"I don't know why, Father," I say, and my voice sounds so

little, and I wish I knew the answer, but I don't. I don't understand it myself.

I don't tell the priest about how I sometimes hate William and how I sometimes pinch him like Julia pinches me. I don't tell about how William asked me once why I didn't like him and how I told him that I thought Owen was cuter, which I said to hurt his feelings. I did not tell about how William's face lit up when I told him this, as if it all made complete sense, and how he went running off to my mother screaming, "Mom, Mom! I know why Maureen doesn't like me! It's because Owen is cuter." And I didn't tell the priest how this answer seemed to make him so happy, because at least now there was a reason and no longer a frustrating riddle that must have kept him up all night as it sometimes did me when I thought about why my sisters pulled my hair or pinched me or made me sleep in the hallway.

As I told the priest about William and the glass pile, I saw my brother in the dark room with me sitting on the floor with the broom sweeping against him, and heard the screaming of my mother's voice, "My good Waterford crystal. Is nothing sacred anymore?" His face red with all the tears and confusion, and a hard knot closes my throat. My lips begin to tingle and shake and my eyes fill up, and even though I don't think the priest can see me, I hang my head.

"So you lied to get your brother in trouble?" I nod and fight back the tears 'cause only a real sinner will leave the booth crying.

"Well, what other sins have you done?"

"Other sins? There are no other sins, Father. That is all." There is a pause and a heavy breath, and I feel like he knows about "my laying on of hands," which he certainly could, due to the fact that the priest lives within earshot of my sisters' screams, "Mom! Maureen is lying on her hands again." But I am not sure if lying on my hands is a real sin. It wasn't one that was listed, and even if it were, I would die before confessing that to the priest. Besides Jesus did something called "laying on of hands," so maybe I am safe.

"There must be more than the one lie about your brother and some stolen candy. Have you used the Lord's name in vain? Have you used bad language?"

"Oh yes, Father, I have used bad language, but never the Lord's name in vain."

"And what about stealing, was it only the candy?"

"Jesus, Mary, and Joseph," I think to myself. *"He'll have me in here all day."* Where would I begin, and where would I end? The change from my mother's purse, the sweater from the mall, all the candy from Leo's and all the pretty things that could fit into my pockets from Nancy's house, the Ayds candies? The more I think, the more I remember, and I start to feel a little dizzy under the weight of all my sins.

"My mother's purse," I tell him, "I have stolen coins from my mother's purse and that is all." I add in the last part 'cause I figure he is going to ask, and I want to cut him off before he tries to pry deeper. Besides, the bad words and stolen goods meant nothing to me. I knew that if I were to leave that black box and step into the church to find it empty except for a collection basket filled with offerings, I would be the first to fill my pockets if I knew no one was looking. Or at least I know I would think about it, and thinking it is just as bad as doing it. So no matter what, I am guilty. And I am fine with that guilt; I can live with it. The only sin that I could no longer carry was the picture of my brother in the pile of glass and his sweet voice asking me, "Why don'tcha like me, Marine?" His huge brown eyes with their thick black lashes that fluttered like the wings of baby black birds on his face. The look in his face and the sound of his voice as he pleaded with her, "No, Mom, it wasn't me."

How could I ever be forgiven for this? This is the cross that I need to leave with the priest, the sin that I need to give to Jesus to take from me and forgive me my trespasses and the bearing of the false witness against my neighbor who is actually my brother William. This is the only sin that is too heavy for me to carry, the one that buckles my knees and punches me in the gut with powerful guilt every time I think about it.

"Are you sure that's all?" he asked again.

"Yes, Father, I am sure."

There is a long pause, and then comes a prayer about forgiveness and absolving of sins, and he tells me to say ten Hail Marys, and I tell him thank you, and the dingy window closes, like the abrupt gatekeeper in the *Wizard of Oz*. Once again I am in the dark with the warm feeling of silence and the smell of old Christmas trees. I want to lean back and rest for a bit, but I know the kids are all waiting and checking the clock on the back of the church wall to see who the biggest sinner of all. They turn their heads pretending to hear someone as they glance up to see the distance the minute hand has traveled from the nine, to the ten to the eleven and now how it's making its way to the twelve, and I could be the winner of the biggest sinner contest.

So I pull back the heavy red curtain and keep my eyes to the floor. I can feel them all watching me, so I make the sign of the cross to show how holy I am, and I walk to the front of the church where we are to kneel and say the prayers. At the altar,

I kneel beside Susan O'Malley and bow my head to the bloody Jesus on the cross. I work my way through the ten Hail Marys. "Holy Mary, mother of God, pray for us sinners, now and at the hour of our death. Amen." I am not sure what it all means, but I do feel better about my brother. I am not sure why, but I do. I stay kneeling and do a hundred "I am sorrys" to my brother William. I know he can't hear me, but I am sorry and it just helps to say it over and over. I am not really sure if I got to a hundred, but the number is not as important as the feeling. Finally I just bow my head right into my hands and make a promise to be a better sister. When I finally look up, things look different, and I know I am ready for the first Holy Communion and the pretty dress. There is now an opening where my heavy heart sat, and now there is a space for Jesus.

On Sunday we are "invited to the table" for our first holy communion.

"It tastes like a cardboard Necco candy," my sisters tell me.

Mom lays three dresses out on the bed and I get to pick. They are the Communion dresses from my sisters who have gone before me. One is very plain and straight, and I can't imagine why anyone would choose it. One is pretty and soft with puffy sleeves and a sash at the waist.

"How about this one?" she asks, pointing to the middle one. But I have my eye on the last one. It's not so much white, more a yellowish gray; still, I know it is the one for me.

It's made of some strange net-like material that goes in at the waist and out like a princess. The sleeves are puffy as well, but it's the front that seals the deal. There are little sparkling diamonds sewn into the material... at least they look like diamonds. It's the very dress that Marian wore, and that was ten years ago, so it's old.

"Are you sure you don't want this one?" She asks again, holding up the middle white dress. "I am not sure how to get that one white again. I could try bleaching it, but that might make the dress fall apart." My eyes grow wide.

"Oh please don't let it fall apart. It's so beautiful."

She shakes her head at me, and the dress soaks in the tub with a bottle of bleach, and no one can take a bath for a whole day. But I don't care. I will also wear a veil and carry a bouquet, like a bride going off to marry Jesus.

Mom holds open her closet door, and we both peek inside.

"Go ahead, pick one for me, too," she says. I look up at her, and she nods. There are so many different colors and patterns, and I move through each one, wanting to make the right choice. There is a long gown with beads around the neck that looks magical.

"This one?" I ask.

"Hum," she moves her hand to her mouth, "That is a pretty special dress, maybe too fancy." I nod my head; okay, that's true, after all it is my day. I look again, taking my time.

Then I spot it. A blue dress, the color of the blue in Mom's good china that we only use on special days. It wraps around her waist, and looks perfect, perfect, perfect. She'll wear it with her alligator sandals, two matching earrings and an extra splash of Jean Nate. She smiles at it and me, sending tingles from the top of my head to the soles of my feet. In the bathroom I watch my dress dance in the smelly water. I too have been washed clean of all my sins, and I am so happy that I want to jump right in the tub with the dress, and get the whole thing started already, but I don't. I get close, but the water is so smelly it makes my eyes water.

The next day, the dress is hung out to dry. It is now a faint shade of grey but all the gems are still in place and that's what's really matters.

I gently pull the dress over my head; it's stiff and scratchy and still smells like bleach. As soon as the zipper is up I run to the front door.

The front door of our home opened to a vestibule the size of a confessional. On one wall hangs an old mirror with curvy edges. It had been there for years before I discovered it. But once I do, I spend hours jumping as high as I can to catch a blurry glimpse of the top of my head. Today I can stand on my tippy toes back against the opposite wall, and there I am, from the chin on up. There is a little veil on my head and I am so happy that I begin to hold a concert. I start out with *"Let there be peace on earth,"* 'cause it seems to go well with my white dress and clean conscience. Then I spot the door knocker and its…*"Knock three times on the ceiling if you want me, twice on the pipes if the answer is no"*, and *"Ben, the two of us need look no more."* But my favorite is *"You're so vain you probably think the song is about you."* I sing to myself in the mirror, and I know that whoever wrote this song is right. I do think this song is about me, just like I think every song is about me…does that mean I'm vain? Do I need to go back to confession?

I asked mom a while ago what "vain" meant.

"Go look it up," she suggests from behind her book.

I go to the attic and ask Annie, 'cause I'm lazy and she's smart. Aunt Caroline would have jumped at this opportunity.

"It means you love yourself," Annie tells me and in such a way that I get that you are probably not supposed to love yourself.

Bridget begins to sing a song from Camp Madeleine Mulford and Riddle joins in. There is a little dance that goes along with the tune and they perform it like synchronized swimmers.

"I love myself. I think I am grand. When I go to the movies I hold my hand. I put my arms around my waist and when I get fresh, I slap my face."

I am mesmerized by their song and dance. It's like I am living with two of the Radio City Rockettes. "Do it again," I plead, and they hit it again without missing a beat.

I run back to the front hall mirror to do my own version of *"I do love myself and think I am grand."* Even though the girl in the mirror is boney and buck-toothed with short hair that looks like it was cut with a dull scissors, because it was. Still, I imagine I look like Shirley Temple, so in my mind I do.

Irish Grandpa comes to see me off.

"I've been in your home for five minutes without anybody offering me a drink," he shouts as he comes in the door. The adults laugh as my father hands him a glass of scotch on the rocks. They have heard this joke so many times that they know to have it ready.

"Give the Mister his drink," the Giant instructs. He calls him "Mister" and when Grandma was alive. She was "The Mrs." It seems strangely fancy for the Giant, and also kind of sad, like they are always meeting for the first time, and he is not sure of their names.

Gifts arrive for me, and it's like having an extra birthday, except none of the gifts are all that great—a new pair of rosary beads, a little Bible and some money tucked in holy cards that the Giant will hold on to for me. He puts it in the bank and writes a number on a little card in his wallet. I watch his short pencil cross out my old number and write in my new number. I wish I could take the dollars to the candy store, but I also like that my wealth is growing.

Before we walk down to church, we'll get the pictures taken in the front yard. Grandpa has a camera.

"Okay, say cheese," he instructs as he snaps off a shot. I am smiling from ear to ear till it hurts. "Hey Charlie," he calls to me from behind the lens. I know he is talking to me. That's just what he calls all us kids. We're all "Charlie." Like the Giant, I don't think he is so good with the names. He pulls the camera away from his face and stares at me. "You want to look beautiful? Smile with your mouth closed."

His words push me back, and I try my best to pull my upper lip over my crooked teeth. I try to smile without showing my teeth, but closed mouths don't feel like smiles at all. The sun is in my eyes, and it's hard to keep them from getting watery. I don't want to cry on my special day. I mash my lips together and grab a piece of my dress in my hand. The material is stiff and scratchy, yet it makes me feel better. My mother soaked it in bleach just for me, and that means something.

We have a special place to sit in the church, and when it is our turn, we go to the priest in single file. He will say "the Body of Christ" and we will say "amen" and then we open our mouths and stick out our tongues to the priest which is sort of funny, but it's not supposed to be, and then the priest will put the round wafers on our tongues. There is also an altar boy standing by with a little round plate that will go under our chins in case the wafer falls. But if it should fall, we know not to pick it up. Only the priest can touch the Eucharist.

I stand and join the line of girls and boys. We hold our hands together in prayer as we walk so that everyone can tell how holy and pure we are. I make my way up to the priest and stand before him. "Body Of Christ," he says.

I come in with "amen" and stick my tongue out to him. The wafer is placed, and I am dismissed with a sign of the cross. The wafer gets caught on the roof of my mouth and I make a face at all the other little kids who make faces back at me even though we are beaming with pride. My sisters are right; it does taste like cardboard. I get back to my seat and kneel just like we practiced. I bow my head to pray, but I do not say the Our Father or the Hail Mary. Instead I say the prayer I learned from my sisters: *"I love myself, I think I'm grand."* I repeat this prayer over and over as I stare down at the diamonds on my dress and smile with all my teeth.

Patty takes a final drag, holds open the heavy church door, and stubs her cigarette out on the ground with one foot while propping the door open with the other. She kicks the butt to the side and steps inside. She turns and with a smile she waves before heading into mass. I wave back because smiling girls with crooked teeth need to stick together.

23

Heading Down the Hill

I HEAD DOWN SORROWS HILL. OUT IN THE DISTANCE, there is a hill that goes from one side of the horizon to the other. It changes with the seasons, and on this early spring morning, it's making its way back to pale green. At the bottom of the hill is a chain link fence that surrounds the parking lot of Our Lady of Sorrows. And I know exactly what it sounds like when struck by a fast moving shopping cart.

A car drives by, some high school kid pecking their head to the radio. *"I felt a rush, like a rolling bolt of thunder, spinning my head around and taking my body under."* As the car rolls by, I am nine and back in our living room staring out the window, my sisters beside me leaving breath circles on the window.

The Four Seasons sing to us from the TV as we stare out the window at Eddy Kelly's go-cart. All summer long, he's been

170

dangling it in our faces, racing it up and down the block, giving everyone and their brother a ride except for us. "None of those Muldoon kids get a ride," we hear Mrs. Kelly instruct him. She doesn't like that we run on her property on our way home from school or that we pick her flowers. So we sit on our stoop and devise different ways to execute Eddy Kelly and confiscate his go-cart. His father, Mr. Kelly, is the chief of police, so we need to put some serious thought into the plan, getting it just right, so it will go undetected for years.

The Kellys live to the right of us. Eddy is the youngest of five mean and troubled siblings. Tommy, the oldest, is the worst. At eighteen he was already known as the town derelict. He shuffles by us kids, spitting curse words and tobacco juice. Once, after a Kelly family fight, we woke to find him pitching a tent in their backyard.

"Not under your roof?" he yells at their back door as he staggers and bobs like a punch drunk scarecrow. "Well, that's just fine with me. I am out of here and nobody's gonna stop me!" We watch from our window as he wrestles with the tent poles and tarp. It takes him all morning, but by lunch he is the wrathful ruler of his own fragile kingdom. Every so often we hear him let loose an angry barrage of curse words and accusations. He pops out in a fit of energy and paces around the entrance like a boxer revving up for the next round. There is something sad about his show, like watching a shark in a fish tank.

Because he's the oldest kid on our block, we make it our business to study how one goes about moving out. We dare to get a closer look and head to the backyard. From within the safety of our chain-linked fence, we witness his awkward attempt at cutting the apron strings. At sundown, we learn about the etiquette of house warming parties. We pretend to be enjoying our rusted out swing set and watch carefully as a small tribe of scraggly teens descend on his "new pad." Great billowy puffs of smoke drift from the top of the tent like a wigwam. "Better leave them alone," Marian warns. "That's more than just tobacco he's burning." But we stay transfixed. This is a great show, and we don't want to miss a thing. Tommy comes out from the tent, walks to the side of his parent's garage, and takes a piss in his mother's daffodils. We burst into laughter till we realize we now have his unwanted attention. It's startling at first; like having the bad guy in a movie turn his attention off screen to the audience. We stand there for a moment thinking, "Can he see us?"

"What are you little queerbaits looking at? Huh? Huh, you little turd-bags?" When we don't answer, he starts toward us with a crazed look in his eyes and we scatter like church mice.

It is hard to be the cop's kids. Mr. Kelly has a bad temper, but what made the Kelly kids' lives even worse was the coldness of their mother. If Mrs. Kelly were my mother, I think I would pitch a tent, too.

We lost more footballs, Frisbees and hula-hoops to that lady. She is the original burgermeister. Our homes are so close to each other, when one of our toys lands on her yard, she bolts from the door, grabs it, and hauls ass back inside. It's shocking how fast she moves and useless to try to rush her for the toy, because she can out run us by a long shot. "It's as if she's been specially trained in ambush techniques by the secret service," William suggests. And we stand there dumbfounded, toyless and in complete agreement. That lady can hustle.

We tell our mother about the confiscation. But she takes it as an opportunity to teach the word of God.

"Jesus says to turn the other cheek. Here, give her this." She picks up the wilting houseplant that is being used as a centerpiece on our dining room table and hands it to us.

"Give her this plant?" we ask, as we stare at her in disbelief, not sure if she is actually in the right conversation. "She took our ball, Mom!"

"Go on, go bring her this plant. Love your enemies."

This is the last thing any of us wants to do, but now that we have involved Mom, it is our only choice. Pushed by the fever of my mother's passionate love for Jesus Christ, we file out the door. At the Kellys' house, we assemble ourselves neatly on the stoop and knock on her door.

"This is for you," we say, holding out the gift. She stares at each of us in the eye trying to figure out the riddle. We have no answers either. In an uncomfortable attempt at graciousness, she takes it. Her head nods angrily and we can tells she feels caught off guard.

"Thank you," she stammers. As the door closes on us, we hear her add, "You're still not getting your toys back."

From that point on, it's war. We go around the neighborhood gathering anything that even resembles a toy. Neglected tennis balls we find in the gutter, chewed up dog toys we steal from the Gabiola's mangy mutt, a broken airplane made from the soft balsa wood that makes its lifespan so brief in our rough hands.

We pile out to our front yard and make a big show of how excited we are to have this new toy.

"Let me hold it!"

"No me! It's my turn!" We smile at each other in delicious delight. Then we begin the toss. Passing it from one to the other, laughing and whooping it up to ensure we've caught her attention.

"Monkey's uncle, monkey's uncle!" we cry. On this cue, the toy is strategically tossed on to her property. Out like a cuckoo bird she pops, a well-trained dog pouncing on our bait. But instead of groans, we send out a howl of cheers and laughter. Julia yells out, "Three point two seconds!" and we cheer some more. The first time this happens, she gets so thrown off that she trips slightly before getting back up her front steps. This misstep sends screaming jeers of victory from our camp and our feet dance in circles with the thrill of revenge.

These withheld go-cart rides are for sure her return blow.

Oh, she is good. Striking us at the bullseye of our soft spot. For days, we stand stymied on our stoop, working and reworking plans of revenge.

Marian's arrival is a sight for sore eyes. She comes hollering down the street, pushing a rattling metal shopping cart.

"Hey! Look!" she yells, "We've got our own go-cart." We run to meet her, and although I recognize the metal basket on wheels as a shopping cart, the minute she introduces it as a go-cart, it magically transforms before my eyes. It is like the pumpkin for Cinderella's coach, and I know in that moment my sister Marian is not only our fairy godmother, but she is also the most clever person on earth.

We begin to pile into the shopping cart and hang off the sides. She tries to push us, but with all the weight we barely move.

"We need a hill," Annie suggests.

"A hill!" we cheer and nod gratefully at Annie for her brilliance.

"Sorrows Hill!" she continues.

"Yes, Sorrows Hill!" We agree.

"We are going to take this baby for the ride of its life," Marian announces as she takes off down the block. We joyfully follow our beautiful Pied Piper and her rumbling go-cart, our feet racing, and our hands holding firmly to our shiny shopping go-cart.

At the top of the hill, we look out over the steep gravel top parking lot that sits beside our church and school. Standing in cut-offs and T-shirts, we stare down at the beast that we're about to conquer. Silently, I wish I remembered to grab a pair of shoes. Riddle is in her signature orange tube top and my pink bedroom slippers with the fur lining that I got from a box of clothes that showed up on our stoop. They were pretty worn already, but her big dirty feet hanging out the back make me angry. I would ask her to give them back, but that's a losing battle. William has on a pair of Julia's sneakers four sizes too big for him, but at least they're both prepared. I stand with my soft soles to the gravel, a slight flutter in my gut warns me, but I brush it aside and climb into the basket.

"This has never been attempted in the history of the world," Marian announces. "Evel Knievel himself has not accomplished it."

"We should call Guinness Book of World Records," Annie yells while running laps around the cart as a warm up, her wild hair catching wind and making her seem more like a frantic cartoon character than ever.

"No time for that," Marian instructs. "They'll find out about us soon enough. Get in. On the count of three, I am going to push off, then it's every man for himself." She lifts her hand to us and makes the Vulcan sign for "Live long and prosper."

"May the force be with you," she adds for good measure. "Okay then, one, two, three!" We join her voice in shrieks, screams and squeals as she pushes off. The weight in the basket sends our cart speeding downhill into a chaotic flight, hitting bumps and dips that send the cart bouncing up and down. We hold on for dear life. The little fence at the very bottom of the hill is barreling toward us and growing by the second. Cars making their way up the road that lay adjacent to the hill slow to stop and watch the historic flight of our cart. They honk and cheer us on over their blaring radios.

"I see a little silhouetto of a man. Scaramouche, Scaramouche, will you do the Fandango? Thunderbolts and lightning, very very frightening me! Galileo Galileo, Galileo Figaro Magnifico-o-o-o! I'm just a poor boy, and nobody loves me. He's just a poor boy from a poor family. Spare him his life from this monstrosity!"

Our pounding hearts fill with the excitement. The wind whips through our hair; the rush of adrenaline warms our cheeks. The cart is a speeding basket of proud human parts as we take in the quickly approaching gate. Three-quarters of the way down the hill we hit a pothole, and the cart goes airborne. My heart flutters and tickles my throat. Seconds later we land with a crash as the cart goes topsy-turvy but reconnects with the gravel. Marian's high-pitched call confirms that we are far from safe.

"Jump! Jump! Jump now!" she screams in complete hysteria. I stare down at the fast moving gravel, unsure of how to navigate her demands. From the corner of my eye, I watch the obedient bodies of my siblings fly through the air with complete abandon. Seconds later, I hear the thud and groan of bulk meeting gravel. The gate rattles toward me, as Marian's words rip through me like an unavoidable bullet. "JUMP!"

So I do.

With my arms out, I catch air for a brief and rewarding

second, and then I crash with the black unforgiving gravel. The weight of my body pulls me across the pavement. I look up in time to see the empty cart crash into the fence and fall sideways. It sounds like the clashing of a cymbal. There is silence except for the rattle of the cart's wheels that continue to spin on their side and the final words from the radio, of *"Nothing really matters, anyone can see, nothing really matters to me."* I turn my head to the street as our faithful fans honk their horns in approval and pull off. Casualities speckle the parking lot. Riddle is the first to speak. She sings out an annoyingly happy tune.

"I stepped right off," she informs us. "Not a scratch." She dances proudly around our bodies as she adjusts her shifting tube top. She had been saved by my beautiful princess slippers. Those slippers, my slippers, raised her above the rest of us roadkill. Like the glass slippers that had saved Cinderella from a life of scrubbing floors and the ruby slippers that saved Dorothy from a life of munchkins. From then on I would be sure to pick my footwear more wisely.

We peel ourselves from the pavement and pick the gravel from our skin, slowly making our way to the top of the hill. For all the blood and pain, there are very few tears. Instead, we proudly compare our wounds. Bridget got it the worst, one bloody scrape from her chin to her toes. William comes in a close second with a body rash that lit up both legs. My knees are ripped open, and the palms of my hands are two pink throbbing melons. We begin laughing, high from the thrill. Like conquerors, we return, louder and prouder than when we left. Each of us tells the story from our own point of view, rehashing all the details—the slowing cars, the crash, the pain and gravel. With each retelling, the story grows and spreads its wings, and we take flight with it.

By the time we pass the Kelly house, we are at full pitch. She peeks from her shade and I wave, forgetting all about our war. She is, after all, the reason that we ended up taking that ride down Sorrows Hill. Eddy's go-cart sits vacant in their driveway that leads to the smoking tent. But we just pass by, none of us even try to steal a ride. That was kid's play, we had moved on.

I watch the fence at the bottom of the hill get closer with each step as I remember the day. But something pulls me back to the memory. I can almost feel the coolness of the air as we walk back to the house—the creak of the door, the sight of Mom on the phone. She hardly looks up as we pour in, and when we try to tell her about our adventure, she brushes us aside with her hand. There is smoke coming from the kitchen, and Marian goes to save the dinner. I stand in the room and watch my mother because something feels different. Something has arrived, and it makes the room feel hollow and my mother appear small.

"That is what he said. I need to go back in tomorrow," I hear her say through all the commotion. There is a heaviness that sits with my mother. She is holding her head in her hand at the end of the table. She is drawing circles with her pen on the newspaper.

24

Kneeling at the Blessed Mother

AS I WALK DOWN SORROWS HILL, THE SONG IS NOW STUCK in my head. *"Nothing really matters anyone can see, nothing really matters to me."* I look out at the fence. To my right is the statue of the Blessed Mother. There is still a bit of the black paint on her head from when she'd been defiled by some hoodlum with a can of black spray paint. The church has done its best to scrub her clean again, but she is still left in a sad state of gray.

I go over to the statue and kneel and pray. This is our agreement, and I want to hold up my end of the deal. I don't actually do too much praying when I get there, mostly just think. I look up at the gray statue and wonder if someone was mad at the Blessed Mother or maybe someone just wanted her to be black. Like the black Jesus we have in one of our nativity sets or the black Barbie that Anita brought to our house.

She stands at the door; shy, slender and pretty in an old-fashioned dress that hangs loose from her lean frame, and she is black. She came on the bus with Aunt Caroline, who is coming with us when we go down the shore.

The screen door slams shut behind them, and the little black girl jumps. Her eyes dart around the room as if someone's been shot. This makes us giggle, and she returns her gaze to the floor. She thinks we are laughing at her. We are, but also we're not. We just laugh at anything and everything, and she qualifies.

"What's your name?" we ask. But she gives us nothing, just stands in silence staring at her feet.

"Her name is Anita, and she is coming on vacation with us," Aunt Caroline informed us.

"Yea! She's coming with us! She's coming down the shore!" we repeated to each other, like a small school for the hard of hearing.

As with all unfamiliar things that cross our threshold, we want to devour her—see what she sounds and smells like, what she thinks about, and where she had been. Her quietness makes her all the more intriguing, but no more safe from our scrutiny. We pile on her, waiting for the words to come. Our enthusiasm causes her to clamp down harder.

"Can we look in your suitcase?" we ask and take her silence as permission.

She is still like a garden statue in our front hallway as Aunt Caroline explains how this girl named Anita would come to spend her vacation with us down the shore. We take in Anita and the story all the while rummaging through her belongings. She didn't have much. The suitcase is packed as if she's spending the night, instead of two weeks. There is a pair of shorts, a T-shirt, pajamas, a toothbrush, a hairbrush, and a Barbie doll.

"Look!" Julia demands as she holds up the doll for everyone's inspection. And several of us blurt out,

"It's black." I've never seen a black Barbie doll before. We look at Anita sheepishly for two reasons; one for having stated the obvious and two, we all silently agree that this girl was a little too old to be playing with dolls. The room is silent as we take in the black Barbie. Even Aunt Caroline pauses a moment from her story. In the silence, Anita gently takes the doll from my sister's hand, places it back in the case, and closes it in such a way that tells us it will be a long time before she'll be willing to share that doll with us again.

"Why don't you show Anita where she will be sleeping tonight," Aunt Caroline suggests in an effort to break the silence.

"She's sleeping with me!" we all yell and race upstairs to try to seduce Anita in to our beds.

The older girls grab Anita and rush her to the attic and slam the door on me, so I go to the steps and listen to Aunt Caroline's version of the story.

"Anita's mother is Bridget Brown who works with me." Aunt Caroline works at the Newark Evening News. "Bridget is in charge of the classified section. She has eight children just like you; except they have seven boys and one girl and they live in an apartment."

"All of them in one apartment?" my mother asks while shaking her head.

"Yes, and during the summer the kids will be out of school

while Bridget is at work. And Mr. Brown is out of town."

Just like Dr. Seuss. *"Mr. Brown is out of town."*

"She's got her hands full, Rosie. The boys can handle themselves, but little Anita, alone with all that roughhousing. It can be tough, being bossed around by all those boys. They pick on her. So I told Bridget not to worry. Anita will spend a few weeks with my brother's family down at the Jersey shore."

"Well, I hope she's okay with sleeping on the porch with the rest of them."

"I think she'll be fine with that."

At dinner, Anita uses her bread to clean the inside of her bowl of soup. My parents beamed with admiration.

"Look at her!" they demand. Anita lowers her head not wanting the attention. But my parents continue on. "She doesn't waste a drop. Now that's how you eat soup!"

In the morning, Anita piles into the van with us along with the usual handful of neighbor kids. There was little Anthony Gabiola and his pee-soaked sleeping bag, fat Maureen McLaughlin, and her secret stash of candy, our cousin Lisa, who also had eight kids in her family and a built-in pool, but she seemed to prefer slumming it with our pack of gypsies, and of course, Aunt Caroline.

My mother sits in the passenger seat, her free arm shoots out sporadically to brace herself against the dashboard when the Giant stops short.

Aunt Caroline sits in a folding beach chair in back, and the rest of us sit balled up in little bundles on a platform that the Giant has built. It is like a big table that fits in the back of the van. The bags go underneath, and we all sit on top. No seats, but lots of blankets and pillows and songs to make the ride softer.

We go through every song we know and some we sing twice. *"Doe, a deer, a female deer. Ray a drop of golden sun. Me, a name I call myself. Far, a long, long way to run."*

I watch Anita as she looks out the window of our van. Everything passes quickly when the Giant is driving, and there is so much to see. Her fingers wipe her upper lip and then rest beneath her chin. She holds her hand there, taking it all in, and I can tell she is like me—not just a quiet girl, but a real thinker. I wonder what she sees, 'cause I am pretty sure it is very different from what is actually out the window.

25

Walking Down the Hill

I GET UP FROM THE BLACK MADONNA WITHOUT HAVING prayed at all. But I make the sign of the cross in case someone is watching.

Right past the Blessed Mother are the doors to the church basement. The church basement is my favorite thing about the church. It's where we go for choir, where I had my first audition, where I got my first part in a play where I got to sing, *"I am Sixteen Going On Seventeen"* in *"The Sound Of Music"*.

Walking past the church basement doors, a cool wind blows by and I am back, seated in the music room of the church waiting for my turn to audition.

The place is so cold it feels like an icebox. Today we can actually see our breath, and the music teacher is wearing gloves with the fingertips cut off so she can play the piano. But even in the chill of the room, I am sweating, and I am not alone.

Kate wipes the beads from her upper lip and turns to me. I can see her mouthing the words *"when the dog bites, when the bee stings."* She wants the role of Maria Von Trapp, and she just might get it. She can really sing. We are called up one at a time and from the front of the room, I hear my name. The director nods at me, and I begin to walk to her. It's like walking through Jell-O. Everything is in slow motion and thick. My heart is screaming, "No! Don't do this." But my feet keep walking and before I know it, I am up in front and holding tight to the piano music. My eyes lock with Mrs. Tedesco, the director. She smiles at me like she wants me to do well, and that makes me want to please her. Still, my heart is pounding out of my shirt, and my mouth is so dry, and I can't figure out where all my spit has gone.

"Look at her knees," someone whispers behind me, and I look down to see my knees knocking together, like in a cartoon. They are knocking so hard that I can actually hear them. I try to make them stop, but they have a mind of their own.

She nods and smiles at me again.

"You want to play Liesl?" she asks. Her perfume drifts by me and sets me at ease. It's warm and rich like Christmas dessert. She is dressed like a mannequin in a fancy store window, everything new and matching, even her earrings match her necklace, and her lipstick matches her nail polish. Her eyes are dark and lined, like Cleopatra, in dark brown and purple, and her hair is a cap of black swirls and twirls that frame her face. It's very easy to imagine her on a soap opera or holding a glass of wine at a museum or fancy party.

"Do you want to play Liesl?" she asks again, and my heart sinks as I realize that I have been staring at her and have already blown my first cue. I nod my head frantically hoping to catch up.

"Not Maria?" she asks. I shake my head in the other direction and manage to add,

"No, just Liesl."

"Okay."

She smiles again and looks back down to her sheet music. I take a deep breath as she flips the pages. I like Liesl. I know all the other girls are auditioning for Maria, but not me. Maria has too many lines, too much to memorize. Liesl's part is just the right size, plus she has her very own song. The music begins, and I start to sing. Mrs. Tedesco looks up at me, smiles and bobs her head as her fingers continue to dance on the keys and push out the music, all without even looking at the keys.

"Okay, let's try again and go a bit higher."

I can't tell if she likes me or is just being kind, but really either option is fine with me. "Okay, very nice, honey, very nice," she says, and I imagine there is an extra nod and wink that I had not seen her give to the others.

When I get to the steps of our house, Julia is sitting on the front stoop peeling potatoes. "I got the part of Liesl," I tell her.

"What?" she asks.

"The part of Liesl in the *Sound of Music*, I got the part and I get to sing, *"I am Sixteen Going On Seventeen."*

Suddenly she is dragging me in the house by my arm. "Maureen got the part!" she screams out to whomever will listen. "Maureen got the part of Liesl!" They come down from upstairs and out from the kitchen with smiles and cheers.

"You did?" they ask, nodding their heads enthusiastically at me like they already know the answer. I stare back at their faces, not wanting to disappoint.

"Well, no actually, I don't know why I said that. I just auditioned that's all, and she said I was good...twice."

"Maureen!"

They all moan as Julia drops my arm in disappointment and returns to the front steps.

The next day there is a paper taped to the music room door, and we gather around the church basement to see our fate.

"Maureen, you got the part of Liesl," I hear someone say. But I keep scanning the paper to be sure. And there it is, right up there for all to see—next to the word Liesl is my name. I stand there for a moment looking up at my name as the other kids push and shove to get their turn.

At home, it's much harder to convince them this time. But whether they believed me or not, I am Liesl.

Like my mother's one hundred rounds of *"There Is No Business Like Show Business,"* I sing *"I am Sixteen Going On Seventeen"* non-stop. It feels a little funny 'cause I am actually twelve going thirteen, but that does not stop me from singing. This is serious business! I am in a show! We eighth graders spend every day after school in the gym at rehearsal. I have to be ready. This is the same stage where Mom had her glee club biff. I have to clear our name. I rehearse and rehearse, staying late to run lines and practice my songs. The school auditorium, the stage, the green room, the piano, the costumes, the music, the role—it's all the perfect distraction, the perfect escape from the chaos and Cancer at home.

On opening night, I go to Claire's house to get ready and put on makeup. She has a huge case of cosmetics that she has been collecting. Half she got with her allowance, and for the other half, she used her five-finger discount.

I put on a little of everything: mascara, eyeshadow, lip gloss, blush. Mrs. Tedesco says it's okay to wear "stage makeup" and that we will not be asked to go wash it off in the girls' room, like we are when we are caught wearing it at school on a regular day.

After I am done, I look at myself in the mirror. *"I am sixteen going on seventeen,"* I sing while Claire sings along with the Bay City Rollers. *"SATURDAY Night!"* At Claire's house we are free to do as we please—make grilled cheese sandwiches, drink cokes, and sing at the top of our lungs to the radio, and when we are done, we can make a few prank phone calls if we want. With her father living in the city and her mother never home, it's like we have our own private place. Sometimes it feels like we're Laverne and Shirley with our own apartment.

Prank calls are one of Claire's favorite things. "Let's get into some mischief," she says, holding up the phone. "Let's do some pranks!" When she is super bored she even prank calls her own father. "I know it's bad, but I just wanted to see what he was doing, or if he'd answer and when he does, he sounds so sad so I just hang up. Is that bad?" she asks me. I am not sure how to answer, so I just shrug.

"Look, you're stuck here by yourself, what do they expect you to do?" I offer. Even though I know it doesn't really make sense.

"No, it's weird," she tells me. "I should not be making prank calls to my dad no matter what."

"Yeah, I guess you're probably right." I say, putting on another coat of mascara. Aside from being mischievous, she's smart even though she makes bad choices. She is wicked smart. She uses words I've never even heard of, not even from Aunt Caroline. I am pretty sure that her father being a professor at

Columbia University is what makes her so good with the words. "I have to get my obligations done," she says. "The onus is on me to do my chores before we go."

"You talk sort of like a queer-bait," I tell her.

"What's a queer-bait?" she asks with a thirsty smile. We spend nights swapping words and other stolen goods. She has taught me the word "depression," which seems like the saddest word in the world. I like "pranks," and "mischief" and even "onus" better, even though onus sounds like anus. Anything seems better than "depression."

"I hate that my parents are divorced. My poor Dad living all alone in the city just makes me so depressed," she whispers to me in the dark when I sleep over at her house. I don't ask for the definition of "depressed" cause A: I don't want it, and B: I don't need it. Sometimes when I look at her, it seems like she is being pushed down, with something heavy on her back. It's good she has that word. It seems the type of thing that might be even worse if it were nameless.

Before heading down to the school auditorium, I stop by my house to show everyone my makeup and remind them to sit in the front. "Front row so I can see you," I tell my sisters. From the dining room I hear my mother call my name. She is up in bed taking it easy. It's been a little harder for her to get around these days. I bound up the stairs and stand in the entranceway to her bedroom, and when I see her, I stop. I can hear her breathing from the hallway, and suddenly I don't want to go into her room. I know that it's wrong, but a part of me wants to stay in the hallway, safe from her discomfort. She calls out for me again,

"Maureen?" My sisters who are downstairs hear her and they scream up to her,

"She is here, Mom. She is on her way up." So I have no choice but to go in.

"Yeah, Mom?" I say softly as I stand in the doorway. Her face is still and sweet. She moves to take my hand but I stand too far from her reach and make no effort to help her out. I have no idea why I am being so distant. She is making eye contact, reaching out to me. I've been waiting for this type of attention for a while, but for some reason, now that it is here, I feel unprepared and stiff.

"Maureen, you got your play tonight," she says, like I may have somehow forgotten. I just stand there, not knowing what to say. "You're gonna be great." I muster a smile, and we both look at each other. "Maureen, I don't think...I won't be...I can't get up," she finally manages. I am not exactly sure what she is saying...

I hate this memory, and I try to fight it from running amok in my head. I look at the fence and the school building and the cars passing but I can't seem to escape the words and her look and my guilt. The guilt is what pulls me back into the nightmare.

"I called the principal," she says, and my face feels funny, warm, and worried. Why would she call the principal? On the day of the production we shouldn't be calling the principal. That may even be one of the rules that they handed out to us. No taking the costumes home, no showing up late, no talking backstage, no extra tickets for extended family members, and no bothering the principal on the day of production. I am pretty sure that is one of the rules, and I start to tick them off in my head. I try not to think about how she said she can't get up. Besides, even if it's not a rule, it seems pretty obvious. Today is a big day. Everyone knows that. There is a ton of stuff to get ready. You just don't want to be calling the principal on a day like today. As all these thoughts roam my mind, my mother wets her lips and keeps talking. "I've explained the situation, and we've figured out a pretty good plan B. After the show is over tonight, you'll come back here in your costume and give me a private show of my own." She says it in a strange, cheerful way like she has just invented something new and wonderful. "Plan B."

"Back here?" I ask, pointing to the floor of her bedroom. "In costume?" I added because it's not really making sense to me. Why would I do that?

"Yes," she smiles. "It's just that I can't get up right now, and this seemed like a pretty good solution. A private show, and the principal said it would be fine. How does that sound?" I want to ask her why she can't get up and why she keeps telling me that she can't get up. But I don't.

I think it has something to do with the chemo she got a few days ago, and she keeps looking at me.

The window in her bedroom is half open, a breeze goes through the leaves, and I watch the white sunlight and the pale leaves on the green trees dance with each other. Her eyes stay on me like they are asking me something, but I am not sure what. It feels like she is waiting for me to give her something. But again I have no idea what that something is. I dig my hands deep into my pockets and feel only lint. I try to think, to really remember all the movies that have this moment, where the mother can't get up, but none come to mind, and I am left without a script, speechless and slipping.

"Okay," she says for me and shakes her head like we have a deal. I nod back at her, not because I agree, but because it seems the right thing to do. She smiles and adds, "Good, okay, tonight I'll be waiting for you after the show."

Walking down the stairs, the walls fold in on me. I move past the dining room and my sisters call, "Break a leg, Maureen."

"Okay," I call back without looking. On the way out the door I pass the mirror. I don't stop to check my makeup or practice my song. I don't want to see.

Claire is waiting for me on the sidewalk. And I try not to cry, I shake my head like an Etch-A-Sketch hoping to erase Plan B. This is not how I had imagined things going. Not at all.

My sisters are great at getting the front row. They go down extra early and stand outside for the doors to open. Once they do, they go right up the side aisle and place things on every seat in the front row 'cause that is usually how many we need. So that is how I figured it would go today. In my imagination, things get even more distorted. Mom is in the front row with all my sisters, there is a spotlight on her so that I can see her every reaction from the stage. My show and my singing is so wonderful that she begins to glow in perfect health and when I come out for the bow, she is up on her feet, clapping, crying, and healed.

I step out the door to our stoop. The lawn is spotted with bald patches and broken toys. There is a home with a daughter who leaves for her show. There is a lawn that is vibrant green, like on TV, and a mother who waves from the door. "I'll see you there, sweetie," she calls. " I'll be right there in the front row." That for sure is Plan A, the one we would all choose if we could.

Out on the sidewalk I tell Claire the news, doing my best to keep it short and casual. "My mom can't come to the show," I say and then, against my will, I bow my head and the tears come hot and heavy. I try to fight them, try making my body hard and closing it down, but I can't. It's all too much. These tears have been building since the day Annie kept her gaze from me, since Julia informed me of the horrible thing that would be done to our mother, since I listened to Riddle drowning in her own tears. They've been building for three years, and now they come and sweep me away with them.

Claire wraps her arms around my jerking body, and the sadness leaks out like a rusty faucet, brownish and squeaky. I lean into her and let it go. I don't even care if the neighbors see me. In the middle of my meltdown, I am grateful that Claire's parents are divorced and that her father lives a lonely life in New York, 'cause I can tell by the way she tries to comfort me that she completely understands.

I wipe my face and tell her that it's not a big deal.

"Yes it is," she tells me, "when it's your mother and your show, and your life, it is a really big deal." I nod at her, but say nothing. She has said it all. We walk the rest of the way to school in silence. And the truth is I won't mind staying in silence forever. I don't care about the words and the lines and the show and the song, and the thought that anyone should care seems crazy.

I meet the rest of the cast in the green room, and we change into our costumes. But I don't feel like I am the one doing the changing. I am just going through the motions. The curtains go up and we sing and say all the words we rehearsed, perfectly on cue. My first line is, "I'm Liesl... I am sixteen and I don't need a governess." But the truth is I am thirteen, my mom is dying, and I do need a governess or at least, "someone older and wiser." At intermission, I change into the next costume and start to cry again. I just can't help it. The other girls gather around me and tell me, "Don't cry Maureen, you're doing great." I bite my lip and nod.

After the show, Mrs. Accardi, invites us all to go to Grunning's Ice Cream Shop. She pops her head backstage and calls, "Get some money from your folks, and we'll all walk to Grunning's." I stand still as the other kids cheer and scramble out of their costumes.

"Ice cream! Grunnings!" At that moment nothing sounds better. I don't want to leave the green room in my costume. I don't want the other kids to ask, "What the heck are you doing going home in your costume? What, have you lost your mind, Maureen? You know the rules!" We all have been told that these are rental costumes, and we are not to take them home under any circumstance.

I watch the kids file out and then, before it's too late, I change back into my street clothes and join them.

At Grunning's the ice cream is cold and sweet and numbing. The place is packed with kids. Mrs. Accardi tries to keep them quiet, but then she joins the commotion when she realizes that no one has any money and she will be stuck with the bill for thirty sundaes.

I take my time walking home. The house is dark, and I am hoping she is asleep. I try to sneak past her room, but her voice catches me in the hallway.

"Maureen? Maureen? Is that you? Maureen, what happened?" I let it hang there, 'cause I don't know what to say.

"Oh, I, ah, I just forgot," I mumble. There is more silence, long and weighed, that neither of us knows how to fill. In the awkwardness, I slip into my room. I lay looking up at the ceiling, not sure how many minutes or hours pass before I hear the Giant make his way up the stairs. From my bedroom, I hear their voices.

"How was it?" she asks in a voice thin and sad.

His answer's like a warm trombone, "It was great, Rosie, really great. That Maureen has a real voice on her, a real gift."

As I stare up at the ceiling, the old man in a wizard hat gives me a gentle wink. I realize that the Giant is talking about me, that he was there, in the auditorium. It doesn't make sense to me, and I try to imagine him in a suit sitting with the other parents.

"Such a gift," he says again. And there is something in his voice that I don't recognize. He is happy, excited...proud. Has that been there all along, living just beyond the wall of fear that I hold up for my father?

Hot tears roll down the sides of my face and drip into my ears, but I just let them roll. It's hard to breathe, hard to hold in the tears, hard to get comfortable with my horrible selfishness.

That is another reason I really don't pray when I see the gray-faced Blessed Mother. I know she knows, and I feel terrible. How can I expect a miracle from her when I am not willing to play my part. "Maureen, what happened? Maureen, what happened?" The question runs circles in my head, and no matter how many ways I think to answer, it doesn't matter, because there is no going back.

26

Meeting Up with the Twins

BEFORE THE CORNER, I PASS THE WALL THAT JULIA USED to stop her bike one day when her brakes gave out. She lay on the couch, moaning and distorted after a terrible face plant. I sat near her on the floor, her face red, swollen and rashed. "Are you okay?"

"Get away from me, Maureen!" she mumbled through her swollen bloody face.

"Let your sister alone, Maureen," Mom called from behind a book in the other room.

To my left is the chain link fence that caught the cart. It's like a Bermuda Triangle of accidents, and I know bad things come in threes, so I cross the street and keep walking.

Down the block from church and one block closer to the train, I spot the Bradley twins, Sandy and Dina. Dina sucks away on a cigarette as Sandy waves. They wait for me at the corner. Sandy and I became friends the hard way.

In first grade, I watch her red shoes walk in from the playground. They are beautiful, and I can't take my eyes off them until I see our sweet teacher, Sister Jacqueline. Sister Jacqueline is sweet like a cookie and warm like an oven. For her, I rush to school and pay attention. She has skin like Snow White, and I am pretty sure that is who she looks like under the heavy black table cloth that she and all her other sisters wear over their heads. She never raises her voice, not even when I spill glue all over the table, and she marks all our papers with happy faces. Every Monday we have "song time" and she teaches us the best ones. *"Kookaburra sits in the old gum tree, Merry merry king of the bush is he. Laugh, Kookaburra, laugh, Kookaburra, Gay your life must be!"* But the best thing about her is that at the end of the day, she stands with a jar of treats and trades us kisses for candy as we leave the classroom. This is first grade. This is heaven, except for one thing; Sandy Bradley's shoes. It's not just that they are beautiful, the real problem is that at least once a day they come crashing into my shin.

I grab a Sugar Daddy, and it's unwrapped and in my mouth before I even hit the sidewalk. Just two blocks to my home, yet by the time I reach our walkway, it's more of a sugar baby.

Sweet caramel is the exact medication for the torment that has been plaguing me for the last few weeks. Sandy Bradley sits across the room from me with curly reddish hair and freckles. Along with the standard blue plaid jumper and saggy knee-highs, she wears the most beautiful pair of red Mary Janes. Since my first day of school, I have had my eye on those shoes like the Wicked Witch to her Dorothy. But lately those ruby slippers have gotten even more of my attention. At least once a day for the past few weeks, one or both of those shoes have been aimed directly at my shins. This is the latest crisis in my life, Sandy Bradley's red shoes.

I put my hand up to tell Sister Jacqueline, who gives Sandy a sad pout, shakes her head, and uses her baptism name. "No, no Sandra. That is not how we treat each other." My eyes narrow in on Sister Jacqueline as I rub my sore shin. Is that it? No wrap to the head with a newspaper? No standing in the corner for Sandy? Each day follows like the last, and the front of my legs become so black and blue that when my knee-highs slip to my ankles, it looks like my legs are dirty.

As I make my way to our stoop, Annie runs by and grabs the wet stick from my lips. When she sees that the candy part is all but gone, she stops.

"What was it?" she asks. Her hair is wilder than ever today. Riddle leaps off the steps and quickly joins Annie's interrogation of me. We've all inherited our mother's sweet tooth. They watch my mouth and wait on my word, like the mere description of the candy will somehow quench their desire.

"Sugar Daddy," I confess as I try to grab my stick back. Annie is quick, and in her mouth it goes. Like a wild haired caveman, she gnaws on it, trying to suck any sugar from the paper.

"Gross, Annie! Cooties!" Riddle warns and shakes her head in disgust like I have leprosy. Annie and I just smile at each other. We have shared popsicles, lifesavers and scraps of gum, and we know Riddle is only sorry she didn't get to me first.

"What happened to your legs?" Riddle asks, her face still stuck in disgust.

"Sandy Bradley's been kicking me." They both stare at my legs and then me and then back at my legs again.

198

"You gotta tell the teacher," Riddle instructs.

"I do! I tell on her every day, but Sister Jacqueline doesn't do anything."

"You have to kick her back." The words hang over us, like the voice of God. It's our older sister Bridget. We wait in reverence for any other gems she may toss our way. Looking up at Bridget's perfection, I imagine that this is how those children at Lourdes must feel like. Her blonde hair catches the sun; her Catholic school skirt is hemmed way too high, and her white button down fits snug across her breast. She is like a Catholic school girl superhero.

"The next time she kicks you, you wait till she gets back to her desk, til she thinks she's in the clear. Then get up, go over to her, and kick her as hard as you can. Don't miss. That will be the end of it."

She sashays up our front steps, and my mind is in a tangle. What about "love your neighbor" and "turn the other cheek"? This is in direct opposition to everything our mother has ever told us! It's confusing, especially since Bridget is the one who assures us that eating carrots will not actually make our hair curly, as my mother had promised. And it was Bridget who clued us all in on the ramifications of picking our noses in public and shaving our legs without using lotion. She had always been right, and yet it all seems so wrong.

"The Bradley's are tough, make sure you don't miss," Riddle adds. She flips her hair and turns to leave. Annie handed me back the chewed up candy stick as some sort of consolation.

"Do you think I should kick her?" I ask Annie. I can tell that she wants to say no. That she wanted to advise me differently.

But she looks down at my dirty shins and shrugs.

"You'll know what to do," she says and then twirls around and takes the stairs two at a time.

The next day comes; it's the same old story, but this time she has caught me off guard. I had been daydreaming, and now I am wincing in pain and groping my shin as she returns to her seat. My sister's words ring in my ears clear as day, "You'll know what to do. You have to kick her back." And I realize they are right. I have no other choice.

I wait until Sandy is settled, and then I wait a bit more. My heart's still pounding from the pain, and now it continues because of the anticipation. This is important, and I want to make sure I do it right. I pick up my pencil and pretend to make my way to the sharpener across the room. Out of the corner of my eye I watch her, amazed by how completely she has moved on from her attack, as if it were just another task she needed to cross off her list of things to do.

The world is moving in slow motion, and the rest of the room starts to fade, until there is just Sandy and me. I tap her on the shoulder and she turns. I eye her leg for only a second before I take aim and with all my might, I ram my foot into the front of her shin. I watch her double over but don't wait to witness her pain. Instead I head to the sharpener and over the grind of my #2 pencil, I enjoy the sound of her moan. Her hand is up, and she is calling the teacher. "Maureen kicked," she calls out.

Sister Jacqueline gives me that pouty face and slight shake of the head. She points her beautiful slender finger, and it's like a blue bird will land on it.

"No, no, Maureen. That is not how we treat each other." She is so beautiful and sincere, and I lower my head, pretending to be ashamed, but really I don't want her to see my smile. I can't help but smile. Poor Sister Jacqueline is wrong; this is exactly how we treat each other.

From that day on, Sandy and I have been friends.

Although the morning snow has all but melted, it's still bitter cold out, a frosty wind whips up the street. But they wait for me, because being cold together is so much better than freezing on your own. Dina's hair is thick and mangy; it covers her eyes like a mutt but fails to cover her anger. Not really sure what she is so angry about, and most times we sum it up to her not being a morning person.

I greet them with, "Hey."

"Hey," they answer, and we begin walking.

"You got an extra cigarette?" I ask Dina. She growls back at me, takes the pack of Marlboro's from her pocket in a huff, and holds it up for me to consider.

"Does it look like they come with an extra cigarette? Do you see one taped to the outside of the box?" I don't answer. I've heard this monologue before and just wait patiently for the ending when she hands me a cigarette. "Yeah, Maureen, each pack comes with one extra for this very reason. You mooch." She huffs and snorts as she hands me one.

"Thanks," I offer, placing the cigarette in my mouth and search my pockets for a light that doesn't exist till she flicks a lighter in my face.

"You want me to smoke it for you, too?"

Then Dina begins her early morning sermon of doom. Sandy and I have never talked about our endurance of this ranting, we both just go along with it, too lazy to get up and change the channel.

"Our Aunt Patty is a nurse who works in intensive care in New York and she says that there's this terrible disease that is killing gay guys left and right. It's like pneumonia, only worse, because they get sores all over their bodies, and they get so thin, and the doctors don't know how to cure it!" This current rant pulls my attention because it sounds so horrible. Watching men suffer and grow thin with sores sounds like how my mom is right now. And it doesn't seem good for anyone to suffer like that. It's odd that it would just happen to gay guys. I think about Steven and Michael, our neighbors, and how nice they are to me and how horrible I would feel if either of them should get sick like that.

My mother doesn't care for the gays. She says they are out to take down the educational system and teach nothing but porno and smut. Sometimes we spend Saturdays picketing. Most times we picket at the abortion clinic or we take the bus to Washington. We hold up signs with little baby feet and sings songs about giving life a chance. But recently we've been picketing the gays. The gays are apparently harder to find, so instead of an establishment, we hang out on a street corner and wave our signs.

Mom doesn't want the public schools to be teaching about homosexuality. We don't go to public school but she says, "Once they get it in the public schools, we are all going to hell in a handbasket. They will have the gays and the perverts running the place." So we make signs that say, "Good education not Gay education" and "Beware! Party time for Satan" and any other brilliant saying she can come up with. We dress like we're going to church and spend the day on the street corner as traffic goes by and honk their horns in approval.

Since Steven and Michael moved in directly behind us, my

loyalty has been divided. Steven and Michael do not seem like smutty perverts, but they are different. Different from anyone I know, so maybe that is what being a smutty pervert is like. They have parties like the hippies, but their music is different, and the parties aren't as messy or smoky. And unlike the hippies, who look pretty ratty and smell like burnt paper and sweat, Steve and Michael look shiny and new—like two beautiful Ken dolls right out of the package.

Plus, their parties are extra pretty. They've strung lights around their backyard like Christmas, even though it's summer, and every weekend their backyard is filled with the most beautiful people.

Smoke from their grill smells like heaven and makes my mouth water. And as if that were not enough, they have an above-ground pool. Not that it does me any good. They moved in when I was eight, and now two years later, I have still not gotten a toe in their pool. From our bathroom window, I can see the clear blue water, and on hot days I imagine jumping in the pool from our roof. It's far, but the risk would be worth it.

The people at their parties are not just beautiful, they are artists, opera singers, and painters, but not the kind who wear painter pants and work from a truck. Once there was even a ballerina who leaped and pranced around their yard. William, Owen, and I watched her leave the ground and sail through the air. "Hey, hey, hey!" I call out, unable to control myself. I can fight off the temptation of the pool and the wonderful smells from the grill, but when the dancing lady shows up, I am overpowered. Michael comes to the fence and smiles down at us. "What is she doing?" I ask, before he even says a word because I have never seen a person move like that. I've seen kids get tossed in the air at the public pool or Cathleen Casey, the little cheer-leading mascot, who is flung into the air like a human firework. But this ballerina is different. No one is tossing her. She goes up all on her own. She flies like a featherless bird, and we can see everything, every muscle, every bone and almost every vein.

"Well, she just finished a show in the city and this is what she needs to do to stretch out. This is how she takes care of her body." Talking to him is like having our own personal Mr. Rogers in the backyard. He makes eye contact and explains things in sentences and somehow makes us believe that it really is "a beautiful day in the neighborhood."

"She just finished a show in the city?" I repeat, wanting to make sure I heard this right. "What kind of show?" I asked.

"She is a ballerina." My stomach swirled as I stare at her. A ballerina, real live ballerina? Like the kind I've been dreaming of one day being? As terrible as it was finding out there was no Santa, finding out there were actually real live ballerinas made up for it tenfold. "Would you like to go see her dance sometime?" he asks.

"Me?" I search his eyes to make sure he is not kidding. He raises one shoulder and gently bends his head to it so that they almost meet.

"Sure, all of you could go." My knees go weak a little and I am not sure I can stand it.

"Yes, yes!" I want to scream, but only bob my head in a frantic nod.

"It's not a big deal," he shrugs. "She'd be happy to have you as her guest." She would? Her guest? I look at my brothers to see if any of this is making sense. But they don't take their eyes from the beautiful ballerina in her nude-colored leotard flying through the air in our neighbor's yard. "I'll talk to your father about it, but you guys have to stop screaming and staring through the fence, okay?" Michael asks as he folds his arms across his chest and grins down at us. I nod my head in agreement and try to imagine Michael talking to the Giant, but I can't. I think about explaining the Giant to Michael. His dirty work boots and his T-shirts with built-in air conditioners, his bristly face. But I don't want to scare Michael off, so I just usher the two boys back inside the house.

"Come on, we can watch from the bathroom window," I whisper, "get a better view."

Later that week the Giant comes in the door with a bottle of wine and a note from "the gays" as he calls them. A bottle of wine is perfect, and maybe I didn't need to explain the Giant to Michael after all. The Giant places the little note on the table as he tries to twist off the cap. "The gays want to bring Maureen and the two boys into the city to see a play," he tells our mother as she places the meatloaf on the table.

"Who?" she asks.

"The gays in the back. Michael and the other fellow who moved in the place behind us," he replies. I sit on my hands, and hold my breath. She stands staring at the wine bottle and the note, as a silent year goes by. Our mother, who spends half the day with the telephone surgically attached to her head, is speechless. "What do we tell them?" the Giant asks as he gets up to find the corkscrew.

Being gay is not okay, but we are supposed to love our neighbors. I wait for her to hand us a depressed houseplant and send us over to Michael's and Steven's. I wait for her to bake a cake to welcome them to the neighborhood like we usually do. I wait for her to say something, but she doesn't.

The Giant opens the bottle of wine and pours a glass as my mother sits at the other end of the table and silently shakes her head. He takes a drink and looks up at her. His head leans to one side near his raised shoulder. "What are ya gonna do, Rosie?" She breaks her silence with prayer, and we join her.

"Bless us, O Lord and these thy gifts which we are about to receive from thy bounty through Christ Our Lord Amen."

I bow my head in prayer a little longer and put in a special plea with God for "these gifts of going to the show as a guest of the ballerina" that I am hopefully "about to receive."

27

Climbing the Stairs to the Train Platform

THE BRADLEY GIRLS AND I CLIMB THE CEMENT STAIRS that lead to the platform where we wait for the train. The one we take heads to Convent Station, away from the city, and is filled with mostly girls and boys dressed in turtlenecks and Docksiders on their way to prep school. They stand in groups and look like they were all ripped from the pages of *The Preppy Handbook*.

Dina continues to talk on about conspiracy theories, all beginning with "My mother says," and "my mother told me," and "my mother knows a guy who…" She is nervous and suspicious. Her dark hair hangs in her face, and her abrupt gestures and harsh manners make you think she is more boy than girl. She continues on with her monologue about what her mother said, and I want to ask her if she has ever had an original idea for herself. But she is generous with the cigarettes, so I nod my head and pretend to be interested. Sandy is different than Dina in almost every way. Like the Tevlin twins, you can easily tell them apart. Sandy is fair and open, where Dina is dark and closed down. I imagine Dina as a shop with a "Not Open for Business" sign on her door. Since the kicking of the shins, Sandy and I have endured quite a few adventures. First cigarettes, first shoplifting (If you don't count the Brachs candy... and who does?), first ditching school, and best of all, first drunk—that is if you don't count the tea party mom and I had back in kindergarten.

I look out at all the other clusters of kids waiting for the train, but instead, I see our living room filled with smoke and laughter. I'm at the Giant's meatball party, which happens every New Year's day without fail. *"Bottle of red, bottle of white. Whatever kind of mood you're in tonight."*

The Giant is throwing his annual New Year's Day meatball party. Everyone is invited, and they all show up. So we have to make a lot of meatballs. Most people who come are still drunk from the night before. That's the reason we have it on New Year's Day, so that everyone has a place to continue the party. All my relatives come; the neighbors, the priest, the nuns, the whole parish, teachers, classmates, relatives of friends, boyfriends, ex- boyfriends, the fire department. The police department isn't actually invited, but they usually show up.

The Giant's best friend, John Boy, comes with a bottle in a bag and a booming voice. "Yeah Boy!" he hollers in the front hall. He tells a joke about our mother's terrible cooking. The joke goes on and on and has about sixteen other jokes built right inside it, so by the time he gets to the real punchline, everyone is already howling and holding their guts. Our poor mother tries to cover her smile as she shakes her head and turns red. Seeing her so happy makes us all forget a little.

Gap-Grin Gary, the Giant's other friend, is also in full spirits. He has more children than teeth, and the Giant says his checks are made of rubber. But tonight he is forgiven, and he comes with all his kids to share the spirits and song. There is a slight hesitation when they show up at the door, but Mom moves in for a hug. "It's New Year's Day," I can hear her say, "and we can all start from scratch."

The living room furniture is moved out or pushed to the side. Card tables with red and white-checkered tablecloths are set up throughout the first floor. We have saved the Giant's wine bottles and melted candles into them. Whenever a bottle is emptied, another candle gets lit. Billy Joel sings from the record player, *"A bottle of red, a bottle of white. Whatever kind of mood you're in tonight. I'll meet you anytime you want in our Italian restaurant."*

The air is thick with onions, garlic, tomato and grease from cooking all those meatballs. I know what they will taste like before I even take a bite.

We've been rolling meatballs for weeks. This is how we spend most of our Christmas vacation. It's been a family tradition for years. The Giant loves meatballs and parties and games, so the meatball party idea is perfect. Every year he breaks his record from the year before. We are up to five hundred meatballs, and growing. The game is that whoever guesses the exact number of meatballs will get to eat the first one. That's the idea anyhow, but it's just another neighborhood myth, because the meat rolling team has been eating them as we go.

I've invited Sandy to the meatball party even though she

is a vegetarian. No meatballs for her, but we have other plans, a New Year's resolution. Tonight after the party, after everyone has left or is passed out, we are going to get drunk.

Mom is in bed early, but that doesn't put a damper on the evening. Everyone wishes her well as she wobbles up the stairway. It's pain, not liquor, that has her off balance. The drinking, debating, and drunken banter goes on for hours. Especially when John Boy and Gap-Grin Gary are in the house, and a lot happens before the final toast. Somebody gets in a fight, someone passes out. Someone falls in love. Someone gets sick in the bathroom. Someone else does not make it to the bathroom, but throws up on our front porch. The Giant tosses a bucket of water out the door to clean off the steps, but the weather is cold, and a few guests fall on the icy puke, and ride their asses right into the snow. They wrestle around in the new fallen drifts before laughing off into the night. Their bright colored coats and hats disappear into the darkness. But as I watch from my bedroom window, I can hear traces of song and laughter echoing back to me. They are completely gone, and I can't wait to join them. I watch for a moment as the light from the street corner makes the snow turn yellow and red. I don't wait for green 'cause we have waited long enough.

Sandy and I stand guard at my bedroom door to make sure the coast is clear. She will stay in the room, and I'll sneak down to get the drinks. The stairs creak so much in our house, it's safer this way.

Down the stairs I go...slowly. I know most of the major creaky parts, but I can't be sure if my mother is asleep. Pain makes her sleep light, and she has good ears. I am at the bottom of the stairs now, and it's smooth sailing. I pass through the dark house like a shadow. There are empty beer bottles everywhere, plates of half eaten food, and what was once our cute little Italian restaurant now looks more like a brothel. Even some of the pictures on the walls hang crooked. Our poor little house has been raped and left to weep alone. But I have no time to console her. I head straight for the liquor cabinet. There are all sorts of bottles, different shapes and colored glass, and I have no idea what any of them are. I pour some brownish liquid into two glasses, making sure they are even. I don't taste it. I want to wait for Sandy because we are doing this together.

Back up the stairs I go, lighter, swifter. I have accomplished the task and just need to deliver the goods. Soon we will be drunk and off on our own adventure.

I wish Claire could be with us, but we have been banned from hanging out for a while. We were playing around, harassing the folks at the local Chinese restaurant. Claire went in and flipped the light switch as I raided their complimentary mint bowl. I didn't know they knew the Giant, which was foolish on my part. It was a bar for God's sake; of course they knew the Giant. When the news got back to him, he grabbed me by the hair and told me I was forbidden to see Claire for a month. I was used to being held hard by the hair, but not seeing Claire was devastating. As I pulled the loose locks from my head, I wondered how we would make it a week, let alone a month. I try not to think about her prank calling her father. Besides, I am glad in one way that she is not here, 'cause two glasses seem like more than enough to handle.

At the top of the stairs I hit a soft spot, and a loud creak escapes from the floor.

"Who is that? Who's there?" Her voice comes at me like a

jack-in-the-box; I fumble a bit, catch myself and try to keep still. She cannot get up without assistance, and my father is out cold. I weigh my options.

"Who is it?" she demands.

"It's me, Mom, Maureen, just going to the bathroom."

"Get to bed," she demands. Quickly, I duck into the safety of my room. I lean against the door with glasses in hand, and exhale a breath I can't remember holding.

After the high stakes adventure, the room is unexpectedly cold. Sandy has been smoking out the bedroom window to kill time. I hold up the two glasses like Olympic gold. She takes one and smells it.

"What is it?"

"I don't know," I confess, "but it had a cool picture on it," I add, not wanting to sound clueless.

"Okay," she says as she closes her eyes, brings the glass to her lips and takes a sip. Instantly she pulls the glass away as her face puckers up like she's sucked a lemon. It's exciting and dramatic and all so forbidden.

"It's gross," she finally manages as she holds the glass at a distance.

"We should just drink it back," I suggest. She nods and pulls the glass back in. But as she moves toward it, the smell catches her again, and she pulls away with a groan. "Over the teeth over the gums, watch out stomach here it comes," I sing in hopes of coaxing her forward. She nods again with more commitment. We raise our glasses in unison, smile at each other over the rims, and toss them back like two synchronized swimmers. Before the liquid clears our throats, there is coughing, gagging, and shaking of heads. It's powerful. When we get control of our senses, we stare into each other's eyes, searching our faces for clues of drunkenness. Sandy's mother is a heavy drinker, like the Giant. When it comes to drunkenness, we know it better than our own reflections.

We wait a short minute that feels like an hour. Swiftly it is agreed that more is needed. I am back down the stairs and in front of the liquor cabinet. I've seen the adults mix things together. Maybe that's what makes this drinking thing bearable. I pick up a clear bottle and tilt it toward the glass. It pours out like water. Seems harmless enough, so I top it off with something from a green bottle. Out pours a golden liquid. I swirl the two around and head back up the stairs. The ritual continues, and on three, we toss back the drinks. It's just as hideous as the first, and still no effect. It's hard not to doubt the whole process. But I am a trooper, so again I make the pilgrimage downstairs. As I hit the last step, something has changed. The living room takes on a holy glow, and as I approach the liquor cabinet, the light is like Christmas morning, and there is music, like in the movies. I step into the spotlight as I stand before all the bottles, like a host on a cooking show. It's fantastic. I take my time like a scientist, smelling, tasting, and talking to my absent audience. "Um, maybe a splash of this, and a swirl of that." I find some soda and cherries; I'm on a roll. Time no longer exists, and it doesn't matter anyway, Sandy will be so happy that I have found the secret to making this stuff taste good...sugar!

Up the stairs I go, but the walls keep knocking into me. The stairs have magically transformed into a fun house, where the floor rises and falls unexpectedly. I have to take breaks along the way up to keep the liquid from splashing over the rim and spilling over the steps. It's all so delightful, and the laughter pushes against my lips, but I bite the sides of my mouth to help secure the dam. Slowly I make it back to my bedroom, one step at a time. Step and rest and focus, and steady and up, and step and rest and focus, and steady as she goes, all the while trying not to laugh. Once inside, a sight that bursts the dam greets me, and a powerful wave of laughter crashes through me, sweeps me up, and topples me over. I cross my legs in hopes of preventing another threatening flood. The crossing of my legs throws off my balance, and again my masterpieces are at risk of spilling upon the floor. I fall back against the door, and try to focus on my friend. She is sitting up in my bed and projectile vomiting across the room. I have never seen the body perform this amazing feat, and I am amused, astounded, and most importantly, drunk! Mission accomplished. I set the drinks down carefully, and slide into bed with my friend.

"I'm drunk!" I exclaim. She meets my enthusiasm with a moan. I pull the puke-soaked blankets and sheets from the bed.

"I have to go to the bathroom," she manages. I laugh at the thought of the two of us creaking through the hallway. Sandy doesn't know about the walls that bang into you. I try to tell her, try to convince her to pee in the potted plant in the corner, like Bridget once did when she came home too late. I don't even think twice about how effortlessly I have crossed the line of wondering why in the world would Bridget pee in a potted plant, to wholeheartedly endorsing it. But Sandy can't hear me. Her head is wobbling and her words are slurry and there is no arguing with her.

"I need to go to the bathroom," she repeats. I have no choice but to escort her down the hall, past my parent's bedroom, to the one bathroom that all ten people in my family share. I send a silent prayer that the bathroom is available. If we have to wait in the abusive hallway, my mother will wake for sure. She will yell out with that high-pitched call, and wake the Giant. He will get up, grab me by the hair, and once he sees that I am drunk, he will beat me.

My prayer is answered, and the bathroom is free. We have made it safely to the bathroom, so in celebration, I start to laugh again. But this time I can't seem to help it or even want to try. The laughter makes me weak at the knees, and I grab the towel rack to hold myself up. The towel rack snaps under my weight, sending me sailing to the floor. I look up dazed and still holding onto the broken bar that used to be the towel rack. Now Sandy is laughing too. The walls are spinning, my body is loose and fizzy like club soda, and life is wonderful. But before I can really enjoy it, her voice pierces the air. This time she knows who it is.

"Maureen? What're you doing in there?" I close my eyes and try to be still, try to still the fizzle and spinning wall.

"Nothing, Mom," I call out with eyes closed. "I was just helping Sandy go to the bathroom." It comes out of my mouth before I have a chance to think, and as I look with amusement into Sandy's eyes, I am at once delighted and embarrassed that at twelve years old, I've told my mother that I am helping my friend take a piss. Sandy and I crouch to the floor and try to control our howling laughter, and I am so happy that she is here to join me in my state of amazing disgrace.

"Get back to bed, the two of you." It is late now, and my mother has been softened by the long night. She will have to let this pass for now. Sandy and I stumble back to my bedroom, clutching at each other for safety. We have no concern for the creaks that escape the floor or the giggles from our lips.

I pull a clean blanket from a chair, and we lay down on the bare mattress with the blanket for comfort. When we are just about to surrender to sleep, there is a noise at the window, a scratching sound, and slowly it begins to open from the outside. Sandy jumps and lets out a yelp; but I nudge her and whisper, "Bridget." Sandy knows I share this room with Bridget, or she with me. It's the ultimate punishment in our home, to share a room with me. Being the youngest girl, with my room closest to my parents, not to mention I am the leper who lies on her hands.

The only good thing about this room is that it has escape possibilities. By climbing a ladder to the roof, and crawling across the ledge, Bridget has ensured herself no curfew. She is seventeen and is just returning from a secret date with Bob.

In through the window she slips like a seasoned cat burglar. Her fair skin is red from alcohol and forbidden love. Blonde hair spills over her face, as her green eyes take in the scene like a hawk. She knows we've been drinking and smoking, like a whore knows the smell of sex. She comes at me; her words and rage could take down a prizefighter. My mother has tried to protect her with braces and bad haircuts, but her beauty, like her spirit, cannot be contained.

So despite all of my mother's best efforts, Bridget has turned out defiantly beautiful. As she yells and ridicules me, I can't help but be mesmerized. She unlocks her closet door; it's actually our closet, but since she is the only one with the key, it has become hers. It's just another survival technique she has learned in our over-populated household. Boundaries. Stake out your territory, lock it off to anyone else, and defend it with your life.

She grabs a pack of smokes from her carton of cigarettes in the closet, locks the door, takes a last look around, throws a few more well-landed darts my way, and slips back out the window into the night. Sandy is understandably impressed. She goes to the window to witness Bridget's final exit as her blonde head drops like a sunset past the top of the roof. Still Sandy stands, watching the darkness, like a well-fed audience too full to move. After a few minutes, she breaks her standing ovation, sits at the edge of the bed and lights up her own cigarette, making use of the open the window. I offer one of my liquid masterpieces to Sandy, but she declines. After the violent dance the last drink put her through, she sits this one out. Before long she is asleep. I smoke the rest of her cigarette and finish off her drink. "Waste not, want not."

The next morning comes on loud and powerful like a train, and I am a penny on the track. Pain, nausea, sunlight, and my sister, Julia, crush me. She stands in the doorway with brooms and pail.

"Get up, shithead! You have to help clean the house." I turn and groan as she throws something at me. "Get up." I can't seem to move. I keep my eyes closed and hope it's all a bad dream or that death will come. Either will do. She walks around to my side of the bed, but before she gets to me, she steps back in disgust. "Gross, who puked?" I open one eye and peer over the bed. There on the floor, is a puddle of puke.

"Sandy." I answer my sister's question and try to wake my friend with one word. Conservation is key this morning. Sandy sits up, rubs her eyes as Julia puts down the pail and lets the broom fall on me.

"Clean it up, and then get downstairs."

She exits to the attic, on to her next victims.

I hand Sandy the rags.

"I can't do it, Sandy. I cleaned up your vomit last night." I roll off the bed on her side, avoiding the puddle altogether. I stand and the stench moves in on me. My head goes light, and I sit back down as I pull on my shoes. Sandy crawls over to inspect the puke puddle as I push the plate of ash and butts under the bed. The house is alive with noise already. The Giant is yelling for the two boys, as my brothers in the next room scurry to their feet.

"We're coming," one of them shouts as they scramble to get down the stairs. My forehead falls into my hands, the pain is unbearable. I hear Sandy gagging in the corner.

"Oh God," she mumbles as she passes by me and tosses the rags at my feet. She collapses back in the bed across from me.

"It's not mine."

"What?" I ask.

"There are meatballs in that puke. It's not mine." I look up at her in confusion.

"Well, then whose is it?" I don't actually speak the words, the thought is enough work for me to muster. She reads my eyes and answers.

"You puked last night, Maureen. That's why it's on your side of the bed. There are meatballs in that puke, and no one else was here, so you do the math." I still don't get it. I am sure I didn't puke. I would have remembered it. Again she reads me. "You probably blacked out." I've heard about blackouts, but never thought I could have one. Like fainting, it was always just something that I fantasized about. It's strange to think it actually happened, like time travel or falling down a rabbit hole. How could I have done something and not be there to remember? I remember everything. I know that I should feel unsettled by this, but oddly I don't. Instead I feel accomplishment and a sweet sense of relief. I like living in my own little world, and now I have another way of getting there. I can go somewhere safe, where time stands still, somewhere over the rainbow, where I don't have to remember a thing. A dreamy, little, blurry place called blackout.

28

Standing at the Station

I WATCH THE SMOKE AND STORIES FLOAT FROM DINA'S mouth. Down the tracks, John-John Chapman is waiting for the train. He is surrounded by a group of boys making small talk. Across the track a young man holds a boom box. *"Everybody was kung fu fighting, those cats were fast as lightning."* The music blares as John-John fakes a few kung fu moves to the delight of his friends. He looks over at me, we make eye contact, and suddenly I am ten, standing with my brother William in the front yard.

"I want to take you on. I want to take you on. I want to take you on." Jerry Segal, surrounded by a small gang of the usual suspects, glares down at William. "I want to take you on." He says, and although I had never heard it put that way, I was pretty sure I knew what he was asking. For the new kid on the block, Jerry could harness some power. He gathered the troops to meet at our yard and "take on my brother." Eddy Kelly, the cop's son, is three years older than most of us. He stands a good head above the rest. John-John Chapman, the adopted only child from across the street, is there as well. Our mother warned us about John-John. And although she warned us about everything, when it came to John-John, we tended to take her word.

"That kid is going to end up in a wanted ad on the post office wall. A bad egg, a bad seed, an evil streak and not in line with the Christian spirit." I am not sure what he ever did to earn all of this, but I don't want to find out.

Vinny Gabiola rounds out the group. Vinny is practically a brother, and William's best friend. We made room for him on all our family trips, and put up with his pee-soaked sleeping bag. He hangs in the back, aware of this blatant disloyalty, and tries not to make eye contact.

William looks up at them from his metal fire truck. His round, freckled face squints in the sun.

"What does that mean?" he asks. The question that seals his fate. They chuckle and nudge each other.

I step closer, taking it all in.

My kid brother William is an oddity to me. He is a boy and younger, and until he arrived our family was six little girls. Even though William is a boy, he is also still a baby—a sweet baby boy who calls me "Marine," like the ocean. He looks up to me, which I am not used to, and I continually let him down. As much as Jesus has forgiven me for the Waterford Crystal event, I still cling to my guilt. Even now, when I promise to play cardboard house with him—a game you play when someone in the neighborhood gets a new washer or refrigerator, and you cut out some windows and sit in it till you get hungry or bored—his whole face lights up. My mother calls his face "the map of Ireland." But no matter how hard I try to find it, when I look at the map of Ireland that hangs in our dining room, I never find his mischievous little smile, turned up pug nose, or his twinkling eyes.

Whenever a camera is taken out to document a wedding, funeral, or baby shower, William is there with both thumbs in the air, his head cocked to one side with a smirk. You can almost hear him saying, "AYYY!" He is our little Irish Arthur Fonzarelli.

However, there is nothing cool about seeing him sitting in this child's toy with these smirking boys crowding him like city skyscrapers. The whole scene makes my skin prickle and sweat, and there is the taste of cold metal in my mouth, like how I felt before I had to kick Sandy. My heart is pounding, and I am not really sure why, but I sense a wave coming, and if I time it just right, I might be able to ride it in, instead of letting it thrash my little brother and me.

"It means I want to fight," Jerry explains with a confident shrug. "I want to take you on." Before I even see William's reaction, I hear my words hit the air. They are as much a surprise to me as they are to the boys.

"No, Jerry, he won't take you on, but I will." I watch this all like a bystander. There is an anger in me that leads the way. I have no choice but to follow.

Jerry and I are exactly the same size. He's a skinny little boy, and I, a skinny little girl. He looks me in the eye as I watch him register this unplanned turn of events. He's here to take on William—a good head shorter than him, and a few years younger- an easy target. But now he has to face me. In his mind, I am sure he believes his chances are still pretty good, after all, I am "just a girl." But we both know it's certainly not going to be as easy.

He's come to our yard for a little entertainment, a way of passing the time and showing off at my brother's expense. For me, the stakes are higher. I am clearing my guilt and defending someone I love. Jerry wants some fun; I want nothing short of death.

I feel my face grow calm as I watch the boys shift and sway in the unexpected news. Jerry hesitates. We know if you hit a girl, you're a bully, and if you cower to a girl, you're a sissy. So I have him beat either way, though secretly, I am hoping he goes with sissy. My heart beats out one strong pump after the next. Like a giant walking slowly; thump, thump, thump. My knees are weak and gently vibrating, but I don't let on. I just stand facing him, without a flinch, and wait for his reply.

Jerry cocks his head, his skin is translucent and fair, his eyes a pale baby blue.

"Okay, I'll take you on."

He smiles. His eyes turn cold. I exhale the fear I held for my brother and inhaled a new gulp just for me.

We walk to the sidewalk in the front of my house. Tall bushes protect us from any adults, and the other boys gather around us to close off the circle. I have no idea how a street fight actually works. I stare back at Jerry, who raises his fist to his face like I've seen on TV, his cold blue eyes looking back at me over his knuckles. I stand motionless taking in his every move, the shifting of his weight, the quick lick and bite of his lip. I think about lifting my hands to my face like he has done, but my arms feel too heavy.

Eddy calls the fight, telling us when to stop and start. The other boys shove each other a bit to give us room, but I stand still, my feet planted to the earth. Between my sisters and Sandy Bradley, I had been training for this match my entire life.

"Okay," Eddy calls out. "On the count of three." Everything is done on the count of three: birthday candles blown out, races begun, bedtime announced. But life is far from fair in this neck of the woods, and you'd be a fool not to jump the gun. By the time I hear three, I already have Jerry by the hair, a good solid hold, from the roots, my thirsty fingers firmly entangled in his locks and pulling him down. It's a technique I learned the hard way.

My teeth are clenched, my gut is tight, and my hands hold fast to Jerry's head. It's not easy, but I am suddenly aware that there is more power in my little body than I have ever known before. I plant my feet firmly, and with my free hand, I make a fist and begin swinging in direct upward jabs, straight into his face. I got him at arm's length. His low and wild swings come at me from the sides but make no contact, or at least none that affect me. I feel nothing but the cold harsh contact of my fist to his face. I make no real attempt to land on his eyes or nose or mouth, but just swing hard. Jab. Jab. Jab. Like shooting fish in a barrel. I can't miss. I have him, and he knows it. They all know it, and the longer it lasts, the more threatened I feel as the other boys move in closer. A thought crosses my mind about how strange it feels to plow my fist into the flesh of someone's face, but also how strangely easy.

Jerry grunts and sputters each time my fist meets with his face, and he dances wildly trying to free himself from my hold.

"Ugh!" he yells. "Wait! Stop!" I ignore him and continue swinging, realizing, for the first time, that I have no idea how to stop. I am on a fast moving train with no way off. If I stop or jump free I, will certainly be swept under. The other boys are breathing down my neck. One weak move and I'll be taken down for sure. Then it happens…he folds. "Hey guys, help me out."

With those five words, he declares defeat, and the whole house of cards tumbles quickly.

Within seconds, I'm pounced on. There is the clawing of someone's nails in my sides and the prying of my fingers from Jerry's hair. A hundred hands pull and lift me from the fray, and then it's over. The boys disperse slowly, joining Jerry in his stumble of shame. They no longer hang as close to him, their loyalty weakened, feeling tricked into having bet on the wrong dog. John-John looks back at me with a twinkle of newfound respect.

That night the Giant gathers the offenders to our home. Jerry and family are no shows. I'm embarrassed that such a fuss is being made. I won for God's sake.

"You're not supposed to hit little girls," I hear the Giant tell them, which made no sense. I know firsthand that he has no problem with it.

"You're not suppose to hit anyone," Mrs. Chapman adds.

"No one hit her," John-John Chapman pipes in. My father raises my T-shirt to display my scratches and ensure further humiliation.

"Well, you should see Jerry's face!" John-John continues. But his statement is met with a smack to the back of the head delivered by his mother, Mrs. Chapman, who looks like a human circle on pretzel stick legs. I often wonder why she doesn't just topple over.

Eddy Kelly comes to John-John's defense.

"We didn't hit her. She beat the hell out of Jerry, and we were just trying to pull them apart." I am very happy with this account of the story and proud to hear I had left a mark. I wanted an announcement. I wanted a plaque; let it be known throughout the land, I beat the hell out of Jerry Segal. It felt rewarding, even though the whole thing confuses me. Jerry tries to hit William, but I hit Jerry, and then I get scratched up by John-John, who gets hit by his mother, who tells us, "It is not okay to hit anybody."

William and I sit in silence, taking it all in, trying to figure out the right and wrong of things. And just when we think things have gotten off track, Mrs. Chapman takes a paddle shaped like a large hand out of her purse. It's attached to a long wooden handle, and on one side the words "Mother's Helping Hand" are written in red paint.

"Do you need some help?" she asks John-John and shows us all the wooden hand with pride.

"This is what I use on John-John when he needs a lesson."

John-John's face gets hard, and I can almost see what he will look like on the side of the post office wall. He gradually lowers his gaze to the floor. I am embarrassed for him, and scared of his mother, and confused about when it's okay and not okay to beat up kids.

Eddy leaves first, and the rest follow. My father and Mrs. Chapman share a few parting jokes at the door. As they leave, John-John looks back at me as I stand behind the screen door. It's the same look that he gives me at the station, it tells me something. It tells me that he knows me, that he holds a piece of my story and I hold a piece of his. We could use it against each other if we wanted, but that we probably won't. We can trust each other not to tell.

29

Boarding the Train

FROM DOWN THE TRACKS, I HEAR THE LOW WARM
whistle of the train, like the early hum of the teakettle, and I
lay aside my memories to watch the massive train pull in. It's
powerful, old and intense as it slows to a stop with a grumble
and a yawn. The conductor hops off and invites us aboard with
a wave of his hand. "Get your tickets out," he calls with a smile,
"nobody rides for free." The Bradley girls and I climb aboard the
Erie Lackawanna, a beautiful old train that smells of metal, cedar
wood, and cigar smoke. The leather seats are worn and soft and
bolted to the train with decorative metal. We pile into our very
own car. There is another car for the boys, and the rest are for
business people. But sometimes people either don't know about
the segregation or maybe they don't care, and you might find a
few businessmen in the wrong car or a few schoolgirls in the
boy's car. But it's best to stay with your own. The businessmen

like quiet. The girls like to sing. The boys like to roughhouse.

We settle in as the train lurches back and then forward and then back a final time, and then we are off. Outside the window, a new song plays from the boombox, *"See that girl, watch that scene diggin' the Dancing Queen."* The train moves forward as the music fades back under the rumble of the engine. Some of the girls have grabbed hold of the tune and won't let it go. Their voices rise above the rumble and they begin swaying in their seats. The misplaced businessmen look annoyed as the prep school boys look intrigued. The song dies off after the chorus and the girls settle into laughter and red faces.

There is a moment when I can almost feel the letting go of everyone on the train. I blame it on the rocking. We are held in this warm vibration of the engine. It hums so loud that you need to raise your voice if you want to be heard. Instead of making the effort, we all just tuck back in our seats and let the train have its say as it rambles on to our destination.

Out the window, we pass by Newstead, with all the big houses, where Bob lives, and where I once hit an all-time high score on Pong. I go there with my sister Bridget to visit Bob. Beautiful, blue-eyed Bob; Bridget's forbidden Jewish boyfriend.

"If Bob calls, tell him I am not here. I am not home. I am out," she informs us. Later that night in our room, she wrestles me to the floor. At first, it's just a game and we are playing, but suddenly it's not. She is on top, and I'm pinned to the floor.

"Why?" she is asking, "Why don't you have your period?" I look at her face, she is laughing but not in a happy way, more like someone has socked her in the stomach and she doesn't want to show how much it hurts.

"I'm only nine," I tell her. "I'm not supposed to have my period." I am not even sure if it's okay for me to know what a period is. She rolls off me and starts to cry again. This has been the way for a while now, since the last time we walked home from Bob's and I made the mistake of trying to help.

I am not sure what really happened, but I know they didn't have a fight. Or maybe they did and I just wasn't paying attention. I'd been thinking a lot about my trip to New York to see the ballerina and her show. I'd been thinking about what I should wear. Is it like church or a birthday party, would I wear a prom dress like my sisters? I haven't heard a word from Mom. She has swept it under the rug where we keep all things of vital importance.

"What do you think?" I ask Bridget, "Do you think she will let us go? And what do you think I should wear? You think we will sit in the front row? That is what I was thinking because we would be her guests and she is pretty much the star. At least, that is what it seemed like." Bridget is not answering, so I go on with my questions. "Do you think it's on Broadway or just in New York? Either way would be just fine with me. Going to New York with Michael and Steven, I'll bet they know everyone there. Do you think Mom will say yes? What do you think, huh?"

"You're not going, Maureen! Wake up."

At first I am not sure what she is talking about or if she is even talking to me. We share a room together, and even when she has to wake me up, she is never mean or abrupt. But lately things have changed. Her eyes are red and worried.

"Over her dead body! When pigs fly!" She lights a ciga-rette, wipes her eyes and keeps walking. Neither of us says a word as we walk down hill, but it's not silence we walk in. There are too many thoughts running in my head to notice the silence. "He is such a jerk," she mutters under her smoky breath, not really to me, but just sort of out loud, like Mom when she is trying to find her purse. Or the lady in the park who pushes the shopping cart.

"Who?"

She's just stares straight ahead, her arms crossed up over her chest so that her cigarette is close to her mouth and she flicks at it nonstop.

"Bob. Bob is such a jerk, that's who," she says, including me in the plot. My mouth falls open and my forehead furrows.

"A jerk? Not our Bob," I want to say, "not our dreamy, handsome, Colgate smiled, a hundred times cuter than Greg Brady, Bob?"

"He's not a jerk; he loves you," I blurt out, trying to cheer her up and defend him at the same time. "And he is going to get you a ring!" I remind her. She stops and turns to me.

"Why would you say that?"

"Because he is," I tell her.

"What do you mean he is going to give me a ring?"

"Well, that's what he said." I continue walking, but she has me by the arm and turns me about.

"When? When did he tell you that?" Her drippy red nose is so close I can smell the tobacco on her breath.

"When we left, you were right there in his front yard. Remember?" I say, and imitate him in hope of jogging her memory. I lean my weight on one foot and lean back holding up a pretend bat and take a swing at a make believe ball. I don't even attempt his smile. Only he has that smile. His smile makes his eyes twinkle and my knees weak. He flashes it at her, looking over his invisible bat at us and says, "All right baby, I'll give you a ring."

She shakes her head and throws her cigarette to the ground.

"No," she screams at me. "No!" And now the tears are filling her eyes, and her breath is stuck in her throat, and she looks like she might want to slap me or someone. But instead she takes off down the hill.

"What?" I ask, running to keep up with her. But her stride is quick, and now it's me who has caused the tears, and I feel a hot lump in my own throat. "What?" I ask again.

She turns back to me, her face damp and red. "That means he is going to call me! 'I'll give you a ring' means 'I'll give you a phone call.'" She is trying her best to keep her chin smooth, but I can tell she would rather be anywhere but here interpreting modern day English to her nitwit sister.

"Oh," I manage. "I thought it was a ring, ring." Her face turns as her blond hair gets swept up in the wind, and she buries her fists in her jacket pocket.

We walk the rest of the way home in this damp, dreary sadness. It's far. Twice as far as the Shop-Rite, but Bob's house has always been worth the hike, what with the Pong and the candy. She cries off and on the whole way home, and I wish I knew how to make her stop. But the last attempt was such a disaster, so I just stay quiet the rest of the way home.

The back of her jacket moves swiftly down the road, and her right arm that moves up and down to her face to wipe her eyes. I have never seen her cry so much, and it makes my stomach hurt. It will be okay, I want to tell her, even though

I have no idea what "it" is. I am just another burden on her back, misleading her with unfortunate interpretations, making the already long walk seem like eternity.

That night the phone doesn't ring and her tears continue. I make my bed on the floor in the hallway outside our room. She doesn't have to ask me. I just go there, knowing she needs some space. I tuck up against the laundry bin so that no one sees me, 'cause The Giant does not like kids sleeping in the hallway. If he sees me, she will get in more trouble than she is already in. She spends the night blowing her nose and listening to the man on the radio singing about how love is higher than a mountain, love is thicker than water, and pleading about being wrong, and how he is not able to live without her love, and how he wants her back, and he was a fool.

And it all sounds right, but still the phone doesn't ring.

And I fall asleep thinking about what would happen if Bob really did give her a ring, not just a phone call but also one for the finger. I dream about their wedding. Mom is laughing, Bridget is beautiful, and Bob winks at me with the smile that makes my knees weak. We dance all the way to Jewstead, even Michael and Steven and the beautiful ballerina are there. Dancing our way to Jewstead, where there is music and kissing and candy and Pong and above-ground swimming pools with Christmas lights. But in the middle of the night I hear her crying again. It's squeaky and strained and painful. I roll over on the hard hallway floor by the laundry basket of dirty clothes and try not to think about the smell of dirty socks. Love is higher than a mountain, love is thicker than water.

The train moves from station to station, and with each stop more girls file onto our car, and by the time we pull into Convent Station, there is hardly a free seat to be had. Dina lights up a cigarette, and I close my eyes to try to stop all the memories.

30

Riding the Train

AT THE SECOND TO LAST STOP, MAEVE LAWLESS GETS ON, and she lives up to her name in every way. Her wild waves of hair and easy smile cause a stir as she makes her way down the aisle to me. There is something almost tribal about her. It's easy to imagine her on a record cover wearing a poncho, puka beads and a tan. Maeve Lawless is my big sister at school. Riddle set it up. "You need to have a cool big sister." So I lucked out. She walks down the aisle of the train like she in shopping is a fancy store. Slowly and thoughtfully she moves, with full blown entitlement, before she stops at my seat.

"Hey kid," she says, wrapping one hand around the handle on the back of my seat.

"Hey," I reply, hoping she doesn't notice how dumbfounded I am by her presence.

"I got you something for your birthday. It's coming up, right?"

"Yeah," I say, watching her pull a package from her backpack. "It's May 20th." My head feels foggy and embarrassed that she has remembered my birthday, especially since I've forgotten it. My birthday is in a few weeks. I'll be fifteen.

The package is wrapped up real nice with a bow and everything. She leans over and whispers in my ear.

"There's a little something special in there for you, but don't open it at school." Her eyes are smiling, turquoise blue with flecks of amber. "A little something to get you through."

"All right. Thanks," I say, bobbing my head at her and mirroring her knowing look even though I have no idea what she is talking about. I feel like I should say something like, "Right on. Very cool of you." But I don't, I just keep giving her as meaningful a nod as I can muster.

"All right kid, take it easy," she says and moves on as smoothly as she arrived. We stare down at the birthday package sitting in my lap.

"You gonna open it?" Dina asks. I start peeling back the wrapping paper. It's a music box with a little puppet clown behind the glass window. It has a knob in the back that you wind up and when you open the little drawer at the bottom, music starts playing, and the clown begins to dance. I love it. In the drawer is a little package.

"What's that?" Dina asks, reaching in and grabbing it. I try to get it back, but she is swift.

"Holy crap, it's weed."

"Seriously?" I ask, while flashbacks of the Cat screaming, "Open it!" ring out in my head.

"What are you gonna do with it?" Sandy asks me.

"I have no idea."

235

But I wish I didn't have to take it to school after what happened with Riddle.

"I'll take it," Dina volunteers. That seems too easy. The truth is, I wouldn't mind getting rid of it, but I feel bad tossing it out, since it was a gift. "How 'bout I trade you my smokes," she adds, and we have a deal. She passes me a half full pack of cigarettes, holds onto the little bundle of weed, and before the train pulls into our final destination, I have completed my first successful drug deal. Dina and I are each happy with our end of the bargain.

"Your big sister is pretty cool," Sandy says. She looks at me knowing that a small act of thoughtfulness is going a long way today.

"Seriously," Dina adds, "my big sister didn't get me dick on my birthday."

"Convent Station," the conductor calls. We grab our bags and file down the aisle and off the train. From the station, we can see the top of the school. It's still two football fields away, and the final leg of the journey we will make on foot. Dina sings, *"We don't need no education, we don't need no thought control. No dark sarcasm in the classroom. Teacher leave them kids alone."*

She rocks her head with each line of the song. The bell rings, and we scurry for the door. The halls of the school are lined with dark decorative wood, and the floors are shiny cold marble. It's like a beautiful old library. The buildings, the lawns, the people are all like the marble; cold and shiny. I don't like it.

Sandy and I are in the same homeroom, and because of our long trek, we usually arrive late. We settle into our seats as a room of pale faced girls in turtlenecks and blue knee-highs stare back at me. There is not a hint of lace or ruffle, not a scent of gloss or shine, nothing teased or unruffled about this clan. I have entered a factory of Plain Janes, a breeding ground for librarians.

The teacher is talking about an assignment I didn't do. Something about reading an article from the newspaper and writing a report on what it's about. I am pretty sure I can fake my way through this one, till I see the other girls pulling actual newspaper clippings from their notebooks and unfolding them on their desks. "We were supposed to bring them in?" I whisper to Sandy. "I forgot mine at home."

She takes her clipping and unfolds it. She folds the edge of the newspaper over the side of her desk, makes a crease and then a clean tear down the middle and hands half of the newspaper page to me before the teacher takes notice.

I tried to read the article about the first shuttle to reach space. But I don't care about it at all. It makes me think about my mom, and how I have been avoiding her, and how maybe I should have taken off, and maybe I shouldn't have come to school. I try not to think about not being there. I stare down at the paper, and it begins to go blurry, and I can't find my breath, and a warm heat creeps up my back. I rub my eyes and look over at Sandy.

She is busy writing about some guy named Bobby Sands who is a prisoner in Ireland and is not eating till he gets his demands met. She and Dina know all about it because their mother is very politically involved. The picture of Bobby Sands makes him look pretty, like a woman, or like Jesus with his long hair and perfect skin and kind eyes. Bobby Sands has long hair and a beautiful smile, and he looks so happy as he smiles off the newspaper at me. His skin is white as snow, and it makes me think of when we had our picture in the paper. It was Halloween, and I was six. As I stare down at Bobby Sands, I hear the librarian.

"Snow White and The Eight Dwarfs? Well, I'll be."

The library is my favorite place 'cause you don't need money, and you always leave with a treat. We walk to the library dressed like Snow White and the eight dwarfs. Mom doesn't want us to fight over who gets to be Snow White, so she gives the part to Maureen McLaughlin. Maureen makes the fattest Snow White I have ever seen, but she looks like a movie star in Mom's wedding tiara. We want to win the contest. So we dress as Snow White and the eight dwarfs. William also wears a wolf mask. So, really, we're Snow White and the seven and a half dwarfs, and half a wolf man.

"Snow White and The Eight Dwarfs? Well, how do you like those apples? There are eight!" The librarian says, smiling as her finger pokes the air trying to count us.

Little Bo Peep stands in the corner with her mother. She raises her hand to the librarian like we were in school.

"Why do they have pillow cases tied to their heads?" She asks, pointing in our direction while keeping her gaze on the librarian, as though making eye contact with us would give her the cooties.

I glare back at her.

"These are not pillow cases. They're our beards!" Julia yells at her directly, cutting out the middleman.

"And we stuffed the pillows under our shirts to make us look fat!" Annie, who is practicing doing jumping jacks, announces proudly to the librarian hoping to gain extra points for cleverness.

We are there to win. The stakes are high; the winner gets a book and their picture in the newspaper.

After we devour all the candy in the jack-o-lantern and chase each other around the library for a few rounds of tag and hide and go seek, the winner is announced. I stare at Little Bo Peep from the corner of my eye as my heart races. I want this! I want to be famous and in the newspaper. She stands in the corner in her perfect costume, under the protective arm of her mother, one child to one mother. Her mother uses her free hand to dig in her purse and find a hairbrush that she uses to smooth her daughter's perfectly waved hair. I look to my mother, but her hands are full with trying to keep the two boys from taking down the entire library, the re-tying of pillow cases that had come loose, and re-adjusting the pillows that have slipped down from beneath our shirts, all while doing her best to juggle a conversation with the librarian or whoever else will make the effort. She even engages the enemy.

"What a little dolly! Isn't she sweet?" My mother beams as my bearded heart swells with envy. I wonder if my mother wants to be the mother of one as much as I'd like to be an only child.

When her name is called, Little Bo Peep slowly saunters up to the librarian to accept her award. My heart flutters and falls, and our mother shushes our "boos." Little Bo Peep is handed the book and turns with a smile that should have been mine. Then the librarian, obviously wanting to avoid a riot, announces that we can all be in the picture, which sends a pirate's cheer up from our camp. My arms fly to the air and I dance in a circle. We are going to be in the newspaper! We are going to be famous!

"Say cheese," says the man with the big camera, even though I don't need to be coaxed. A smile is plastered across my face. I couldn't take it down if I wanted to. It is so embedded that it makes my cheeks hurt. I can't fight it.

From the picture in the paper, it looks like we're the first place winners. Bo Peep and her staff are pushed to the side. Her costume is store-bought and perfect, but we have her outnumbered. We're famous. It would have been a sweeter second place victory if there had been a third place winner, but no one else showed up. So second place doubled as last place.

Our mother buys extra copies to clip out the picture and pins it to our refrigerator so we can see ourselves every time we go to get a glass of milk.

Back in the classroom, I wonder if Bobby Sands's mother clipped his pictures from the paper and put it on their fridge. The teacher passes by me to make sure we are working on our papers. I pretend to be writing, but actually I am just doodling out words, 'cause the truth is I am not sure what I am supposed to be doing. In fact, I am not sure of anything anymore.

"Are you okay, Maureen?" my teacher asks.

"I am," I answer. Suddenly there is a tingling wave that swells right up from my toes. A feeling of a fast approaching tidal wave, and then the bell rings. It rings in every cell of my body. It feels like it is ringing on the inside. I lay down my pen, take a breath, and gather my things. Without thinking, I follow the school of fish out into the hall and onto our next class. Then our next class, and the bell rings, and our next class, and the bell rings, and we pass again, until the final bell comes, and we are free to leave for home.

31

Heading Back Home

SANDY AND DINA ARE ON THE FIELD HOCKEY TEAM, so I take the train home alone. There are others girls who travel with me. But I don't trust them the way I trust the twins. A couple of girls ride by on their bikes. I watch them turn the corner and think about living close enough to school to be able to ride a bike instead of taking the train that can sometimes take an hour.

There is a fancy car parade the pulls out of the parking with radios blaring and horns honking. Riddle's friends pile into a rusted beater and pass by. If Riddle were with them, she would make them stop and give me a ride. Even if there were no room, she would squeeze me in. A few more girls pass by on bikes. As I watch them go, one turns her head back toward me and calls out. I imagine they are my sisters, Riddle and

Annie, and their hair goes flying in the wind, and I am eight, and more than anything, I want a ride.

"Use the black bike, Maureen. The black bike, use that one." Riddle's voice drifts through the air, and suddenly Riddle and Annie are circling me on their bikes, screaming like banshees.

I run to the sidewalk and beg them for a ride on the handlebars or to let me sit on the tip of the banana seat. They just keep going, without even stopping. They crane their heads to scream, "No, Maureen! You're too big! You need to learn to ride by yourself." I don't let up. Each time they pass, I beg even harder.

"Use the black bike," Riddle screams at me again, while standing up on her pedals and swerving the handlebars to both avoid me and show off her latest tricks.

"But I don't know how to ride a bike," I scream back. They ignore my pleading and continue chasing and circling each other like crazy squirrels, and I want in.

The old black bike is in the garage. It's a clunker with a banana seat and half of a broken ringer. The spokes and chain are rusty, and it creaks and cracks when I pull it to its wheels. I know that it's time I learn to ride a two-wheeler, but it's hard. I have the pushing off part down, but I can't get both feet on the pedals at the same time without dropping to one side. I try to get a running start, but my feet don't reach the ground. The bike wobbles and shakes; I fight to keep it up. It's heavy, and I am awkward, and I go crashing into the hedges to break my fall. My legs are lined with pink scrapes as I pull myself from the bushes. My sisters slow down. They pull up and lean in on me with squinted concern.

"I need help," I tell them. "You guys gotta help me." Now with the tears and the scrapes, it's hard for them to say no.

Riddle slowly climbs off her bike. "Come on, Annie," she says, "you hold her on that side, and I'll get her from this side, then I'll run with her. Maureen, you pedal, and don't stop." Annie does her best to keep me propped up as I tilt back and forth like John Boy Byrnes after he has spent too much time drinking wine with the Giant. On the word "go," Riddle takes off with me, and I do my best to stay up and not lean too hard on her. "Pedal! Pedal!" she screams, her heavy breath on my cheek, her shaky arms holding me steady. I push down hard on the pedals that creak and whine. I stand up straight, putting all my weight into it. Even with all my effort, it's hard to get the pedals to move, we jingle and jangle down the block like a glass jar of rusted nails. Riddle is running the whole time. "Good job, Maureen. Keep pedaling," she yells, and I wish my legs would move faster. We pass the Kellys', then Pennys', but by the time we get to the Segals' house, Riddle falls to the grass.

"Okay, you're on your own. You just gotta keep your feet on the pedals and keep moving. That's it." I make it to the Segals' and stop before the dip in their driveway.

Riddle runs to meet me there. "I got a good idea," she tells me, as we stand at the top the Segal's steep driveway that leads to the street below. Annie runs to join us, and watches from the safety of the sidewalk.

"You're not suppose to ride in the street," she reminds us. We don't even look at her, 'cause we already know the rules.

"When you have to stop, use your feet, 'cause the brakes don't really work so good, okay?" I nod at Riddle and take a deep breath. "On the count of three, I am going to push you off down the drive and.in to the street. Are you ready?" We check one last time that no cars are coming, and then she begins to count. I stare down at the silver banana seat between my legs and the tips of my toes trying to hold my balance on the bike. I try saying a prayer, but her counting is quick. Before I know it, "three" is called and she pushes me off. My feet jump to find the pedals as the bike goes flying down the hill straight for an oncoming car. It comes out of nowhere; charging like a bull, horn screaming. The air rushes at me so strong that it's hard to keep my eyes open, like I am holding my face too close to a fan. My hair stands up, and my skin wiggles on the bone. My feet can't find the pedals, and they stick out on either side. In the blur of watching my life end, I hear Riddle's scream, her voice high, her words getting lost and mangled beneath the blare of the horn.

The driver flashes before me, his white knuckles clutch the steering wheel, eyes wide, shocked, and angry. I squeeze my eyes shut, grip the handlebar and my sister's voice comes again, but this time I hear the words, "Turn the wheel. Turn the wheel!" So without thinking or looking or knowing, I push the handlebars toward the curb. The bike hops and pops over the cracks and potholes, my teeth bang together, and I know I am going to die. I see his mouth open, yelling as he pulls on his steering wheel. The car swerves, tires screech. Instead of a crash, I hear a whoosh, and a blast of air moves me closer to the curb. I pull my feet in, find the pedals, and begin pumping. My knees shake, but I keep peddling without thinking about staying up, without even thinking, "I am riding a bike." At our driveway, I turn the wheel again and bump over our cracked cement. At the sidewalk, I toss the bike to the ground and collapse on the grass and listen to my heartbeat against the dirt. I feel its loud thump in my chest and in my throat and ears. Boom, boom, boom like the big drum at the parade. Boom, boom, boom, that's my heart, I tell myself. I am still alive, and then I feel my breath and the sting of water in my eyes.

My sisters come running and fall beside me on the grass. I keep my face to the grass and try not to think about being dead.

"You did it, Maureen! You learned how to ride a bike."

I press my face into the dirt and grass, so they don't see my tears. I don't want them to call me a baby.

Annie pokes me in the side to try to make me laugh, but I am not so ticklish.

"You either have an army of angels or you're part cat," she says, poking me again.

"A cat?" I ask, looking up at her.

"Yeah, cats have nine lives," she says and stops poking when she sees my tears. I lay my head back down and think about how Tom, the cat from Tom and Jerry, always gets back up after being hit with a frying pan or smashed by a big rock.

I don't think I am part cat, or that an army of angels has saved me. I know that it's my sisters. It's always my sisters. Everytime without fail, flying in like superheroes. They catch me, warn me, cover for me, and protect me. They are the ones to count on, the sure thing, who steer me in the right direction, and walk through blizzards to buy me a Coke. If it wasn't for my sisters, I would be a dead girl for sure.

"Well, if she is part cat, she sure is going through those lives pretty fast," Riddle adds as she pulls on a blade of grass. "You should probably stick to the sidewalk till you get a little better." Uncle Harry's car pulls to the curb, and the girls take off to get in one more ride before Mom rings the dinner bell. I stand to watch them mount the bikes like horses, smooth and fierce they ride the wind. The Giant slams the car door and passes by me. I move in his shadow as we make our way to the house. At the stoop, he turns to me. I think about telling him about the car and the horn and how I saw my death. But my dad is so big and it's hard to find my words, and before I gather all the thoughts, he brushes his chin and says, "Don't leave that bike out on the curb." I turn back as he makes his way into the house.

32

Back on the Train

ON THE TRAIN HOME, THERE IS A LITTLE COMMOTION. Susan Divine is crying and telling us that she is going to slit her wrists with a knife that she carries in her backpack.

"Go for it," I tell her. I've seen this act before and am not convinced. The other girls gasp and stare at me in shock like I am a horrible monster. I am not sure why I don't feel anything, I am not sure why I am so angry.

"Maureen! How could you say that? You are so cold!"

"She doesn't even have a knife," I say, calling her bluff. Susan takes a pocketknife out of her bag and fumbles around to open it. It's about the size of my thumb and so old and dull, I doubt it could cut butter. I smile and sit down across from her. I take a drag from my cigarette and exhale smoke rings at the closed window. "Why do you want to kill yourself, Susan?" I ask, in as kind a way as I can muster. I am not trying to be compassionate.

I am morbidly curious. I pull another long drag and keep my eyes on her. I hope to make her squirm a bit.

"It's just my parents and school. It's just so hard." Her round face is red and wet and honest. A part of me wants to slap her and toss her off the train, but another part of me still cares about what people will think. I stub out my butt and reach to light another. I offer her one even though I know she doesn't smoke. She shakes her head at me, appalled at the assumption. I sit back and stare at her a while. I can see she is uncomfortable with me, and I am glad because I am uncomfortable with her, with all of them. Their crisp white shirts, ironed by mothers who can still stand. The frowns that crease their brows over the stress of homework. There is an empty place in me that goes even more hollow around them. At the bottom of this empty place is a sadness so deep I am afraid I will fall right through, and it will swallow me whole.

"Don't kill yourself over homework, Susan," I tell her." "That would just be so lame." I lift myself from the seat. I wish I could hit her with the hot end of my cigarette butt. It seems fair pay back for the way her eyes have branded me.

I move to a seat by myself, lean against the dirty window, and watch the towns pass by. Each stop takes me closer to home and farther from escape. Susan sits surrounded by sympathy and concern. Part of me wishes I hadn't called her bluff. Watching rich girls attempt to draw blood was demystified for me last year. I remember when it still intrigued me, when it called me to the attic stairs in quest of answers.

Looking up the attic stairs, you can only see to the landing. Beyond the landing, the stairs turn, and there is a second set of stairs and then a landing, and you have reached the attic, which is much like reaching Oz. The attic is all VIP. I creep up the stairs slowly on tiptoes. I don't want them to know I am coming. My arms extend out to either side of the stairwell and move along the walls as I make my way up. I turn the corner and take a breath. Music leaks out from beneath the door along with the faint smell of burning tobacco.

I push on the door and it opens. They are all there on the other side. Annie, Riddle, and Julia are lounging around and smoking cigarettes to Billy Joel's "The Stranger," *"And it seems such a waste of time, if that's what it's all about, Mama, if that's movin up then I'm movin out. Mm I' movin out, mm oo oo uh huh mm hm"*

Annie sits on the makeup bench with her back to the dressing table. She has one knee bent up to her chest, and the other dangles to the floor. Her bare toes tap away to the tune as she pushes smoke rings by her mouth. On the dressing table is a huge array of lipsticks and powders and perfumes. Most of it was given to us from our Uncle George who works for Revlon. Against one side of the room are a stereo and a turntable and a ton of albums. On the walls are posters of Van Halen for Riddle, Billy Joel for Julia, and the Eagles for Annie.

There is a fan in the window that blows air out so that the smoke from their cigarettes does not finds its way down the stairs. This room is set up like a living room with a small couch and a few chairs. The cat rests in a ball on the couch. I can tell it's one of her favorite hangouts by the halo of fur that surrounds her on the pillow. She lifts her head to me, as I stand in the doorway, waiting to be invited in.

I look around the room for Nina, Julia's friend who is spending the night.

From the corner of my eye, I see her placing her bags beside my sisters' beds and adjusting her gloves, black evening gloves that go all the way up her arms and make her look like she is going to the prom or some other fancy place. But she isn't, she is just hanging out in our attic. She moves into the room and goes straight for the turntable. She causes such a stir when she walks that no one objects to my crashing the party. I find a spot beside Annie on the bench and wait.

Billie Joel is tossed to the floor, and now the Blondie record is playing, and Nina begins to dance in a way that makes me feel weird about watching. *"Call me any day or time, you can call me, call me anytime."* Blondie sings out as Nina raises her long arms in the air and slowly peels off one glove. We sit still and watch as the smoke from my sisters' cigarettes mingles with her moves. When the song is over, she sits on the arm of Julia's chair like a graceful bird perched for a while but always ready to take flight. Her long legs twisted around each other as she grabs her purse.

"How did you learn how to dance like that? Are you a stripper or something?" I ask.

"Maureen!" Annie and Riddle snap at me at the same time.

But Nina doesn't seem bothered. "Stripper?" she repeats, as she takes the lighter from her purse and flicks at it like she's clicking a pen.

"Stripping is vulgar. I just tease," she informs us as she shakes out her long black glove, lays it across her lap, tilts her head, gathers her straight locks of white gold to one side of her head, and lights a long menthol cigarette that she holds between two gloved fingers. It all so smooth and calculated, and I am not quite sure if the dance is actually over or not.

"What's vulgar mean?" I ask. She takes a drag with a slight nod to my sisters and then blows the smoke into my face.

"That's vulgar," she whispers with a slight smirk, proud of her perfectly executed teaching opportunity. My sisters grin out of obligation and fear that they may get the smoke shower next. Nina leans back casually as I blink away the sting and wave away the stink. My questions are getting to her, but I can't help it. I have a desperate need to know, and I am not above asking. That's just what I do. I am the reporter, "Brenda Starr." I am the one who will ask the questions. My sisters know it, too. That is why I am here, why I am even allowed to stay and not get kicked out of their rooms and sent downstairs. They know I will ask what they are too polite to ask, and I don't let them down. I want the whole story, the one about the cutting, and I won't leave till I get it. It the same reason they take me to the thrift shop. They know I will dig for the gold, I will unearth the place. I have no problem rifling through a bin, or crawling the dusty floor for the other shoe, and at the counter I feel no shame in haggling. I have watched the ladies who ride the bus do it, so why not? My sisters blush and turn away, but I enjoy game. So in the safety of our converted attic, I begin to ask Nina about the marks on her ungloved arm. She answers, not so much bragging at first, but just an off-handed explanation.

"It brings me comfort to see the blood. It's how I know I am alive."

"But doesn't it hurt?" I ask. She pulls back a bit.

"Pain is truth. Do you get it? Pain is truth. If you weren't such a half-wit you would be able to understand." Half-wit? She is so refined even in her insults. I can't help but smile. Calling me a half-wit is giving me half more credit than I am used to getting. She sighs heavily and continues. "It's a rush of truth, and it's beautiful, because it's something you know, 'cause you feel it when you know it. When you experience real truth, you don't have to ask so many asinine questions." She says "real truth" and I want to know what the hell that means. "Real truth." Like is there "fake truth," and how would you know the difference? She rolls her eyes to the ceiling and says something about mailing her blood to a guy named Bob Dylan.

"Is he your boyfriend?" I ask, instead of asking about the different types of truth. She snorts at me and rolls her eyes again and looks over my head at my sister Julia. "Is your sister a moron?" she asks. Julia smiles at her boldness and bobs her head in agreement.

"Basically a moron," she adds. I don't like being hung out like this, but I'm a scrapper. I poke my face back at Nina.

"You're the one who needs to see your own blood to know you're alive! That's dumber than being a moron." My sisters go still and Nina blows more smoke at me. But this time she looks right at me, so I keep swinging. "Beside you're just a fat liar anyhow. I'll bet you don't actually cut yourself. I'll bet you're such a fat dumb ass that you got your own arm stuck in a blender." I can tell the word "fat" hits her in the bullseye. My sisters laugh nervously, even Julia, and I'm not sure who's with me and who's against me. "Show us, then. Prove it," I dare her.

Nina eyes me like a zit on prom night. Julia grows a grin as Annie shakes her head at Nina the way you would shake your head at the pretty blonde girl who goes to check out the basement in the scary movie. She shakes her head so slight and slow and scared. We're in uncharted territory. I can feel it, in my sisters' silence, and in the way Nina holds my gaze. So I smile, too. Not a big one, just a little, faint smile, small and still. "Just show us." I shrug softly, and then I add, "Please," 'cause after all, she is a guest.

"Fine, I'll show you, but just once, that's it, one little one, and never again. It's sacred. It's a ritual."

She presses her cigarette into the large shell that they use for an ashtray and reaches for her purse. It's so small that I can't imagine it holds much of anything. But she seems to have all the essentials. She removes each item slowly like a ceremony. Cigarettes, lighter, wallet, keys, a few slips of notepaper and a neatly folded bundle of clothes. She sits cross-legged and begins to replace all the items except the cloth and a single slip of paper. She takes a deep breath and unfolds the beautiful cloth. It's a handkerchief of dark blue silk, like something a fancy man might wear in his coat pocket. She lays it out on her lap, and there, in the middle, is a sparkling rectangle of sharp metal, a razor blade.

She runs her fingers up and down her long arms slowly, takes her time deciding where to make the mark... and again. It's like a never-ending dance, the way she roots around her body.

"This is the most important part," she explains. "You want it to look clean and simple." Her words are light and filled with air and absence, like she is in a dream state, so beyond fear of pain, she is asleep to it. Finally, after much frustrating foreplay, she lays the razor to her skin and slices a clean, straight line on her arm. The blood shows up right away. A bright red liquid line appears on her skin. I wait for something else to happen, for some of the "real" truth and beauty to show up. There is nothing but a girl with a cut and a thin line of blood. Blondie goes on singing, *"Color me your color, darling, I know who you are. Come up off your color chart, I know where you're coming from..."*

I look up at Nina to ask her about it, but she shakes her head at me.

"Look, look at the blood." So I do. I watch it puddle and begin to form a drip on the back of her arm. I am not sure why I expected something different.

It doesn't look like it hurt at all. Her face is flush as she soaks up the blood with a clean piece of white paper that she pulls from her purse. She opens an envelope, slips the paper inside and then licks the glue like it's candy. I feel tricked and tormented, and I leave the attic with more questions than I came with and no desire to ask them. Back down the stairs I go, and even Crazy, the cat, has the sense to follow me...

The train pulls into my station, and it's time for me to get off. "South Orange!" the conductor calls. I grab my bags and head for the door. The consoling sorority of sisters that circled Sue has all disbanded. Most of the girls get off earlier in towns closer to school. I pass their vacant seats; I still feel my hatred for them.

33

Walking through the Village

I TAKE THE LONG WAY HOME, WALKING THROUGH THE village of South Orange, passing the Shop-Rite, with its wonderful display of Brach candy, and Town Hall Deli, where you can get a buttered end for five cents. I pass the dancing school where I eventually got to take classes, thanks to hoarding away my babysitting money, before getting kicked out for talking too much. I pass by Gruning's Ice Cream Parlor, where I tried to gulp my guilt down on scoops of rocky road ice cream. I pass shops with nice dresses where I have never shopped.

Glass store windows display a beautiful arrangement of outfits. Window-shopping is like flipping through one of the magazines in the dentist office. I take my time as I pass.

At the edge of town, where the shops meet with houses, I pass the Jewish Council Thrift Shop, my saving grace and guilty pleasure. It's like clothes porn, a warehouse of other people's prom dresses and tossed off designer jeans. It's social suicide to shop here.

"You don't shop at that thrift shop, do you, Maureen?" Beth Duncan, the most popular girl in eighth grade, asks with a sour look on her face that tells me what my answer should be.

"No," I lie and mimic her look.

"I would never wear someone else's clothes. That's just gross," she continues, and I nod my head even though, with five older sisters, I have been wearing "someone else's clothes" my whole life. And I don't mind it at all.

I take in the block to make sure no one of importance is around, then I slip into the shop, and right away I feel at peace. Being in the thrift shop is worth all the damage it might do to my reputation. There are rows and rows of clothes, ball gowns, cocktail dresses, men's suits, acid washed jeans, cowboy hats, Halloween costumes, books, boots, and all sorts of beautiful and unusual items. I drink in all the diversity of the materials and shapes and colors. I take a deep breath 'cause I could easily get lost in here for hours. It is a welcome distraction from going home.

Down the rows I go, examining the line-up. The colors and patterns and textures—it's like being in a rich lady's closet. The wealthy women of Newstead donate most of the items. On one of the dresses, I can still smell perfume. It smells musty and beautiful. This dress has gone somewhere. It has a story woven through the paisley print of deep greens and blues. Did someone wear this to a party? A wedding? Did she grow out of it or out of love with it, or did she die? The paisley print and pretty scent begin to make me feel nauseous, but I can't seem to let it go. On my way to the dressing room, I find a brown leather jacket with fringe that looks just my size, so I grab that, too.

The dressing room is not fancy, just a simple booth made from plywood, with a bench and a few mismatched hooks on the door and walls. A long mirror hangs a little lopsided on one wall with a thin crack in the corner. I lock the door using the hook and eye and turn back to the safety of this little booth. Instead of hanging the items, I hold them to my chest and sit on the bench. A deep breath takes me as I bend my head. The next thing I know, I am crying. It just comes, soft and slow and warm and thick, like syrup, and I let it pour out of me. It feels almost as impersonal as going to the bathroom. These tears are just something that my body needs to release, so I don't try fighting them. They come rolling down my cheeks and hanging off my nose. I am not sure why, but they bring release and peace, and I think my aunts may have been right about not going to school. Maybe I should have stayed home and said goodbye to my mother another hundred times. Trying to hold onto ordinary is exhausting, and I am worn out by all the pretending that everything is normal when it's not.

I pull my legs up onto the bench and make myself into a small ball. Wrapping my arms around my shins, I begin to rock, back and forth, hugging my knees and some rich lady's dress. My face presses against the fabric until everything has run out of me, and I close my eyes and lean against the wall.

The beautiful dress drapes over my knees. The paisley swirls begin to dance like the waves on the ocean. And I see it all, the sucking in, the drawing up, the crashing down, the pattern. It's all the same, all the same thing, all the giving and taking is all the same. It's all just the ocean. "Tenfold, Maureen, it will be returned to you." I don't want to think about my mother not being there when I get home, not today, not ever. I see my reflection in the mirror, and suddenly I am back in eighth grade.

I have been invited to an end of the school year party. It's a girl/boy party, but it's not like those kid parties. It's where you could possibly kiss or get kissed, and it's at night. Mary Ann Kelly is having it. She is new at our school and has not yet figured out that, in a regular situation, I might not make the short list, so I am invited to my first boy/girl party. I am going, once I figure out what I am going to wear. Aside from the school uniform, I have two pairs of pants. One pair are floods, according to Maureen McMartin who goes to public school and knows these things. The other is too big. I got them at the thrift shop, and I love them because they look like corduroy or velvet. I keep them up by tying a shoelace through the belt loops.

"Why is she wearing those pants?" my sister's friend asks, loud enough so that I can hear the question and soft enough to let me know she's not really interested in an answer. I hadn't realized that the shoelace was a bad idea. I thought I was being clever and resourceful.

I stare into the mirror. I am too small to fit into anything nice that my sisters may have, and too big to fit into the Saint Vincent De Paul's box. I am off to my first boy/girl party. There will be no trips to the Children's Cottage or gifts from Aunt Julia to save me. I lie on my bed and decide that I won't go to the party. Because I would rather not go than go and be made fun of.

"Maureeen!" My mother's voice chills the air. I try to ignore her, but she continues, "Maureeen!" I follow the sound of her voice downstairs to the front door. It's spring, the smell of fresh cut grass, sun, and children's laughter floods into our front hall. My mother is standing at the front door adjusting her turban. Her back is to me, but as she throws a glance to the mirror, she catches me behind her. "Look Maureen, tenfold!" She leans against the door so that I can peek past her. On the other side of the door is Cathleen Casey smiling back at me like a gorgeous centerpiece on this spring buffet. She's surrounded by sunlight and the chirping of birds. She is smiling one of those smiles that can't be contained. It takes over her whole face. She is the younger sister of five brothers, the only girl in her family, and a little runt of a thing, like me. I've seen the older girls toss her around the cheerleading events. She is their mascot. She can do splits and flips, and with her pretty little face and permanent smile, it's like she was born to be tossed in the air in a short skirt.

"I told you it would be returned tenfold." She's pointing to something at the bottom of our front stairs. I lean in closer to gather the view. There, at the bottom of the stair, stands the Cadillac of baby strollers. It's no doubt nicer than the one I was pushed in as a child. "Didn't I tell you?" my mother continues, as if only a few days have gone by since I stood in this very spot and waved goodbye to my childhood.

The carriage sparkles in the sun and sends off a glare. There's no debate, this stroller is ten times nicer than my stroller, but what difference does it make now? What difference does it make if it were twenty times nicer? I had no use for a baby stroller. I was on my way to my first girl-boy party! What was I going to do with a baby stroller?

"Look inside," my mother is saying and smiling now, just like Cathleen. The insanity is contagious, I think, but I go down the stairs to look in the baby stroller, half expecting to find a live baby from the way my mother is glowing. Just what our house does not need, another baby. I go and I look. In the stroller is a neatly folded stack of clothes. They lie there crisp and clean and cared for. I look at Cathleen, and she smiles.

"I can't fit into them anymore. I hope you like them."

"They're mine?" I ask. She nods as I lift up the top pair of pants. They are white painter's pants with a loop for a hammer. Beneath them is a dark blue pair of Levi's. I continue to lift what seems like an unending supply of clothes, a whole wardrobe of clothes, exactly my size. Because she is the only girl in her family, they look like they have never been worn. There are T-shirts, and peasant skirts, and jean jackets—all folded so nicely and smelling so good. It's the disguise of a cool kid, and it's all mine. I look up at my mother, smiling down from the stoop at me.

"Didn't I tell you?" she is saying. From the front walk she looks a bit magical, leaning her weight against the door and beaming out at us. My sisters help me carry the stroller into the house. Bridget has a crush on Cathleen's older brother, and she takes the stroller for a loop around the living room pretending she is married to him and having his baby. I begin my own show, a fashion show, one outfit after the other, and one more beautiful than the next.

"You're so lucky," they say to me. These clothes are all too small for them. Annie and Riddle have a try at it, but they look like the Incredible Hulk bursting at the seams. It is me that these clothes were meant for.

I slip into each item and pose in front of the mirror. I see Mom smiling at me in the mirror. I am not sure how she did it, or if it was really Jesus who returned the carriage to me tenfold, but either way, I have fallen into her faith. It's deep and mysterious and confusing.

After dinner, I head off to the party in my new outfit. At Mary Ann's house, I follow music to the basement and sit between Annie and Frannie Tevlin on the wrong side of a pool table and watch kids take turns spending three minutes in heaven with each other. Turns out, heaven is a closet, and they go two at a time.

Even though we are not in on the action, the Tevlin twins have a way of being the center of it all. They bark out instructions on what music should be played and call out insulting but funny names to all the other guests, like two bantering hosts at a comedy show. Frannie takes it upon herself to be "the gate-keeper" of heaven. She makes sure no one spends too much time there. But if they do, she starts to do the radio voice from "Paradise By The Dashboard Light."

"Okay, here we go, we got a real pressure cooker going here, two down, nobody on, no score, bottom of the ninth, there's the windup, and there it is, a line shot up the middle, look at him go. This boy can really fly! He's rounding first and really turning it on now, he's not letting up at all, he's gonna try for second; the ball is bobbled out in center, and here comes the throw, and what a throw!"

Then Annie, not wanting to be upstaged, comes in with... *"Stop right there! I gotta know right now, before we go any further! Do you love me? Will you love me forever? Do you need me? Will you never leave me? Will you make me so happy for the rest of my life? Will you take me away and will you make me your wife!?"*

Frannie hops up and pulls open the door to the cheers of the crowd. The couple emerges red faced with buttons unbuttoned and zippers unzipped.

I laugh but say nothing. I pull my knees to me chest. I don't want to draw attention to myself. I don't want anyone to ruffle my new clothes. The basement air is thick with pulsating music and pre-teen sweat. But all I can smell is the fresh scent of foreign detergent permeating from my new jeans that fit like a glove and have no need for a shoestring belt. I am so happy not to be the butt of the Tevlin twin's jokes. Frannie returns to the table and eyes me, "Maureen, that outfit is perfect," she confirms and then moves on to her next victim. I sit safely between the twins, and rest my nose on my knees so no one can see my smile.

"Are you okay in there, honey?"

My head jerks up, both legs shoot to the floor and I rub my head.

"Yep, yeah, be right out," I manage. I gather my items and unlock the door. It's kind of like coming out of the confessional, only here no one is watching the clock.

Before making my way out the door I flip through the used record section. Barbra Streisand looks back at me from the cover. She is wearing a white top hat and she smiles, bats her eyes, and begins to sing, "Secondhand Rose."

"They call me Secondhand Rose. I never get a single thing that's new." I jam her back into the pile and head out the door.

34

Walking Back up Sorrow's Hill

I WALK SLOWLY PAST THE CHAIN LINK FENCE, THE WALL that Julia rammed her face into, and the school. I pass the doors to the church basement as I watch the eighth grade file in for graduation practice. They are smiling and nervous and swept up in themselves. I try to remember my own excitement about graduation.

"Somebody's gonna hurt someone before the night is through. Somebody's gonna come undone. There's nothin' we can do"...

Aunt Caroline and Mom take me to the mall to buy a dress for my eighth grade graduation. Mom sits outside the shop on one of those public benches because she can't really stand for too long. We hold dresses up in the storefront glass for her approval. She nods at almost every one of them. Her pain has made her very agreeable. She should not be here. She should be in bed. We know it. We all know it, but no one questions her when she pulls herself from the bed. I wish she had stayed home now. Not just because of her pain, but also because it's hard to enjoy this rare shopping experience. I do my best to ignore my mother's pain, to pretend it's not happening.

The mall is bright and everything is pretty and new. I find the most beautiful dress and hold it up for her. Our eyes meet; she nods and points to her wrist. Time to go. Aunt Caroline and I move to the register. This time, the dress will come home with us the first time.

My school shoes and sneakers look ridiculous with the dress, so Marie Campanelli lends me a pair of Candies! She wears blue eyeliner and rhinestone earrings. She hands over the strappy sandals that make me look three inches taller. "I want them back," she reminds me as my mouth begins to water. Riddle applies my makeup.

I think, when she grows up, Riddle will be famous, like a movie star, because she is an expert with fashion and makeup, plus she treats everyone like a friend. When she gets money for babysitting the neighbors, she spends some of it on me, taking me to lunch on the avenue at The Sandwich Factory. We wolf down toasted bagels with cream cheese and butter and laugh at each other with braces full of bread and cheese. Sometimes she smuggles home boxes of Tastykake Krimpets and stores them outside her bedroom window.

"Come here, I have to show you something," she whispers to me, leading me quietly into her room. She pulls open the window and reveals her secret stash.

"Don't tell anyone, okay?" she instructs as she hands me a treat wrapped in wax paper. The two of us sit and eat in silence.

"What do you think makes it taste so good, the sponge cake or the butterscotch icing?" she asks, as we lick the crumbs from the wrappers. I do my best to try to decipher one ingredient from the next and come up with an exact evaluation of the snack, but for me, the real sweetness comes from her. She calls me Mighty Moe, and she is radical Riddle, and together we will rule the world.

When she is done with my makeup, she shows me the mirror. I am in love with the dark purple eye shadow and the brown mascara and the Bonny Bell Pink Shimmer Lip Gloss and again my sister, Riddle. She has grown from a pumpkin hobo to a hot tomato. Today she is a real live fairy godmother who has waved a few magic wands to get me ready for the big day.

I slowly walk down the stairs so that I don't break my neck. At the bottom of the stairs, Mom turns to see me, and her face goes blank.

"What the hell are you wearing?" Though she is small and weak, she has caught me off guard. I am overpowered. She has me by the hair and is screaming words like "hussy" and "floozy." It is shock more than physical pain that shakes me at the root. I had expecting something so different. I find myself being tossed and turned, and I can't even find the words to reason with her.

"What? What did I do?"

"Get those floozy shoes off your feet!"

"What, Mom? Wait! I have to go! I have to graduate," I plead. Riddle and Annie are with me.

"Stop, Mom. She has to go! She'll be late! Just go, Maureen, just go!"

"Don't you dare leave this house looking like that."

"She looks fine, leave her alone." Then they turn their heads and whisper warnings, "Maureen, just go. Just go now." They turn back to her and do their best to keep her at bay. "Maureen, just go." But I have never openly defied my mother. This will not be easy. It is an amputation of the apron strings, and this time, I am the one with the scissors. There's a look in my sisters' eyes that tells me today is the day; if not now, then never. I am to walk away from my mother, even when she tells me to stay. My heart is breaking. I have no idea what to do.

"Just go, Maureen! Go!" So I do. I stumble out the door, down the steps, and continue down the block to my eighth grade graduation. My legs are shaky, and the high heels are not helping.

We graduates meet in the cold church basement. I keep my head down till I get to the bathroom. In the mirror, the beautiful make up is now a rainbow of watercolors that puddle beneath my eyes. I pull a tissue and do my best to fix it. I try to smooth the mangled hair back in place and begin to feel the pain from her blows. My skin is red and blotchy and no matter how I try, I can't seem to stop crying.

A hussy? Why would she call me that? A hussy is like a slut. I have never even kissed a boy. I am trying hard to get on top of my breath to make sure that no one sees me. Much as I try, I can't stop crying. All the kids will know. I want to die. I can't go home, but I don't want to be here. I don't want the kids to see me like this. I have no choice but to make my way out to the church basement meeting room where all the graduates are waiting.

Out in the hall, Annie is standing with my cap and gown. "Here, you almost forgot these." I take the cap and gown that she holds out to me and begin to put them on.

"Are you okay?" I don't answer 'cause I don't want to cry. I just stand there fumbling with the robe. "She's just upset is all... it's not you," Annie continues.

"Why did she call me...?"

Annie cuts me off. "She's scared."

"Of what?" I ask. She pauses and waits for some kids to pass us by.

"She just doesn't want you to grow up too quick."

"Well, how am I not supposed to grow up?" She doesn't answer me. More kids come bustling down the hall as she turns to go. I stand there trying to zipper up the strange robe as I watch her slowly make her way down the dim lit hallway and push open the heavy church door. There is a moment where the blinding sunlight steals her from my view. I can see her outlined in the light; she is no longer that wild haired hyperactive kid. I guess I could be scared or sad to see her fade into a slow walking girl. But that sure won't stop it from happening. She slips into the light, and the door closes behind her, and she is gone.

I place the cap on my head, and the tassels hit me in the eye and get stuck to my wet cheek. I tuck my head in, so as not to get abused by it.

I find a seat, and try not to attract attention. The last few kids shuffle in slowly, and the chairs begin to fill up around me, but I don't look up. I watch the tears drop off my chin and onto my new dress. I just try to breathe. Then I hear it, a sniffle, and a sigh, and another sniff. Someone else is crying. I look up out of the corner of my eye. Frannie and Annie Tevlin wipe tears from their eyes, next to them Kate is all red-faced, and then Claire blows her nose. Slowly I look around. All the girls are crying. Donny Robertson sits down in front of me and whispers to Brian Holl, "All the girls are a mess cause we're graduating. Karen Dunn is outside hugging everyone, and Marie Campanelli is handing out free kisses. Man, we have to get in on that action." They both head back out the door.

Because we're graduating? That's what all the tears are for? I look around at all the crying girls and suddenly feel relieved that no one will know. No one will have to know that my mother is dying, and that she thinks I am a hussy.

35

Meeting up with William

JUST AS I GET TO THE GRAY-FACED BLESSED MOTHER,
I hear him call.

"Hey Marine! Marine!" William is running to catch up
to me. I forgot that they let him out early so that he can be
at his post to help cross the other kids. I wish I had made
it home earlier. A part of me wants to keep walking, but he
calls and calls till I stop and turn. He comes like a puppy
hoping for a quick game of catch. It's hard to make eye
contact, so I don't.

"Marine, Marine!" He grabs at my arm, out of breath as he
pulls on his bright orange crossing guard vest.

"What?" I say, continuing to walk up the hill.

"Hey, Marine, I gotta tell you two things. You're gonna love
this," he laughs. "I learned a new curse word."

"Really?"

"Yeah! I learned the coolest new curse word. Anthony taught me it."

"What is it?"

"Vaginal discharge!"

I shake my head and look over at the statue of the gray Blessed Mother.

"William! That's not a curse word."

"It's not?" he asks, looking betrayed.

"What's the other thing?" I ask.

The final dismissal bell rings, and we are suddenly swarmed by a sea of blue-and-white uniformed children who charge up the hill with bags and books swinging. He is supposed to be at his post. But he's got other things on his mind.

"Well, ah, I don't know, I think maybe, I think I heard Aunt Caroline say...I think Mom is gonna die."

I come down fast and hard, "No, she's not!"

"Yeah, I know you said, but I heard Aunt Caroline talking and..."

"Aunt Caroline? Aunt Caroline drinks too much beer, William! Everyone knows that, she's crazy." No one has ever mentioned this, but I say it like it is true, and since twenty lies are as good as one, I just keep going. "She lives by herself with no TV, she's gotta make up stories. You know that, William." I say in a way that makes it hard for him to argue.

Aunt Caroline is a wizard; a master magician. She turns used greeting cards in to shellacked artwork. She turns leftovers into a three-course meal. She turns old jeans into new pillow covers. She makes everything better. I feel guilty making up stories about her.

"Yeah, Marine, but what about Father Pete? He definitely said Mom was dying. Why would he say something like that if it weren't true? Why would a priest lie?"

I take a breath and watch the little kids form a crowd at the corner waiting for assistance. I stall for time and hope an answer comes, 'cause even I have a problem with this one, but not because Father Pete lied. It was more his delivery...

He asks us into his office, the very way you think a priest would ask. I never guess it for the bait that it is.

"How is everything at home?" he asks. My brothers remain silent; I am the one expected to speak. I wait a bit, taking him in, trying to figure how much he already knows and how much I should confess. Do I tell him about the dad drills or the sleeping mother? Do I confess about the trips to Jewstead, the laying on of my hands, the stolen candy? No. Each thought brings a wave of heat. No, best to deny it all. Best to keep it short and sweet.

"Everything's fine, Father," I confess, raising my shoulders a little and shaking my head as if to say, "All is well." But my words seem to slap him, and his anger brings him to his feet as he leans toward us.

"No, no it is not fine. Your mother is dying, and it's time you kids grow up and accept it." His hot words wilt us, shrinks us into little balls. I feel my head bend in to cover myself, my head is so heavy and hard to hold up, so I just let it hang.

Owen is sitting beside William, tucked in like a scrawny little rag doll. I watch his legs, as he begins to kick his feet back and forth nervously. They are still too small to touch the ground. I want to rescue him from this, but I am so ill equipped, I am unmatched for this opponent. How does he expect me to explain to him what left me speechless? I want to run and scream and cry, but something very heavy and nameless is holding me down.

Not in front of the children. Not in front of the children!

Suddenly, I can't breathe, I close my eyes only to find that I have jumped from the fire into the frying pan. In my mind, I see it all over again...

My mother bolts up in her hospital bed and begins to moan. My sisters rush in from all directions, still wearing their school uniforms.

"Mom! Mom, what's the matter, Mom!" She doesn't look at them. Her eyes travel the room, like she is following a ghost, and she continues moaning without opening her mouth. She looks scary, like a crazy person in a horror film, and I can't move. Her body jumps and shakes, and it makes her hospital bed rattle.

"She is choking," Bridget yells, as she tries to pry open my mother's mouth. Riddle and Annie begin to beat on her chest and plead with her. It's happening in slow motion, and the light is playing against Bridget's hair.

Her hair is like gold, golden butter that pours out of her head and drips over her face. It takes on a life of its own. It's shiny and alive, and I try to focus on the lightness, so that I don't have to look at my moaning mother.

A wrinkle creases her brow, and worry dances over her eyes, so I go back to her hair. Don't look away from her golden hair, whose strands are a hundred shades of light, and sunrise, and corn, and sand, and daffodils, and baby chicks. My mother moans again, and I'm grasping at straws, and my sister's beauty will not save us.

"Mom, Mom, what's the matter?" I step closer to the bed, reach out my hand and hold on to her toe.

"Open your mouth, mom! Open your mouth!" they scream,

and I begin to scream too. Not words, just sounds—just mouth open and sounds coming out, a human fire alarm. My sisters freeze for a second and look down the bed at me.

"Stop it, Maureen! Stop it!" they scream.

I bow my head, hold my breath and hope that it will all end soon. But the priest continues his blows:

"You kids need to grow up! Grow up! You hear me? Stop being such a burden." The room feels like a horrible, hot trap, and I can't seem to find the way out. There's his large desk that stands between us and the door, and the shame that weighs on me like a wet blanket, but mostly it's the rage in his eyes that makes my heart stand still. I no longer recognize him as a priest or a person. His face is red and bursting with rage. He pounds the desk. My brothers flinch. My mouth goes dry.

The next thing I know, we are back out on the sidewalk stumbling home on shaky legs in silence. I stop for a second to try to get my bearings. My brothers stop with me. We have to stick together, we're all we have. They look to me to say something. So I do, I say the only thing I can think of. "Don't tell anyone what he said. Don't tell Dad."

"Right, don't tell Dad," they repeat.

We nod in silence, and it feels odd to want to protect the Giant from this situation, but we do, and we will with a fierce solidarity. Because when we say, "Don't tell Dad," we don't think of the mysterious Giant who comes home at night. We think of the man who sits at the end of our table with the jug of wine and the need to burst into song.

"And when the war is over and dear old Ireland is free,
I'll take her to the church and wed, and a rebel's wife she'll be.

273

Well some men fight for silver and some men fight for gold,
But the IRA is fighting for the land that the Saxons stole.
And we're all off to Dublin, in the green,
Where the helmets glisten in the sun,
Where the bayonets flash and the rifles crash,
To the rattle of a Thompson gun."

His singing drifts right through the ceiling and between the floorboards and vibrates through the whole house. He has the proud warbly voice of a crooner...

So, when my brother finally asks the question, "Why would the priest say that?"

I feel my blood boil a little, and I answer with the only truth I have, even though I still don't look him in the eyes. I stare just above his head at the gray-faced Blessed Mother, Our Lady of Sorrows. That is her name. That's also the name of our church and school, Our Lady of Sorrows. I am just beginning to figure out why. I zero in on her and let her have it. She should know.

"Why would a priest say something like that? I'll tell you why, William. Because he's evil and crazy. He's crazy evil, that's why. And he doesn't have a wife, so he's jealous, and he likes to torment little children because he doesn't have any of his own. Mom is fine, William. She's just tired is all. If you had eight kids you'd be pretty tired too. She's just resting that's all."

My mouth is feeling thick with all the lies I've been pushing through it, and I feel so tired that I could almost lay down right there on the sidewalk.

Mrs. Accardi, "the pretzels lady" and crossing guard, is waving William over to his post. But he sticks with me, and hangs on my every word. It's all making sense, and I can see that a piece of the puzzle has slipped into place for him. I watch his riddles unraveling, but he's not leaving. She blows her whistle to get his attention, and the kids begin to call. "William! William, you're supposed to be at your post." He is deaf to it all, and I know I won't shake him till I give him what he came for. So I do. But this time, I look him right in the eye. I want to make it real. "She's not dying, William. She is not dying. She's not."

He nods and as he pulls up his heavy book bag, his face has gotten lighter.

"I know, Marine. I don't think so either."

36

Waiting on the Corner

WE WALK IN SILENCE TO HIS POST. AT THE CORNER, THE cars speed by, and I notice my heart is racing too, not sure why. We wait for Mrs. Accardi to find a break in traffic as William takes up his role, extending his arms to inform the kids not to cross till she gives us the noble nod. A car horn sounds in the distance, and suddenly I am two...

Standing in the shadow of the Giant, my arm stretches up so high to meet with his. It's nice in his shade—a relief from the blaring sun. We are down the shore, on our way to the beach, but first we must cross the street. We're stopped at the corner. I can't see to the other side. It's so far. Loud blurs of color speed by, with each one I am shaken like a rattle. I could be blown away like a loose piece of paper, but the Giant has me by the hand. We stand on the edge of this hot, black river as the world presses in on us. He leans back on his heels, his shadow falls away, and I am exposed to the sun. It's bright and burns my head and stings my eyes. The bubbly black tar climbs up my nose. Engines rumbling, music blaring, horns warning, heart racing. The Giant's body shifts forward as we lean off the curb and wait for a clearing. I look up, staring into the light, trying to catch a glimpse of him. I can see the end of my wrist where my hand gets lost in his huge paw. His grip is uncomfortably tight; my knuckles crush into one another.

"We are almost there," he tells me as we hop from the curb, his voice cutting clear through the roar of the traffic. I am not sure who he is, but he has me by the hand, and I feel safe. I run a mile for each of his steps. I have to stay close, keep up, or get swept up into the speeding blur of commotion.

"I am too little," I think. "I won't make it." But I tighten my grip and hang on. I hear him singing something about being a Rambler and a Gambler and a long way from home. His song drowns out all the traffic and almost makes me forget my fear. Somehow I have to trust this singing giant to usher me safely to the other side.

Mrs. Accardi taps me on the shoulder.

"You gonna cross, honey?" she asks with a soft smile. Her sweetness tells me she knows what is happening at home. I have only ever heard her barking orders. "No running, no pushing! And line up single file, or I'll crack yas all in the head." This sweeter version of Mrs. Accardi gives me the creeps.

I watch my feet make their way across the street. Slowly I go, till I reach the cracked cement sidewalk. Spring is poking her head through. The sidewalks around town are all very familiar to me because Mom doesn't drive, and we kids like to roam. But the sidewalk to and from Our Lady of Sorrows, I know by heart. Been walking it since I first found my footing. Have heeded years of warnings about stepping on a crack and breaking my mother's back. Still, in all their brokenness and danger, I have managed to fall in love with them. Their consistency comforts me, and in that comfort I can get lost in thought, like stepping through the wardrobe. They are my odd ticket to my own private Narnia, where I drift like seaweed with the tides of my imaginations. Getting completely immersed is the goal, sinking into my own little world is the only thing that saves an escape artist like me.

I look up to catch a wild flock of children being set free from the kindergarten. Miss Miller is still standing post, and I imagine falling into her warm battle-ax embrace. From a distance she looks almost the same.

"Maureen, you're a crackerjack reader! A crackerjack reader!" She is staring right at me and using my name and connecting it with something good. *"We're all in our places with bright shiny faces. And this is the way we start our new day!"* I watch Miss Miller lock the door of the Kindergarten. She is older and slower as she makes her way down the stairs. "You're a crackerjack Reader, Maureen, a real crackerjack Reader."

She starts to unlock her car, and I think about waving to her, but I don't. I don't want her to ask me about my mother. I don't want to explain. I don't want to turn into that crying baby boy in the back of the class. I see his face clear as day, pink and blubbery and plain out howling, letting snot drip. My mother whispers, "Be a good girl, he just wants his mother." I get it now and my head gets dizzy.

Back on the sidewalk, I wish I could howl and snot and blubber away. But instead, I just turn the corner to our street and keep walking.

When I get home, they are praying the rosary in the living room. But this time there is no funny rhythm to follow. It's delivered clean and clear with a methodical pace, like they are all rowing this prayer without any thought of where it might go. It lulls me into peace, and I sit on the deacon bench and rest my head against the wall.

In the midst of their prayer, the doorbell rings. It's such an odd sound that at first we all just look at each other. No one ever rings our doorbell. They either knock or just walk right it. The doorbell is for salesmen and politicians. "Get the door," someone says and I follow orders because I am the closest. She is standing there with a box and the searching smile of someone who wants to be remembered.

"Maureen," she says, as she leans her head in, "it's me Anita. Do you remember me? Anita, Anita Brown? I came to stay with you for a while. My mother is outside, so I can't... I wanted to drop this off. I heard about your mom, and I wanted to..." She extends the package to me. She moves her fingers across her upper lip and then drops them beneath her chin as she pulls her head back to take me in. "Look how big you are."

I don't feel any bigger. I feel just the same as when she first came with her old-fashioned dress and black Barbie. I smile and stand back, but she doesn't move. "No, I am not coming in. I don't want to stay." And it's almost like she'd wanted to say those words all along. "I don't want to stay."

And I nod, because I understand. I don't want to stay either, but school is over, and there is nowhere else to go. I wish I could escape with Anita, that we could join hands again and roam the boardwalks.

"Line up in two's. Line up in twos. Line up in twos..."

The Giant only comes down on the weekends because he has to work. On Saturday, he walks us all to the boardwalk. We roll like a ball of song, sound and laughter. "Line up in two's," he instructs, raising us as the army raised him.

I look up, and Anita is beside me, obediently taking my hand. Her skin is soft and warm. She keeps her eyes on her shoes, but I look up at her and see right into them. And when I do, she smiles at me. It's so small and yet like turning a light on in a very dark room. The effect is amazing, like peeking into a secret sacred little church.

As we reach the boardwalk, the place is alive. Bright lights and music and the hum of a hundred people talking. Kissing teenagers in tube tops and sunburn. Tattooed carnies with cigarettes dangling from their lips, shouting promises of, "Step right up, everyone's a winner." The smell of cotton candy, popcorn, seaweed, and tar. Our flip-flops pad against the wooden boards that still hold the heat from the day. The crowd is thick, and everyone moves like one big wave of people.

We line up for a cone of soft ice cream. I want vanilla.

"Vanilla!" Riddle snorts. Nobody eats vanilla when they can have chocolate or rocky road or something exciting. But I stick with vanilla and follow the others to an empty bench where we can watch the show.

My sisters begin to play a game called "Walk this Way." One of my sisters enters the crowd and finds someone with an interesting walk, and then strolls behind them and tries to imitate them. We play a couple rounds, and it has us laughing and pointing with mouths full of creamy ice cream.

The success of this game leads to a new game called "Lost in The Crowd." And again, they just make it up as they go along. One of my sisters will walk far enough away till we can no longer see them, and then they have to try to walk past us in the crowd without getting caught. My sisters are good at this game, it's like they were born to play it. It has the Giant laughing and slapping his knees. We sit on the sidelines watching the parade of summer folks stroll by and jump to our feet whenever we catch sight of a sibling trying to sneak past behind a fat man or baby stroller and we laugh and scream till we are all worn out.

The crowd begins to thin out and it is our time to go as well. We pass by all the booths with wonderful prizes, trophies, T-shirts and trinkets. But the only souvenir that our hands will carry is the faint remains of sticky ice cream.

"Find your partner and get in file," the Giant informs. Anita takes my hand, and we slowly head for home. Leaving the stores and sounds of the boardwalk, it seems our voices are left there as well. The stores turn to houses dressed in drying beach towels and sandy boogie boards. At one house, two men swig beers on their porch.

"They can't all be his," one of them says loud enough for us all to hear.

"Well, the black one is definitely not his," the second one answers, as their laughter echoes out at us. Her soft grip on my hand goes limp, and she raises it to her face to swat an invisible fly. I continue to hold my hand up for her, but she's crosses her arms over her chest to inform me that our dance is officially over. Her eyes look extra dark. She has shut the door, and I can tell that I am not supposed to knock. We have, in some strange way, put her at a disadvantage. We have exposed her vulnerabilities and have caused her to be target of the drunken humor of two beerswigging beach bums whose laughter seems to follow us all the way home.

That night, I lie wrapped up in a blanket on the porch. I can hear the ocean rising and crashing and the clatter of dishes being stacked. I turn my head to see Anita looking up at the stars. She feels my gaze and turns her back, and I realize how uncomfortable she must be, not being able to get lost in our crowd...

And now she is here with soup and sympathy. "I am so sorry," she says, as I hold open the door. "I'm not coming in, I just wanted to drop this off. Pea soup, not as good as your mom's." And then, "Your mother was a good lady, Maureen. Don't you forget that." She hands me the package, and our hands meet as we maneuver the exchange. I just smile at her and try to say "Thank you." But nothing comes out. And for a sweet second she looks at me and smiles back, and I can tell how much more comfortable she is on this side of the situation.

"It is better to give than to receive," I hear the priest say as I stand there watching her get in the car that is waiting by the curb and drive off.

"Your mother was a good lady, Maureen." Her words fall soft and slow like morning snow, so I wait in the doorway to see if they will stick. 'Cause it's the first time I've heard my mother talked about in the past tense, and I am not sure I want to go back into a house that she doesn't live in anymore. But the pot of soup is getting heavy, and eventually the strain of my body wins over the pain in my heart.

I bring the soup to the kitchen and make some space for it on the crowded counter. The sink is still full and so is the dishwasher, and I can see that someone has started to use my mother's good china. "Is nothing sacred?" I hear her say. And this time I am in complete agreement. Who has been using the good china? Who has been letting it all pile up on the side of the sink? A song drifts in the window, *"You can go your own way. Go your own way. You can call it another lonely day. You can go your own way. Go your own way."*

Julia and Bridget enter the kitchen and grab a beer from the refrigerator. They are talking about the priest coming for last rites and having to get Annie up. "She has been sleeping in the attic all day," one says to the other. "Is she okay?" they wonder. And then Bridget lights up a cigarette right there in the kitchen. The smoke swirls with the dirty dishes and the song and the thought of the sleeping sister, and suddenly I have an overpowering need to be by my mother, to wake her up to all of this unsacred activity.

I push through the kitchen door and move with purpose to the living room, which should now be called the dying room because that is what's happening. My Aunt Brenda, who has just arrived, stands like an angry ghost at the entrance of the room. She just stands there, staring across the room at her sister, pale faced and holding her purse like she might have to vomit in it. Being a schoolteacher, it has been harder for her to get off work. She brings no morphine, only confused looks and shaky hands.

Riddle is sitting on the long bench at the end of the room, holding her prom dress like a security blanket. My mother's bed is beside her. I navigate all the cots and find my way to her side.

"Hey," she says, as I sit beside her.

"Are you going to the prom?" I ask.

"No, but my friends are coming by to take pictures with me before they leave." I bob my head.

"Oh, that's good," I say. Not really knowing if it is good or not.

"That nasty old Mrs. Kelly came by with muffins," Riddle whispers.

"She did, she came here?" I ask.

"With a plate of muffins. But trust me, I wouldn't eat them if I were you. Even Crazy snubbed his nose at them."

"Why would you give them to the cat?" I ask incredulously. "What do you have against the cat?" She makes a face and we start to giggle, our shoulders shake and rock, and I can't seem to stop.

Across the room, I see Aunt Brenda begin to shake her head. "What? What are you doing? Stop that. Stop that right now, you two." She is looking at us and pointing. "How can you laugh while sitting at your mother's deathbed?" she asks in her best condescending teacher voice. We stop laughing and look at her. "Stop that," she says again, even though we already have. She turns and heads to the kitchen and all I can think of is—wait till she sees the china and the smoking sisters.

"She's a bitch," Riddle whispers.

"Yeah," I whisper back, "she's our mother, and we can laugh if we want to." And then we both look to our mother to make sure she has not heard us. She lies there more quiet and still than I have ever seen her before.

A little while later the door creaks open, and Dolly Zupko is standing there in her prom dress and motioning to my sister. Riddle hops up and heads to the door. I follow her so I can see all girls in pretty dresses. They all look glossy and shiny, and Riddle tucks into them in her jeans and T-shirt. She is still the prettiest and cannot be outshined, but the other girls in their bright dresses and lipstick sure give her a run for her money. I stare in awe at the burst of color that swirls around our front yard till Riddle tells me, "Get the boutonniere from the fridge." And because I am their gofer, I follow orders.

In the kitchen, my sisters are quiet. Aunt Jody and my cousin, Chrissie, are there, too. They all lean against the counters staring at my Aunt Brenda who is crying and shaking her head. As soon as I enter, I wish that I hadn't. Everyone looks different when they cry, and she is no exception. Her eyes become bluer, and her pale cheeks are now pink and flush, and she seems so much sweeter and frailer and softer than I had ever known her to be.

"I had no idea," she confesses. "I just had no idea." And her words hit me like a wave I didn't see coming. I watch her face crumble as she wipes away her tears, and my judgments of her get wiped away too. There is not a dry eye in the kitchen, and we shake our heads with her.

"I know, I know," I hear my Aunt Jody agree. And we all nod along trying our best to tell her with our eyes. We know too, 'cause we had no idea either. Somebody hands Aunt Brenda a glass of wine. Her thin hands shake as she brings it up to her lips, and it takes both hands to do the job. I go to the refrigerator, grab the light blue carnation from our crowded fridge, and head to the front lawn.

On the grass, the couples gather. The boys are in suits; cummerbunds and ties. They look so awkward as they fidget with their ties and jackets and steal expectant glances at the girls. The girls' totter around in high heels and flowing long dresses, their long hair in braids and curls and swept up in all sorts of arrangements. Riddle looks brave as she tries to change gears. I watch all the effort it takes for her to play along. Secretly, I am glad that she won't need to wear that mask all night.

The prom couples arrange themselves in different configurations. All girls, then all boys, then one couple at a time. The longer they stay, the harder it is to watch. Even though they are so beautiful and happy, part of me wants to scream and chase them off the lawn. "Get on with your silly selves. Shoo." From down the street, I see William making his way up the block. He still wears his crossing guard vest and his hopeless smile. I duck around the back of the house. The way things are changing so quickly, it is going to be mighty hard to make my case stick for him.

I cross the patio of handprints and step into the back hall and then the kitchen. Aunt Brenda is now doing impersonations and telling outrageous stories that have them all laughing. The glass of wine has done its trick. She is in better spirits and safe as long as she stays in the kitchen.

"Ah, I love that you kids are smoking," she tells my sisters. "I gave up smoking with my good friend Pat Mcgill when we were twenty. But we have both vowed to take it back up when we're eighty. There is not a day that goes by that I don't wish for my eightieth birthday. There is nothing like the smell of a good cigarette. Here, blow it my way," she coos, waving her hands in the air.

As I pass through the kitchen and into the dining room, the front door opens and Riddle comes in with tonight's dinner lady. A dinner lady has been coming almost every night. Our home has never known such aromas. The dinner lady is never the same lady, but a different one every night, and the meals are just as varied. They are parish women and neighbor ladies and ladies from town. They all wear the same shade of red lipstick, as though they all bought the same "gift with purchase" at the Clinique counter. It's like they put it on before dropping off the meal so that they look perky or happy or something. They present the offering by name as if it is being considered for a prize at the fair. Mexican lasagna, chicken Marsala, beef bourguignon over egg noodles. Like Anita, they don't go in to see my mother. They stand in the front vestibule and whisper confessions, "I am sorry I haven't been by sooner, tell your mother I say hello, she's in our prayers." Their eyes scan the room gathering details, the chaos that clutters our dining room table, the gray circles beneath my sisters' eyes, the strange smell of a souring body.

When we ask if they would like to see her, they smile and shake their heads.

"No, no the car is running, I have to get back, the kids are waiting...best to let her sleep," they say, as if we have a choice. This is all too much for them. They have been brave and dutiful, done their bit, shown up, but now it's too close for comfort. I watch their wheels turning. "This is what it will look like when it is my turn, this is how it will feel." We have colored in the outline of their worst nightmares. And sometimes, against their best efforts, they, too, will begin to cry before they even get out the door.

My cousin Robin shows up with more supplies, and she leans over my mother's bed to check her bandage where the IV is taped to her arm.

Marian and Bridget come through the door with bags of their own. But their story is too heavy to hold, and they start to spill it all out before even putting the bags down.

"You won't believe this," they sing. "We saw not one but a whole army of little girls in white dresses and red roses. A whole parade of them," they continue, finishing each other's sentences. "They are having the first Holy Communion down at the church and there they were! A whole army of little girls all carrying red roses. Just like the sign that Mary asked for. Can you believe it?" My aunts just smile and nod their heads.

Robin smiles up at me as I sit by my mother's bedside. From her necklace, a pearl white charm swings as she talks tenderly to my mother. "How do you like that, Aunt Rosie? A whole army of little girls with roses?" My mother just lays there asleep, she doesn't even wake when Robin pulls the tape from her skin to change the dressing. The charm continues to swing from Robin's neck. The charm is a lovely white dove. Before the day is up, we have seen all the signs, except the rainbow. My aunts have their faith. I begin to wish I had spoken up about wanting to see a rainbow, because more than anything I, too, would like to believe.

Outside the kitchen, Father Moore has arrived with Father Funk. These are two of her favorites. "They are here to give the last rites," I hear someone whisper. This is not the first time they have come to our house. They have come for dinner and drinks and debates many times before. They have dedicated books to my mother and brought her bottles of dead babies...

Be careful with them. You must be very careful. Like Pandora, I suffer from a bad case of curiosity: I just want to look. So up on my tiptoes I reach for the box. It's heavy, and the bookcase sways. But I manage to carefully bring the box down from the shelf and rest it safely on top of the upright piano. I reach inside and pull out one of the glass jars, as I had seen the priest do a few years earlier. It is the size of a large pickle jar. I hold it up to the lights as the little baby floats and bobs. It spooks me, and sucks me in, all at the same time, holding me as a captive audience. I study its tiny hands and feet, its thin arms and round belly, still attached to the floating placenta. This floating fetus has me hooked.

The box of bottled babies arrived at our door a few years earlier, carried by a priest. He brought them to my mother to assist her in the battle to defend the rights of the unborn.

He set the box on our dining room table. We all gathered round to get a closer look.

"You must be very careful with them," he warns, placing each jar gently down. They are labeled: three weeks, two months, and four months. The liquid is the color of murky dishwater, the babies—Silly Putty before it had been pressed to the funny pages. Their faces small and quiet, the skin around their closed eyes tinged blue, their expressions somber. I've never seen such quiet babies, and it seems to be contagious.

Our normally loud and rowdy group has gone still. The bottled babies have us frozen. I know if anything is sacred, it's these babies. They have us mesmerized to the point that we even forget about the wonderful prank concocted for the evening's enjoyment. Under the direction of Bridget and the inspiration of Marian, we have created a little comedy production, called "Freak Out the Priest" which we plan to premiere during dinner.

"You need to protect them," he instructs our mother.

"Protect them from what?" Annie asks, before I can. It seems like a lost cause trying to protect dead babies.

"From the witches. People who practice witchcraft will try to use them for human sacrifices and rituals." We search his face for signs that he has learned about our "freak out the priest plan." Maybe this is his attempt to "freak out the kids," but he continues on dryly educating our mother on the care of dead babies.

Witches? Real witches? Visions of wart-nosed hags on broomsticks fly through my mind. Dark covens of green-faced grannies, hissing and beckoning me with their bony fingers to bring them our bottled babies.

"One human fetus," they smirk, dumping the baby into a huge steaming cauldron.

We stand in fear and awe examining the ominous bottles of floating witch bait. And then it's time to eat. Just like that, life unfolds without transitions. There's never any lead in, or warm up, never any introduction period. Things just happen, all the time and when you least expect. A priest arrives with three dead babies, now what? Oh yes, dinner. Clear the table, time to eat.

The bottled babies are placed on the hutch. They remain there during dinner, sleeping right through our show, though their presence adds to the drama.

It begins innocently. "Pass the pepper," is the cue from Marian for us to start the humming. "Low at first, and then let it rip," she had instructed us.

When our voices reach a deafening pitch, Marian slaps her hand to the table. We hook our feet under the bench and slowly lean our upper bodies back, crossing our arms over our chests, like the dead people we had seen in the caskets at Preston's Funeral Home. When our heads are almost touching the floor, we sing out.

"Pray for the dead, and the dead will pray for you."

"Stop that! Stop it! Jim, make them stop!" my mother squeals.

The Giant, a sucker for show biz, sits back in his chair with a look of subtle pride as the priest stares uncomfortably at the mashed potatoes. If we had known the babies would be here, we may have rethought our song selection, but then again, maybe not.

The next day, the box of jarred babies is moved to the sun porch, the one room in our home that did not get much action. In the winter, it was too cold and in summer, too hot. Crammed with rickety bookcases that overflow with books and papers. There is a forgotten piano, piles of yellowed newspapers, broken toys and trash. The room is a way station, a place to store things we didn't know what to do with. It is the perfect home for three dead babies.

For the next few years, they are sequestered to this quiet orphanage for homeless things. And they seem to be fine in their new surroundings. Time passes without incident. They don't get out as much as the priest would have liked. The trips and conventions that had been planned for them were canceled, cut short by that other unexpected and awe-inspiring visitor, my mother's breast Cancer. Before long, the dead babies, along with the rest of us, would need to learn how to fend for themselves, which is not as easy for them. They arrived when I was nine and now, a full two years later as I sneak in to steal a peek, it surprises me how little they've changed.

A sunbeam slides through the window and sets off the flakes and bits that dance in the liquid. I can't take my eyes off of this sad yet mystifyingly beautiful human snow globe. And then, like a nervous cat, not used to being held, it is gone.

There is an unsettling time lapse between my holding the jar up to the sunlight, and then seeing it smashed into pieces on the floor. My breath is pushed from my lungs as my gasp fills the air. My fingers come together, searching for the cold damp glass that has slipped from my hands as a cold breeze runs up my spine.

I know that our house is haunted. The lady who lived here before us died in my parents' room. My sisters give detailed accounts of run-ins with her spirit. I imagine her beside me— half-ghost, half-angel. I can't blame her for knocking the jar from my hands, but I wouldn't put it past her either. For sure, she was not instrumental in helping me to catch the fumble or give assistance, like angels are supposed to.

I look around but find nothing but the quiet confusion of our messy room. The baby lies at my feet with its body free from the confines of the glass jar. As I stare down at its body, another idea comes. Maybe it wasn't the dead lady's spirit. Maybe it was the angry spirit of this little baby who came and sent the jar smashing to the ground to aid its escape. After all, it had been bottled up for so long. Babies are not supposed to be ignored, even I knew that.

I watch as the formaldehyde gets absorbed into the scattered books and papers, the fineness of the shattered glass, the slivers, as small as splinters, that glisten against the dingy linoleum floor. My gut tightens with the fear of having to deal with the whole mess of this unwanted accident. The guilt, the shame, the moment penetrate my blood. This nameless baby and I are forever bonded.

"What are you doing in there?" my mother calls.

She has not been getting around so good for the last several weeks, but my fear of her wrath leads me to believe that if the circumstances were right, she'd find a way to get up.

"Nothing," I reply, trying to sound innocent as I stare down at the dead baby. It lies on its side, cheek to the floor. A fallen bird amid the jagged glass of its broken shell.

I grab hold of two hardcover books and use them to lift the lifeless infant, trying to be careful so that it won't get cut from all the broken glass. I didn't want to hurt it. But I can't bring myself to touch it. I know that I should just lift it, hold it, honor it, and cradle it in my hands. I know that I should not be so afraid or disgusted. But I am. I protect myself with the two book covers. I lift the baby from the cold sun parlor floor and I drop it, books and all into the big hefty bag filled with junk that had not made its way out to the trash yet.

It's not lost on me that this poor baby now had the bad luck of being thrown away...twice. I try not to look in the garbage at all the trash and wet books. "Ashes, ashes we all fall down." I continue with my job of cleaning and covering evidence. Balling up newspaper like sponges and sopping up the defiant baby juice that knows no boundaries. When it is done, I perform no prayer or ceremony like I had for my dead fishes. Instead, I make the long cold journey outside to the garbage, and bury the bag deep into the bottom of the can. It would not have been my first choice, but at least now the baby is free. Maybe now it could find its way back to the earth instead of being stuck in the strange purgatory of bottled formaldehyde.

After some time, the baby is missed.

"What happened to the baby?" she screams. "Where is the baby? Marian! Bridget! Julia! Get down here all of you. Get down here and find the baby!"

Our well meaning tribe takes up a search. I move stacks of

papers and books trying to appear busy and innocent. How can I tell her that I had threw the sacred baby into the trash? She would kill me. I'd be pickled in formaldehyde for my sins and shipped off to other parishes as an example of what happens to weak young girls who quench their curiosities.

"I don't know, Ma. We can't find it," we all shrug.

"Oh? Nobody knows anything, is that it?" She paces the living room mumbling.

"Dear Saint Michael, please come around. Something is lost that must be found." I walk on eggshells behind her chanting a small prayer of my own. "Dear God, please forgive me." When the search brings forth nothing, she collapses on the couch.

"Jesus, Mary and Joseph, is nothing sacred anymore? How could we have lost a baby, for God's sake?"

She lies back against the couch and stares up at the ceiling. Her confused gaze mentally retracing the steps that led to this moment.

"Maybe the witches came," Annie offers. Mom leans forward and buries her shaking head in her hands.

For the next few days, I can still feel her frustration of how she will have to confess to the priest that, after all his warnings and instructions, she has not protected all the babies from the witches…

The two priests are standing by my mother's bed and speak with my father. Is this the price I pay? I imagine that they are negotiating for my sins. One mother in payment for one bottled baby.

I go back to sitting by my mother and searching for any signs that she is waking up. I watch the blanket rise and fall with each breath and the pattern comforts me. William comes in from school and sits beside me. Owen, who has been taking comfort between my two aunts on the couch, comes and joins us.

I watch as the priest says a few prayers and anoints our mother's forehead with some oils and then says a few more prayers. He begins to say the rosary, and we all join in. It is a long prayer that goes on and on in the saddest way and threatens to drain me of all my faith. Yet I can't let that happen, giving up hope would be a mutiny of the harshest kind.

37

Sitting by Her Bedside

SO WE SIT, MY TWO BROTHERS AND I, BY MY MOTHER'S big hospital bed in the middle of our living room. We watch her sleep and wait in vain for her to open her eyes and tell us to go clean our rooms. My sisters begin to flit around the house preparing for death. That does not mean she is dying; it just means that my sisters like to flit and will do it over anything. It helps to settle their minds and busy their hands.

The Giant sits across from us with the gentleness of a boulder being tossed in a lake. He casts a heavy shadow, and small snakes of fear run down my back.

In the corner of my eye, I see his mouth open and close several times. I don't look at him. I don't want to know about the words he is wrestling with.

"Listen," he says, looking at nobody in particular. I try to stay very still, pretending he is not talking to me. I know he wants me to look at him. But I can't. It's like having to look at a badly skinned knee, you already know how ugly it will be from the pain you feel. So he continues on without our acknowledgment.

"When I was around your age, my mother died. Just like your mother, just like this. Cancer...Breast Cancer. Before she did, she told me I was lucky because there would be kids who would have their mothers forever, and that someday they would have to leave their mothers, move out. But not me, my mother would be there with me forever. In spirit, she would always be with me. And if I ever needed her, in spirit, she would be there."

I hold my breath. I sense a massive wave forming in my father's words. I know there is no place to hide. They will come crashing down, and I am certain I will not survive. I stare straight ahead and try to will him silent. If he tells me that our mother is going to die, I will have to believe him, 'cause I can't imagine why a father would say a thing like that if it weren't true.

He wipes his brow and exhales a breath that tells me everything. I think about running from the room, but my feet won't move. I stare at the flower on my mother's comforter and try and find the pattern till it all becomes a blur. He sucks in a huge breath and refuels for the next group of words. They are heavy, but he manages to push them out.

"Your mother is going to heaven, but she's not gonna leave you. She'll be up there with my mother. You will miss her. I know, I still miss my mother, but it's gonna be okay. You'll all be okay."

I watch from the corner of my eye as he sits back into his chair. The room swirls in silence, and we just sit there; my brothers, my father, and me. Three little and one big kid waiting for Death. Now we know. It is coming.

I stare down at her hand on the blanket, so unusually still. There is a slow, heavy, sinking feeling in my heart as I recognize how lifeless she has become. I feel my heart turn to stone and slowly but surely begin to shatter in slow motion. For all my effort in trying to hold off this moment, it has come, and all I can do is watch her lifeless hand lie on the floral blanket. All the signing of papers, wiping of faces, the stirring of batter, the licking of fingers, turning of pages, the wild gesticulations as she ranted on the phone have all come to an end.

"Marine?" my brother whispers. But I ignore him as I try to blink warm tears from my eyes. I can't bear to look into his beautiful brown eyes, for they will be the eyes of a motherless child, and I so don't want that for my brother. "Marine?" he whispers again, this time with a sharp nudge to my ribs.

"I'm sorry," I want to tell him. But when I look at him, he directs my gaze to my father, who has sat back deep into his seat and fallen asleep. There have been many restless nights and cases of cheap wine that have led to this moment. And now he is asleep, snoring softly like a distant train that has just relieved itself of some heavy cargo.

Without anything preventing me, I study my father's face. I get there finally, past those boots, and dusty pants, up over the well-worn flannel shirt that fit snugly across the broad shoulders of this very big man.

I reach his face, and I let myself rest there.

His hair is a crew cut from his army days, and under the stubble on his face, his skin confesses how young he actually is. Not as young as I had hoped though, and even when I squint my eyes, I can't seem to find that boy he spoke of.

Yet the spell is broken. The spell that had led me to believe his life started with my birth. There had been a past: a childhood, a mother, and a death. He was once a kid like me. He had been to this particular place in hell, and he had survived. And so there is hope.

I sit there for the rest of the day between my two sleeping parents, accepting, maybe for the first time, that only one will wake up. And as I begin to make peace with the departure of my mother, there grows in me an odd curiosity about the strange giant in dirty work boots, who tells me it will be okay.

Later that evening she wakes, but it's brief. As she does, we watch him stand, as if they had both come to an agreement. He leans over her and labors to control his breath.

"I love you, Rosie."

His voice so clear and soft, I hold my breath so as not to miss a moment. Then we witness one of those very rare moments when courage meets fear, and resistance meets love, and they all stand together in one man's shoes. The Giant bends to whisper in her ear, she reaches up to hug him. Her aim is off, her arm weak, she ends up just swiping at his nose. Like a punch drunk boxer trying to get one more in before they ring the bell. The Giant holds her face in his hands.

"Hey Rosie, I love ya," he says again, wanting to make sure it lands. For a brief moment, their eyes meet. They seem frozen there, like a statue, and I can't see where she ends and he begins. I feel my head shaking itself "no" because my mind can't imagine how to separate the two. My breath comes in sudden and hard gasps, and my body begins to rattle. He takes his hands from her face and, without hesitation, he turns to the machine that has been keeping her alive. There is a small pause, and though I can only see the back of his shoulders, I can feel him summoning his strength, his courage, his faith. With a firm and reverent hand, he pulls the plug. My head continues shaking, and my body continues to rattle. I reach for my sister's hand, and we hold tight and do our best to contain the storm that is stirring in our bodies. The room pulsates with pain, swells and swirls with it, and all I can do is to hold tight to my sister's hand.

We watch our mother slowly shut down as odd sounds come from her body.

"Is she still alive? Is she alive?" we ask Marian, confused but still with a strain of hope.

"No, it just the death cough," she whispers. But we watch, still waiting for a miracle. The room grows quiet, and the Giant's head hangs so low that I see the very top of it. It is such an odd perspective, but this time I know what's coming. I remember this all from this morning, when he was out there in the snow. He holds his face in his hands, and his body begins to sway. At first it's like he is dancing to some music that we can't hear. Large swells that sway his massive frame, then the intensity builds, like he is holding tight to a jackhammer. There is a groan, and then another, and suddenly it feels like the whole house begins to vibrate like a volcano about to blow. My aunts usher us outside to the front stoop. We gather to each other on the cement stoop, still chilled by this morning's snow. We huddle together, a soggy choir of sadness. Weeping and worn out, we sit in the shock and snot that make it hard to breathe. My sisters turn back to the door. They murmur and nudge each other, so I turn too. At first it's hard to see, hard to decipher through the screen door. I strain and squint to see the Giant. He is standing there with William in what looks like a headlock and they are rocking, almost wrestling, with each other, with death. It's clumsy and awkward, sloppy and stunning. I can't take my eyes from them. My sisters whisper, "Don't look, don't look, Maureen." But after so many days of death, it's hard to turn my eyes from such life. So I watch unapologetically. I watch my brother in the Giant's arms. I watch with both jealousy and hope. He comforts my brother in the darkness of the vestibule as I stare from the sunny side of the stoop. The low sun hits the mirror on the wall and sets off a prism that surrounds them, little rainbows all around. Little rainbows all around, and I am so glad that I didn't turn away. 'Cause I would have missed my sign. This is the place where troubles melt like lemon drops. Cancer is gone. Our mother is free, and the Giant is not actually a giant at all. I watch as he folds his head into my brother and holds him like a small toy doll as he cries. They stand like this in the rainbow shrine, and I know that I am witnessing something sacred. Then I see him. It's only for a flicker of a second, but there he is, clear as day...that boy that he spoke of, the one with the dead mother. The brave one, the strong one, the one that was hiding in the Giant all along.

And as they rock, I hear a song that seeps up slowly from the cement stoop and swells in the softness of my sisters' eyes. It sighs from the sleeping cat, and serenades me from every direction. And like my brother in my father's arms, I am embraced and held gently in this perfect harmony that vibrates through everyone and everything. I turn my head to look out at our yard, from the cracks in the sidewalk and all the way up to where the trees kiss the sky, there is music. It's a love song. A giant love song. And even though she is gone, she lives in that music. That is how my father could reach his mother, and that is how I will reach for mine, through the music of everything that plays on,

    and on

    and on

    and on

    and on…and it always will.

About the Author

Maureen Muldoon is a writer, author, motivational speaker, and life coach. She spent twenty years working in TV and film as an actress and writer. She lives in La Grange, Illinois, and Madeline Island, Wisconsin, with her husband and their four kids. She is the author of *Giant Love Song*, the children's book *The Life of A Sandcastle*, and *Spiritual Vixen's Guide to an Unapologetic Life*. Her poetry, personal essays, fiction, and creative nonfiction have appeared in *Story Lab, Lit Up, Booby Trap, Story, Actors Access, Voice Box, Risk!,* and *Voyage Chicago*.

As an international teacher of A Course In Miracles, Maureen is part of the new generation of spiritual visionaries and thought leaders. She has trained top artists and executives in empowered leadership and communications and coached celebrities and media professionals, including Grammy and Emmy winners. As the founder and CEO of SpeakEasy Spiritual Community, an incubator of awesomeness, she shares cutting-edge spiritual principles and success strategies to achieve affluence, purposeful productivity and creativity, and happiness. From her global platform, Maureen has touched hundreds of thousands around the planet with her message on finding your voice, your path, and your purpose, and leaving your unapologetic mark of love.

She blogs about creativity, spirituality, and storytelling at MaureenMuldoon.com. Be sure to subscribe to her YouTube channel for more insights and inspirations.